B. J. Barnes

9-15   1,2,3
9-22   4,8
9-27

MATERIAL
REQUIREMENTS
PLANNING

OVERVIEW

PART ONE • PERSPECTIVE
Introduction
Inventory in a Manufacturing Environment

PART TWO • CONCEPTS
Principles of Material Requirements Planning
The Material Requirements Planning System

PART THREE • MATERIAL REQUIREMENTS PLANNING LOGIC
Processing Logic
Regenerative Systems and Net Change Systems
Lot Sizing

PART FOUR • USING THE SYSTEM
More than an Inventory Control System
System Effectiveness: A Function of Design and Use

PART FIVE • DATA
System Records and Files
Product Definition

PART SIX • MANAGING WITH THE NEW TOOLS
The Master Production Schedule
A New Way of Looking at Things

MATERIAL REQUIREMENTS PLANNING

The New Way of Life in Production and Inventory Management

JOSEPH ORLICKY

McGRAW-HILL BOOK COMPANY

New York St. Louis San Francisco Auckland Düsseldorf
Johannesburg Kuala Lumpur London Mexico Montreal
New Delhi Panama Paris São Paulo
Singapore Sydney Tokyo Toronto

Library of Congress Cataloging in Publication Data

Orlicky, Joseph.
  Material requirements planning.

  1. Electronic data processing—Production control.
  2. Electronic data processing—Inventory control.
I. Title.
IS155.8.074   658.7   74-10904
ISBN 0-07-047708-6

    12 13 14 15   KPKP   8987654321

*The editors for this book were W. Hodson Mogan and Carolyn Nagy,
the designer was Naomi Auerbach, and its production was
supervised by George Oechsner. It was set in Rector by
University Graphics, Inc.*

It was printed and bound by The Kingsport Press.

FOREWORD

I am more than pleased to write the foreword to Joe Orlicky's new book on material requirements planning, which represents the "state of the art" in managing production and inventories. We have been witnessing a rapidly growing acceptance of the MRP approach by industry over the past several years, and this has been accompanied by the emergence of a group of articulately outspoken champions of MRP who see the relationship between flows of materials and product structure in a fundamentally new light. The author is one of that group.

I have had the opportunity to work closely with him while he was creating the manuscript, which I critiqued in detail. I have learned more from reading and reviewing the material than can properly be chronicled here, but I would like to attempt a brief evaluation; in the final analysis, it is the degree of personal learning that measures the impact of any book.

This book captures, organizes, and methodically expounds knowledge of the subject that until now has existed only in fragments, as far as business literature is concerned. Coverage is comprehensive and thorough; throughout the text, examples and illustrations are liberally used to clarify each important point. I might add that despite the author's affiliation with IBM, and his extensive knowledge of computer use, the book does not read like a data processing manual.

Material Requirements Planning will prove of interest to at least three differently oriented audiences. The manufacturing management reader will find sufficient depth to understand why "the new way of life in production and inventory management" is possible, and to realize which of the MRP system design aspects are his responsibility. For the more technically oriented reader, the book provides an important perspective: the point of view of the user, his problems, and the skills needed in using the new tools. Finally, the book offers the first truly comprehensive treatment of material requirements planning to academic readers.

It is my hope that this book will help academics to deal with the really significant aspects of the total production and inventory control system, going beyond the usual comparisons of its modules which, to my view, are too often simplistic. Educators and students alike should find this book to be an important source of new material on production planning and inventory control. As an academic person, I particularly appreciate the inclusion in Chapter 12 of a section on research opportunities. It is time for academic researchers to attack those problems that have the highest relevance in the real world, in other words, to work on what would have the largest payoff from success in research efforts rather than what is most "researchable."

In the past, there has unfortunately not been good communication between practitioners in industry and those who teach and write in the production planning and inventory control area. This book will help in improving communication, because the author speaks as a professional with both theoretical knowledge and practical experience. It is time for the subject of material requirements planning to be incorporated into curricula of collegiate schools of business, and one of the really critical needs is for MRP literature. Here *Material Requirements Planning* is a most important contribution.

THOMAS E. VOLLMANN
Professor of Business Administration
Indiana University

PREFACE

Someone had to write this book.

Since around 1960, when a few of us pioneered the development and installation of computer-based MRP systems, time-phased material requirements planning has come a long way—as a technique, as an approach, as an area of new knowledge. From the original handful, the number of MRP systems used in American industry gradually grew to about 150 in 1971, when the growth curve began a steep rise as a result of the "MRP Crusade," a national program of publicity and education sponsored by the American Production and Inventory Control Society (APICS).

As this book goes to print, there are some 700 manufacturing companies or plants that either have implemented, or are committed to implementing, MRP systems. Material requirements planning has become a new way of life in production and inventory management, displacing older methods in general and statistical inventory control in particular. I, for one, have no doubt whatever that it will be *the* way of life in the future.

Thus far, however, the subject of material requirements planning has been neglected in hard-cover literature and academic curricula, in favor of techniques that people in industry now consider of low relevance or obsolete. I suppose one of the reasons for this situation is the subject's position outside the scope of quantitative analysis, and the view of it as being "vocational" rather than "scientific." The subject of production and inventory management is, of course, vocational in the sense that the knowledge is intended to be applied for solving real-life business problems. Like engineering or surgery, production and inventory management is oriented toward practice. Unlike many other approaches and techniques, material requirements planning "works," which is its best recommendation.

In the field of production and inventory management, literature does not lead, it follows. The techniques of modern material requirements planning have been developed not by theoreticians and researchers but by practitioners. Thus the knowledge remained, for a long time, the property of scattered MRP system users who normally have little time or inclination to write for the public.

The lag of literature became painfully evident to me when, in early 1973, I undertook to prepare a study guide for a publicly administered examination on material requirements planning. I chaired the committee of APICS in charge of developing this examination, under the guidance of Educational Testing Service of Princeton, and in preparing the study guide I wanted to list all written material pertaining to the subject. I found that the entire MRP literature consisted of twenty-six items— good, bad, and indifferent—all of which were either articles, excerpts, special reports, or trade-press "testimonials." Tutorial material on MRP basics was lacking entirely. The job of "getting it all together" remained to be done.

Someone had to write a book on "MRP from A to Z," and I concluded I may have to be the one. So I wrote this book.

ACKNOWLEDGMENTS
In writing a book one needs help, and I owe my thanks to many who helped me, in several different ways. I am indebted to my employer, the IBM Corporation, for a "sabbatical" leave from regular duties under its Industry Grant Program, which enabled me to write this book. I wish to thank my superiors at IBM, Messrs. Wayne K. Adams, Edward R. Frick, and Joe M. Henson, for the encouragement and support they have given me. My secretary, Mrs. Kathy McHugh, helped by typing and retyping the manuscript.

My thanks go to Professors William L. Berry and D. Clay Whybark of Purdue University, who critiqued the manuscript in its early stages and who provided many valuable suggestions. I wish to acknowledge a particular debt of gratitude to Professor Thomas E. Vollmann of Indiana University, who spent many hours, throughout the period of manuscript creation, reviewing the material in depth and helping me with the formidable problem of organizing it.

My old friend Oliver W. Wight was the first to urge me to write this book, helped me to design it, and reviewed the manuscript. Over the years, he has conveyed to me so many observations, techniques, and insights into material requirements planning that it is not practical to give him individual credit each time one of his contributions is documented in the text. Finally, I must give thanks to my wife, Olga, for all the things an author's spouse must endure. Only those who have had the experience can possibly know what I mean.

In the text, I am quoting from, paraphrasing, and otherwise making free use of my own past writings on the subject.

A section of Chapter 1 includes some of the material originally published in the *Proceedings of the 13th International Conference of APICS*, 1970, under the title "Requirements Planning Systems: Cinderella's Bright Prospects for the Future." A good portion of this material, including slightly disguised illustrations, surfaced, without attribution, in a 1973 publication. Just so the unwary reader won't reach the wrong conclusion as to who is cribbing from whom, I felt obliged to reaffirm my authorship in a footnote on page 21.

Chapter 5 is largely based on my paper "Net Change Material Requirements Planning," published in the *IBM Systems Journal*, vol. 12, no. 1, 1973.

Some of the material in Chapter 9 is adapted from a section called "The Problem of Data" in my book *The Successful Computer System*, McGraw-Hill, 1969.

Chapter 11 parallels, in part, the chapter called "Master Production Schedule Planning" in the *Communications Oriented Production Information and Control System (COPICS)*, IBM Corporation, 1972, which I helped to write.

Chapter 10 includes most of the material in the article "Structuring the Bill of Material for MRP," published in *Production and Inventory Management*, vol. 13, no. 4, 1972, which I wrote in collaboration with George W. Plossl and Oliver W. Wight.

Finally, Chapter 12 is based on the keynote address I delivered at the 15th International Conference of APICS on October 12, 1972 in Toronto.

November, 1974   JOSEPH ORLICKY
                                          Stamford, Connecticut

CONTENTS

LIST OF ILLUSTRATIONS

MATERIAL
REQUIREMENTS
PLANNING

PART ONE

PERSPECTIVE

It is interesting to note that the number of pages written on independent-demand-type inventory systems outnumbers the pages written on material requirements planning by well over 100 to 1. The number of items in inventory that can best be controlled by material requirements planning outnumbers those that can be controlled effectively by order point in about the same ratio. It is a sign of the adolescence of our field that the literature available is in inverse proportion to the applicability of the techniques.

OLIVER W. WIGHT *in "Designing and Implementing a Material Requirements Planning System," Proceedings of the 13th International Conference of APICS, 1970.*

INTRODUCTION

The purpose of this book is to contribute to business literature a comprehensive, state-of-the-art treatment of a subject of relatively recent origin yet of first importance to the field of manufacturing operations management—computer-based material requirements planning. This approach, its underlying philosophy, and the methods involved represent a sharp break with past theory and practice. The subject, broadly viewed, marks the coming of age of the field of production and inventory control, and a new way of life in the management of a manufacturing business.

The commercial availability of computers in the mid-1950s ushered in a new era of business information processing, with a profound impact of the new technology on the conduct of operations. Nowhere has this impact probably been greater, at least potentially, than in the area of manufacturing logistics, i.e., inventory management and production planning. Until the advent of the computer, these functions constituted a chronic, truly intractable problem for the management of virtually every plant engaged in the manufacture of discrete items passing through multiple stages of conversion from raw material to product. Known and available solutions to the problem in question were imperfect, only partial, and generally unsatisfactory from a management point of view.

The first computer applications, around 1960, in the area of manufacturing inventory management represented the beginning of a break with tradition. The availability of computers, capable of handling information in volumes and at speeds previously scarcely imaginable, constitutes a lifting of the former heavy information-processing constraint and the sudden obsolescence of many older methods and techniques devised in light of this constraint. Traditional inventory management approaches, in precomputer days, could obviously not go beyond the limits imposed by the information-processing tools available at the time. Because of this, almost all those approaches and techniques suffered from imperfection. They simply represented the best that could be done under the circumstances. They acted as a crutch and incorporated summary, shortcut, approximation methods, often based on tenuous or quite unrealistic assumptions, sometimes force-fitting concepts to reality so as to permit the use of a technique.

The breakthrough, in this area, lies in the simple fact that once a computer becomes available, the use of such methods and systems is no longer *obligatory.* It becomes feasible to sort out, revise, or discard previously used techniques and to institute new ones that heretofore it would have been impractical or impossible to implement. It is now a matter of record that among manufacturing companies that pioneered inventory management computer applications in the 1960s, the most significant results were achieved not by those who chose to improve, refine, and speed up existing procedures, but by those who undertook a fundamental overhaul of their systems. The result was abandonment of techniques proven unsatisfactory and a substitution of new, radically different approaches that the availability of computers made possible. In the area of manufacturing inventory management, the most successful innovations are embodied in what has become known as *material requirements planning (MRP) systems.*

When implemented, such systems not only demonstrated their operational superiority but afforded an opportunity for the student of inventory management to gain new insights into the manufacturing inventory problem. The new, computer-aided methods of planning and controlling manufacturing inventories made the true interrelationships and behavior of items constituting these inventories highly visible, thus illuminating the tenuousness of many previous assumptions and revealing the causes of inadequacies (always admitted) of many traditional methods.

It became evident that the basic tenet of the old inventory control theory, namely that inventory investment can only be reduced on pain of a lower service level (and vice versa), no longer holds true. The successful users of the new systems reduced their inventories and *improved* delivery service at the same time. A revolutionary change occurred and a new premise was established. Orthodox approaches and techniques became open to question, and existing inventory control literature—indeed, an entire school of thought—was marked for reexamination.

REEXAMINING TRADITIONAL INVENTORY CONTROL

Specifically, the following mainstays of conventional inventory management became subject to reappraisal as to their validity, relevance, and applicability to manufacturing inventories:

1. The concept of stock replenishment
2. All techniques built around reorder points
3. The square-root approach to the economic order quantity
4. The analysis and categorization of inventory by function
5. The conventional notion of aggregate inventory management
6. The *ABC* inventory classification

Stock replenishment is a concept forcibly grafted onto a manufacturing inventory. It is in conflict with basic management objectives of low inventory and high return on investment. The term *replenishment* means restoration to a state of (original) fullness. But manufacturing inventories should, if possible, be the very opposite of the mentioned "fullness." Stock replenishment systems are based on the principle of having inventory items in stock at all times, so as to make them available at the (poorly predictable) time of need. Stock replenishment is intended to compensate for the inability to determine the precise quantity and time of need in the short-term future. But in manufacturing, the idea is to have the inventory item available *at the time* of need (and, if possible, not before or after that time) rather than to *carry* it just so it would be available when, and if, needed. To the extent that short-term need for individual manufacturing inventory items can be pinpointed in terms of both quantity and timing—and this is indeed possible through the use of modern, computer-assisted methods—stock replenishment techniques in a manufacturing environment prove undesirable and wasteful.

Reorder point techniques, in their various forms, represent the implementation of the stock replenishment concept. These techniques, including the statistical order point, min/max, ordering "up to," and the maintenance of N months' supply, represent variations on a common theme. Whether explicitly or implicitly, all of them forecast demand during replenishment lead time, and all attempt to provide for some safety stock to compensate for fluctuation in demand. Systems based on reorder point techniques suffer from false assumptions about the demand environment, tend to misinterpret observed demand behavior, and lack the ability to determine the specific timing of future demand. These shortcomings, inherent in all systems of this type, manifest themselves in a number of unsatisfactory performance characteristics, chief among them being an unnecessarily high overall inventory level, inventory imbalance, and stockouts or shortages caused by the system itself.

The economic order quantity (EOQ) turns out to be a poor ordering quantity in the typical manufacturing demand environment. The EOQ equation is totally insensitive to the timing of actual, discrete demands (requirements) arising during the period that the EOQ is intended to cover following its arrival in stock. Once future requirements for an inventory item are precisely determined and positioned along a time axis, it can be seen that the square-root approach in the EOQ calculation does nothing to balance the lot size against either the timing or the quantity of actual requirements. For example, demand for an item over a ten-week period may be determined in advance to be, by week,

$$20-0-20-0-0-0-0-0-20-0$$

The EOQ for this item may turn out to be 50, more than needed to cover the first three weeks' requirements but not enough to cover the next requirement in the ninth week. The "remnant" of 10 pieces will be carried for eight weeks without any purpose. Note that the EOQ would still be 50 if the ten-week demand were

$$20-0-40-0-0-0-0-0-0-0$$
$$\text{or } 20-0-0-0-0-0-0-0-0-40$$

In the first instance, the EOQ would fail to cover the first three weeks' requirements, and in the second, the excess 30 pieces would be carried for nine weeks without being able to satisfy the requirements of the tenth week. In any of these cases, the EOQ is determined solely on the basis of setup cost, unit cost, carrying cost, and *annual* usage.

The derivation of the EOQ formula rests squarely on a basic assumption of uniform demand in small increments of the replenishment quantity, i.e., gradual inventory depletion at a steady rate, which then allows the carrying cost to be calculated for an "average" inventory of one-half the order quantity. This basic assumption is grossly unrealistic vis-à-vis a manufacturing inventory, and therefore fatal to the validity of the technique.

The stock replenishment, order-point/order-quantity techniques have predominated in the past, in both actual practice and inventory control literature. The reason for this is historical. The field has been conditioned in favor of the philosophy expressed by these techniques, because the pioneering theoretical work in inventory control has generally been confined to the areas of order point and order quantity.

This work has been stimulated by the fact that problems of order point and order quantity lend themselves to the application of mathematical-statistical methods which have been known and readily available for quite some time. The inventory control problem was perceived as being essentially mathematical, rather than one of massive data handling and data manipulation, the means for which simply did not exist in the past. The fact that the chronic problems of manufacturing inventory management are now being solved, however, is due not to better mathematics but to better data processing.

Inventory analysis and categorization by function, designed to account for a given total inventory in terms of the respective functions of its constituent inventory groupings, i.e.,

- Order sizing
- Fluctuation
- Stabilization
- Anticipation
- Transportation

is subject to revision, not of concept but of the method of determining the value of the respective inventory categories. Of the functions listed, it is the first two that appear in a new light.

Order sizing creates what is called *cycle stock* or *lot size inventory*. But this category cannot be reckoned to approximate one-half the quantities being ordered, which has been the traditional approach. With the discarding of the EOQ in favor of discrete lot-sizing techniques (discussed in Chapter 6), the lack of validity of such an approximation becomes clearly apparent. Actual order quantities for a given inventory item will be seen to equal the (precalculated) requirements for one or more planning periods, without remainder, causing the quantity to vary freely from one order to the next. The number of periods covered by an order quantity will in part be dictated by the relative continuity of demand for the item in question. In cases of pronounced discontinuity, the order quantity will tend to equal requirements for one period. The same will usually be true for all assembled items (subassemblies), because of the typically minor assembly setup considerations.

The second category, called *reserve stock* or *safety stock,* serves primarily to compensate for, or to absorb, fluctuation in demand. In stock replenishment systems, the safety-stock quantity is (a known) part of the order point quantity calculated for each inventory item, and the sum of the item safety stocks, costed out, represents a fair estimate of this category of inventory. In the new material requirements planning systems, safety stock on the item level tends to disappear. It is normally no longer calculated for each inventory item separately but, where used at all, it is incorporated at the end-item (master production schedule) level only.

Aggregate inventory management is a concept, and a set of techniques, used for manipulating and controlling inventory *in toto*. As the term implies, the overall inventory investment level can become subject to direct management control through certain policy variables, to the extent that the policies in question apply to the inventory across the board, or if different policies apply to a limited number of inventory groups. Under the conventional approach to aggregate inventory management, the two inventory categories most susceptible to control by means of varying a policy are lot size inventory and safety stock. When lot sizes are being determined through some form of the EOQ formula, it is possible to exert across-the-board control over them by manipulating the carrying-cost variable in this formula.

Carrying cost, a controversial value, is in all cases semiarbitrary (in practice, the values in use vary between 8 and 35 percent per annum, from company to company) and can therefore be thought of as reflecting management policy. Increasing the carrying cost used in the EOQ computation will result in smaller lot sizes, and vice versa. Thus the inventory carrying cost in use at any given time reflects the premium that management is putting on the conservation of cash.

The idea is entirely sound, and its application is simple and direct. What now must be discarded, however, are the traditional methods of quantifying the results that can be expected as a consequence of a given policy change. In an EOQ environment the theoretical relationship between incremental change in carrying cost and lot quantity change (and, by extension, lot size inventory change) is clean and straightforward. The EOQ varies inversely with the square root of the carrying cost. The value of EOQ squared doubles as a result of halving carrying costs, and halves as a result of doubling this cost. Table 1 shows some typical lot size reductions and the carrying-cost increases required to effect them. For example, a 10 percent reduction in lot size requires a 23 percent increase in the carrying cost.

Once a stock replenishment system, with its economic order quantity orientation, is replaced by a material requirements planning system utilizing discrete lot sizing, an exact mathematical relationship between incremental change in carrying cost and lot size inventory no longer exists. Inventory carrying cost continues to figure in the determination of lot sizes where warranted by the economics of ordering, but other factors (see Chapter 6) exert a more direct influence on the lot size, which usually varies from order to order. Changes in lot sizes and in lot size inventory cannot therefore be predetermined quantitatively on the basis of a change in carrying cost alone.

The other policy variable utilized in conventional aggregate inventory

TABLE 1   Carrying Cost and Lot Size Relationship

Desired lot size reduction, %	Relative values		
	Carrying cost	EOQ	EOQ^2
	100	100	100
10	123	90	81
20	156	80	64
30	200	70	50

management is the service level, which enters into the calculation of safety stock. In a stock replenishment system environment, the quantity of safety stock is computed individually for each item in the inventory, and its principal determinant is the standard deviation of past demands per period from their arithmetic mean. A normal distribution of these demands being assumed, a desired service level — i.e., incidence of item availability — determines the number of deviations represented by the safety stock.

The higher the service level desired, the higher the safety stock, and vice versa. The investment in this inventory category can therefore be controlled by manipulating the service-level value. The principle remains valid, but the technique tends to become irrelevant because, as has already been mentioned, safety stock is normally not planned at the item level in a material requirements planning system.

ABC inventory classification[1] is a popular inventory control technique, which is an adaptation of Pareto's law. In a study of the distribution of wealth and income in Italy, Vilfredo Pareto observed in 1897 that a very large percentage of the total national income was concentrated in a small percentage of the population. Believing that this reflected a universal principle, he formulated the axiom that the significant items in a given group normally constitute a small portion of the total items in the group and that the majority of the items in the total will, in the aggregate, be of minor significance. Pareto expressed this empirical relationship mathematically, but the rough pattern is 80 percent of the distribution being accounted for by 20 percent of the group membership.

The 80–20 pattern holds in most inventories, where it can be shown that approximately 20 percent of the items account for 80 percent of total cost (unit cost times usage quantity). In the typical *ABC* classification, these are designated as *A*-items, and the remaining 80 percent of the items become *B*'s and *C*'s, representing the middle 30 percent that account for 15 percent of cost, and the bottom 50 percent that account for 5 percent of cost, respectively. The idea behind *ABC* is to apply the bulk of the (limited) planning and control resources to the *A*-items, "where the money is," at the expense of the other classes that have demonstrably much less effect on the overall inventory investment. The *ABC* concept is to be implemented by controlling *A*-items "more tightly" than *B*-items, etc.

Today, the principle of graduated control stringency may be somewhat difficult to comprehend, but in precomputer days the degree of control was equated with the frequency of reviews of a given inventory item record. Controlling "tightly" meant reviewing frequently. The frequency of review, in turn, tended to determine order quantity. *A*-items would be reviewed frequently and ordered in small quantities, to keep inventory investment

[1] Introduced by H. Ford Dickie in "ABC Inventory Analysis Shoots for Dollars," *Factory Management and Maintenance,* July 1951.

down. A primitive but fairly typical *ABC* implementation is represented by policies shown in Table 2.

The rationale of *ABC* classification is the impracticality of giving an equally high degree of attention to the record of every inventory item, *due to limited information-processing capacity.* With a computer available, this limitation disappears and the *ABC* concept tends to become irrelevant. Equal treatment of all inventory items, as far as planning is concerned, now becomes feasible. In a modern, well-implemented material requirements planning system, every item, irrespective of its cost and volume, receives the same degree of care, the same stringent treatment.

Possible exceptions are certain extremely low-cost items, especially purchased ones, that may have safety stocks and be ordered in large quantites. These exceptions are made, however, not due to some inability of the computer system to plan and maintain the status of such items, but because of the impracticality of accurate *physical* control. It simply does not pay to do exact counts of lock washers and cotter pins. Physical inventory control continues to be a problem in inventory management, and the *ABC* concept, when applied in this area (to inspection, storage, frequency of cycle checks, etc.), remains valid.

The techniques and concepts covered in the preceding discussion evolved during a time when, due to very limited information-processing capacity, the precise pattern of future item demand could not be ascertained and reascertained; neither could the status of every inventory item be updated and reevaluated with sufficient frequency. The approaches embodied in these techniques and concepts reflect the former deficiencies of information, in attempting to compensate for them by other means. They lost their relevancy and usefulness, however, once it became feasible, through computer-assisted material requirements planning, to establish and maintain the formerly unavailable information.

FOCUS AND ORGANIZATION OF THIS BOOK

This book is not meant to serve as a basic text on the general subject of production and inventory management, or even inventory control. At least elementary knowledge of these subjects on the part of the reader is assumed, particularly a knowledge of the fundamentals of conventional (statistical) inventory control. (See list of references at the end of this section.) The book is written primarily for users and potential users of material requirements planning systems, i.e., for manufacturing managers, materials managers,

TABLE 2 Sample Ordering Rules under ABC Classification

Inventory class	Review frequency	Order quantity
A	Monthly	1 month's supply
B	Quarterly	3 months' supply
C	Annually	12 months' supply

production control managers, inventory planners, systems analysts, and interested industrial engineers. It can also serve the needs of students of production and inventory management when more universities include the subject of material requirements planning in their business curricula, as is ultimately inevitable.

The book's scope is limited to the system of logistics *planning* in a discrete manufacturing (as contrasted with continuous process) business. The discussion does not extend to *execution* subsystems, although it stresses that a high quality of the outputs generated by the planning system is a prerequisite for the effective functioning of such subsystems. A simplified chart, applicable to any manufacturing operation, of the relationships between the planning system and the execution (control) subsystems is presented in Figure 1.

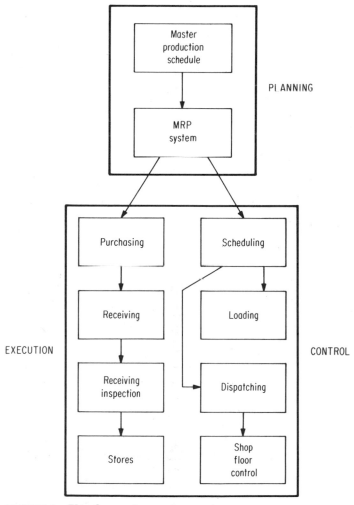

FIGURE 1   Planning and execution systems.

The focus of the book is on material requirements planning systems, and the objective is an exposition of procedural logic, function, and use of these systems rather than programming and other considerations of system implementation. All considerations that are of a purely technical data-processing nature are excluded (they are amply documented in manuals published by computer manufacturers), and the computer aspect of material requirements planning is intentionally downplayed so as not to divert the reader's attention from the really important subject matter. As far as material requirements planning is concerned, the computer's contribution lies solely in its power to execute a host of rather straightforward procedures in a very short time. The computer aspect is not essential to the understanding of the subject in question.

The discussion of material requirements planning concepts, principles, and processing logic is expanded to encompass system inputs and system uses reflected in functional outputs. The input-output chart depicted in Figure 2 can serve as a map of the topics that constitute this book.

The author has tried to avoid a case-study approach to the subject so as not to obscure the general validity of the principles involved and the universal applicability of the material requirements planning approach. Abstract examples are used as much as possible, and there are no pictures of actual forms, documents, and computer printouts.

The book consists of six parts, as follows:

Part 1—Perspective

Part 2—Concepts

Part 3—Material Requirements Planning Logic

Part 4—Using the System

Part 5—Data

Part 6—Managing with the New Tools

The material is organized into an introduction and twelve chapters which are assigned to the broader areas represented by the parts according to subject content. The discussions in the individual chapters cover essentially the following:

Manufacturing inventories, their demand environment, and the alternative techniques available for their management are discussed in Chapter 1. The suitability of statistical inventory control for items in a manufacturing inventory is examined.

Principles of material requirements planning are the subject of Chapter 2. The discussion covers the technique of time phasing, categorization of inventory systems, a review of assumptions and prerequisites to the proper operation of a material requirements planning system, and an examination of applicability, by type of business and by type of inventory item, of such a system.

Common attributes of material requirements planning systems are considered in Chapter 3, which is devoted to a discussion of the central purpose and objectives of any material requirements planning system, and its key inputs and outputs. In a more technical part of the discussion, constraining factors in the computation of requirements are enumerated and described.

The processing logic, i.e., the specific procedural steps followed in the planning of material requirements are the subject of Chapter 4. The com-

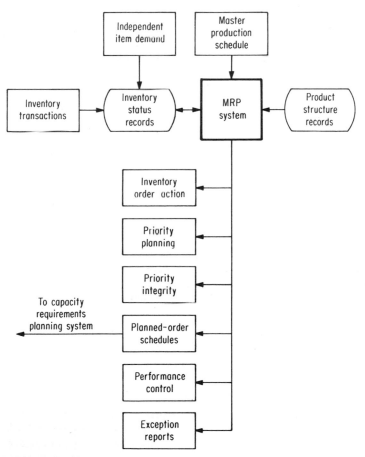

FIGURE 2   MRP system: Input-output relationships.

putation of gross and net requirements is explained in examples, as is the method of coverage and the technique of explosion. The so-called time-phased order point, an adaptation of regular material requirements planning logic for the control of items such as service parts and finished products, is also described.

The two varieties of material requirements planning systems, called *schedule regeneration* and *net change,* are described in Chapter 5 in terms of their differences. An evaluation of their relative merits and a review of conditions for their applicability are included.

Nine lot-sizing techniques that may be used in material requirements planning are reviewed in Chapter 6. Each technique is described and its use demonstrated in an example, followed by a brief evaluation.

The three key functions of a material requirements planning system, i.e., inventory control, priority planning, and providing the basis for capacity requirements planning, are the focus of Chapter 7. Any material requirements planning system possesses an inherent ability to reevaluate the validity of all open shop-order and purchase-order due dates, and thus to keep these due dates up to date. The discussion stresses this important new capability to maintain valid order priorities, which is prerequisite to effective production control.

System effectiveness is the subject of Chapter 8. Such effectiveness is a function of both system design and use. Design parameters are examined with a view toward usefulness of system outputs, and the role of the inventory planner is reviewed.

Data-base considerations are discussed in Chapter 9, including the design of a time-phased inventory record; the updating of this record via transactions; problems of file organization, access, and maintenance; bill of material formats; and the importance of data integrity.

Bill of material structure is the main topic of Chapter 10, in which item identity coding, modular bills of material, and pseudobills of material are discussed. Included is a review of the problem of product model designation and translation of model codes into part numbers.

The master production schedule, which "drives" a material requirements planning system as its prime input, merits a chapter of its own. Master scheduling concepts are discussed, as are schedule development and resource requirements planning. Chapter 11 ends with a discussion of considerations in managing the master production schedule, and managing the manufacturing operation through this schedule.

Impact on production and inventory management thought made by the newly found capability of responding to change is discussed in Chapter 12. Material requirements planning methods have provided this capability, in the light of which we now must rethink a number of traditional concepts and revise some orthodox tenets.

REFERENCES

Brown, R. G.: *Decision Rules for Inventory Management,* Holt, Rinehart and Winston, 1967.

Buchan, J., and E. Koenigsberg: *Scientific Inventory Management,* Prentice-Hall, 1963.

Hadley, G., and T. M. Whitin: *Analysis of Inventory Systems,* Prentice-Hall, 1963.

Magee, J. F., and D. M. Boodman: *Production Planning and Inventory Control,* 2d ed., McGraw-Hill, 1967.

Melnitsky, B.: *Management of Industrial Inventory,* Conover-Mast Publications, 1951.

Plossl, G. W., and O. W. Wight: *Production and Inventory Control,* Prentice-Hall, 1967.

Prichard, J. W., and R. H. Eagle: *Modern Inventory Management,* John Wiley & Sons, 1965.

Wagner, H. M.: *Statistical Management of Inventory Systems,* John Wiley & Sons, 1962.

Welch, W. E.: *Tested Scientific Inventory Control,* Management Publishing Corp., 1956.

Whitin, T. M.: *Theory of Inventory Management,* Princeton University Press, 1957.

CHAPTER ONE

INVENTORY IN A
MANUFACTURING ENVIRONMENT

Manufacturing inventory management is a subject in its own right. It only partly overlaps *general* inventory management as we know it from literature, because it represents a special problem and is governed by unique laws. This means that many of the traditional approaches to inventory management are not properly applicable to manufacturing inventories. When applied, they prove relatively ineffective. The so-called classic inventory control theory does not adequately reflect the realities of a manufacturing environment and makes incorrect assumptions as to the function of, and the demand for, the individual items which a manufacturing inventory comprises.

Failure to distinguish between manufacturing and nonmanufacturing inventories accounts for a measure of confusion or controversy, frequently observed in connection with the question of applicability of a given approach or inventory control technique to a manufacturing environment. So as to avoid such difficulties arising out of a failure of definition, this chapter is devoted to examining the attributes of manufacturing inventories and of the demand to which these inventories are subject.

MANUFACTURING INVENTORIES

A manufacturing inventory is defined as consisting of the following:

- Raw materials in stock
- Semifinished component parts in stock
- Finished component parts in stock
- Subassemblies in stock
- Component parts in process
- Subassemblies in process

Note that so-called shippable items (inventory items ready, at their stage of completion, to be delivered to a customer), such as end products and service parts, are excluded from the above list. They are part of a distribution inventory, as discussed later in this section.

In order to establish those attributes that set apart manufacturing inventories, let us first consider what the functions of a system of inventory management are — any such system, including that of a grocery, museum, or blood bank. Inventory management, or inventory planning and control, comprises the following functions and subfunctions:

1. PLANNING
   - Inventory policy
   - Inventory planning
   - Forecasting
2. ACQUISITION
   - Positive order action (place or increase)
   - Negative order action (decrease or cancel)
3. STOCKKEEPING
   - Receiving
   - Physical inventory control
   - Inventory accounting (bookkeeping)
4. DISPOSITION
   - Purging (scrap and writeoff of obsolete items)
   - Disbursement (delivery to source of demand)

While any system of inventory management can be functionally described this way, *manufacturing* inventory management has its own distinct characteristics and, compared with nonmanufacturing inventories, shows a difference in the content of certain key functions in every one of the four principal areas just mentioned:

1. PLANNING

There is normally no need for a special inventory policy pertaining to a manufacturing inventory as a whole. The least inventory consistent with production requirements which allows manufacturing cost to be at a minimum is always the management objective. Forecasting, within the manufacturing inventory system proper, plays a minor, secondary role, and the type of forecasting being performed (such as the *proportion* of a given optional feature within a future product lot) differs from the usual forecasting of demand *magnitude*.

2. ACQUISITION

The order action function is expanded and exhibits several characteristics unique to manufacturing. Material in the manufacturing process is, from the inventory system's point of view, being acquired and reacquired as it progresses through multiple stages of conversion from raw material to end product. An order for a manufactured item, once started, cannot be cancelled without the penalty of scrap or rework. Neither can it normally be increased or decreased in quantity. Factors that enter into the order quantity determination include allowances for yield or scrap, raw-material cutting considerations, etc. The ordering function includes order suspension, i.e., rescheduling the order to an indefinite future due date. Finally, the quantity and timing of an order may be affected by capacity considerations.

3. STOCKKEEPING

The inventory-accounting function may be integrated into, or merged with, the inventory-planning function (see Chapter 5).

4. DISPOSITION

Delivery of a manufacturing inventory item is always to an in-house demand source. Demand is represented by a production requirement or a production schedule. When an inventory item is completed (or received from a vendor), it is earmarked for consumption in the next stage of the material conversion process. If it is shippable upon completion, it enters a distribution inventory.

The term *manufacturing inventory management* is really a misnomer. In a manufacturing environment, inventory management cannot be conceived of apart from production planning, with which it is inseparably bound up. The function of a manufacturing inventory system is to translate the overall plan of production (the master production schedule) into detailed component material requirements and orders. This system determines, item by item, what is to be procured and when, as well as what is to be manufactured and when. Its outputs "drive" the purchasing and manufacturing functions. It plans and directs purchasing and manufacturing activities, as nothing will be purchased and no component parts will be manufactured without a requisition or order that it generates. The manufacturing inventory system determines (or rather, should have the capability to determine) order priorities and implies the capacities required. All in all, it does considerably more than manage inventory. It is the heart of manufacturing logistics planning.

Manufacturing inventory management can be put into sharper focus by dividing business inventories into two categories, by purpose. The purpose of a *manufacturing* inventory is quite different from that of a *distribution* or marketing inventory such as is found in a supermarket, at a wholesale distributor's, or in a manufacturer's finished goods and/or service parts warehouse.

The purpose of a distribution inventory is to be available to meet *customer demand* (the term *customer* applies to any recipient of items provided from distribution inventory), which tends to be erratic and of limited predictability due to its characteristic of randomness. Total demand over a given period (termed *period-demand* hereafter) is typically made up of many unit demands originating from separate sources. Period-demand can be thought of as a sample drawn from a potential demand universe which is very large or infinite. The inventory investment level is governed by *marketing* considerations.

In contrast, the purpose of a manufacturing inventory is to satisfy *production requirements.* Availability can be geared to a production plan, which means that demand is calculable, i.e., predictable. Period demand typically consists of a limited number of individual demands for multiple quantities of the inventory item. The production plan (including the planned production of such items as service parts) is the sole source of demand, and this demand is always finite. The inventory investment level is dictated by *manufacturing* (process, setup, etc.) considerations. Work in process, an inventory entity unique to manufacturing, constitutes a significant part of the investment, and the level of this inventory is primarily a function of manufacturing lead times.

In comparison with a distribution inventory, a manufacturing inventory represents a means to a different end. A manufacturing inventory, as previously defined, exists only to be converted into a shippable product. Once the product is assembled or, in the case of a service part, finished, it passes into distribution inventory. In many cases, at this point the responsibility for the inventory by manufacturing management ceases and is assumed by a marketing, distribution, or service organization.

The difference between distribution and manufacturing inventories is fundamental. Consequently, the respective inventory management philosophies, systems approaches, and techniques in use are (or should be) fundamentally different.

In determining the desirable level of a distribution inventory, the tradeoff is between investment (and the attendant inventory carrying cost) and sales revenue realized through availability. Under the service-level concept in a distribution environment, 100 percent service theoretically requires an infinitely large inventory investment. In determining a manufacturing inventory level there is no such tradeoff. The investment is dictated by production requirements which, unlike customer demand, are given and controllable. The inventory that exceeds the minimum required brings no extra revenue. A 100 percent service level (between component items and the shippable product made from them) is a necessity, but it is feasible to achieve it with a finite inventory investment.

In a distribution inventory environment, demand for each inventory item must be (explicitly or implicitly) forecast. Uncertainty exists at the item level. The principle of stock replenishment (to restore availability) applies, and the two principal questions are *when* to reorder and in what *quantity*. The first cannot be answered with certainty, whereas the second is answered through the computation of some form of an economic order quantity.

In a manufacturing inventory environment, on the other hand, individual item demand need not be forecast, and uncertainty exists only at the master production schedule level (will customer demand materialize to allow shipment of the product?). There is no need to "replenish" inventory, only to order what is required to cover production needs. Inventory availability can be geared to the *time* of these needs; i.e., it need not exist prior to such time. The existence of any of the in-stock categories of manufacturing inventory signifies, strictly speaking, premature availability. *Ideally, all manufacturing inventory would be in process,* with every item immediately consumed (by entering into the next manufacturing conversion stage) upon completion or receipt. The best-managed manufacturing inventories approach this ideal.

The questions of when and in what quantity to order are being answered, the first one with certainty provided by required date and lead time, the second one through lot-sizing techniques which utilize only known future demand (i.e., planned requirements) and take into account both its magnitude and its timing.

In practice, the question of the "correct" order quantity receives only secondary attention, and deservedly so. It is interesting to note that this question does not arise at all when the demand for an inventory item is either highly continuous (as is typical for large-volume production operations) or highly discontinuous. In all cases, it can be said that it is more important to have the quantity needed *at the time* it is needed than to order the "correct" quantity. In the real world of manufacturing, evidence attesting to the truth of this statement abounds. Splitting lots in mid-production, double setups, teardowns caused by "hot order" expediting, and partial vendor shipments are normal occurrences. They show that it is not practical always to adhere to the most economical order quantity.

The three crucial questions of distribution-oriented inventory management

1. When to reorder
2. How much to order
3. What the investment level should be

appear in a different light in manufacturing inventory management, because the problems and criteria are quite different. The answer to the first question is simply: when and if required—perhaps never. The answer to the second one is often given by the production schedule, but the general rule is to order as much as is needed to cover requirements in a planning period, unless it pays to cover more than one period. The answer to the third question is not a matter of policy, but (where material requirements are properly planned) is dictated by production schedules and lead times. A minimum inventory investment consistent with production objectives and constraints imposed by the manufacturing process is always the goal.

ORDER POINT VERSUS MATERIAL REQUIREMENTS PLANNING [1]

There are two alternatives in fundamental approach and two corresponding sets of techniques that a manufacturing enterprise may employ for purposes of inventory management. They are:

1. Stock replenishment, popularly known as statistical inventory control or order point systems
2. Material requirements planning

Definitions

The first of the above alternatives, called here *order point* for short, may be defined as a set of procedures, decision rules, and records intended to ensure continuous physical availability of all items comprising an inventory, in the face of uncertain demand. Under the order point approach, the depletion in the supply of each inventory item is monitored and a replenishment order is issued whenever the supply drops to a predetermined quantity—*the reorder point.*

This quantity is determined for each inventory item separately, based on the forecast demand during replenishment lead time and on the probability of actual demand exceeding the forecast. That portion of the reorder point quantity which is carried to compensate for forecast error is termed *safety stock.* It is computed on the basis of historical demand for the item in question and of the desired *service level,* i.e., incidence of availability over the long run. In an order point system, some form of an economic order quantity computation normally determines the size of the replenishment order.

A material requirements planning (MRP) system, narrowly defined, consists of a set of logically related procedures, decision rules, and records (alternatively, records may be viewed as inputs to the system) designed to translate a master production schedule into time-phased *net requirements,* and the planned *coverage* of such requirements, for each component inventory item needed to implement this schedule.[2] An MRP system replans net requirements and coverage as a result of changes in either the master production schedule, or inventory status, or product composition.

---

[1]This section, including illustrations, is adapted from material previously published by the author, referenced on p. 29.
[2]For an alternative definition, see Chapter 9.

In the process of planning, an MRP system allocates existing on-hand quantities to item *gross requirements* and reevaluates the validity of the timing of any outstanding (open) orders in determining net requirements. To cover net requirements, the system establishes a schedule of *planned orders* for each item, including orders, if any, to be released immediately plus orders scheduled for release at specified future dates. Planned-order quantities are computed according to one of several lot-sizing rules specified by the system user as applicable to the item in question. In its entirety, the information on item requirements and coverage that an MRP system generates is called the *material requirements plan.*

Order point is part-based, whereas material requirements planning is product-oriented. Order point utilizes data on the historical demand-behavior of an inventory item, in isolation from all other items. Material requirements planning, a radically different approach, ignores history in looking toward the future as defined by the master production schedule, and works with data specifying the relationship of components (the bill of material) that make up a product.

In the face of two alternative approaches to manufacturing inventory management, the question naturally arises as to which of them is preferable. Which of them will yield better results under what circumstances, and what is the principal criterion of their applicability?

Dependent versus Independent Demand

Orthodox inventory analysis and classification techniques are designed ostensibly to determine the most desirable treatment of a given inventory item or group of items. They examine various attributes of the individual items, such as cost, lead time, and past usage, but none of them takes into account the most important attribute, namely, the *nature* of demand. Yet it is the nature (or source) of demand which provides the real key to inventory control technique selection and applicability. The fundamental principle that should serve as a guideline to the applicability of either order point or material requirements planning is the concept of *dependent* versus *independent demand.* [3]

Demand for a given inventory item is termed *independent* when such demand is unrelated to demand for other items—when it is not a *function* of demand for some other inventory item. Independent demand must be forecast.

Conversely, demand is defined as dependent when it is directly related to, or derives from, the demand for another inventory item or product. This dependency may be "vertical," such as when a component is needed in order to build a subassembly or product, or "horizontal," as in the case of an attachment or owner's manual shipped with the product. In most manufacturing businesses, the bulk of the total inventory is in raw ma-

[3]This principle was originally formulated by the author in 1965. See reference on p. 29.

terials, component parts, and subassemblies, all largely subject to dependent demand. Such demand can, of course, be calculated. Dependent demand need not, and *should not*, be forecast, as it can be precisely determined from the demand for those items that are its sole cause.

Forecasting is inseparable from order point techniques. But all forecasting (intrinsic, as well as extrinsic) attempts to use past experience to determine the shape of the future. Forecasting succeeds only to the extent that past performance is repeatable. In a manufacturing environment, however, future demand for a given part may be quite unrelated to its past demand. Forecasting, therefore, should be the method of last resort, used only when it is not possible to extract, determine, derive demand from something else. In cases of dependent demand, forecasting is unnecessary because dependent demand is, by definition, derivable and calculable.

In a manufacturing environment, a given inventory item (subassembly, component part, or raw material) may be subject to dependent demand exclusively, or it may be subject to both dependent and independent demand. Such mixed demand arises in cases of parts used in current production as well as spare-part service. The independent portion of the total demand then has to be forecast and added to the (calculated) dependent demand. Service parts no longer used in current production are subject to independent demand exclusively, and this demand is properly forecast.

In manufacturing operations, the typical relationship between individual items that make up the inventory is as depicted in Figure 3. Material conversion stages create the relationship between raw material, semifinished part, component part, subassembly, and assembly, each of which carries a unique identity (part number) and as such represents an inventory item in its own right that must be planned and controlled. Demand for all these inventory items is being created *internally*, as a function of scheduling the next conversion stage to take place. In the example, (purchased) steel is made into a forging blank which, in turn, is machined into a gear which then becomes one of a number of components used in assembling the gear box, a major component of a transmission. The transmission will be required for the building of some end-product vehicle, which is also an assembly.

The demand for the end product, it should be noted, may have to be forecast. But none of the component items, including raw materials, need be forecast separately. When someone manufactures wagons, for instance, he may have to forecast how many he will sell, and when. Having done that, however, he need not forecast the wheels, because he knows that there are four wheels per wagon. This seems elementary, but the point is that the wagon wheels *can* be forecast independently, and the most sophisticated statistical techniques can be employed for this purpose. Some manufacturing companies do, in effect, just that. The results, of course, are bound to prove disappointing.

Stock replenishment systems are oblivious to the relationship between inventory items, and to their dependence on one another. Order point, in effect, looks at the demand-behavior of every inventory item as though it had a life of its own. That, however, is a totally false premise in a manufacturing environment.

Statistical forecasting, which order point depends on, addresses only the problem of individual item demand *magnitude,* but for purposes of manufacturing an added requirement is that component inventory represent matched sets. When components are forecast, and ordered, independently of each other, their inventories will tend not to match assembly requirements, and the cumulative service level will be significantly lower than the service levels of the parts taken individually. This is caused by the adding up of

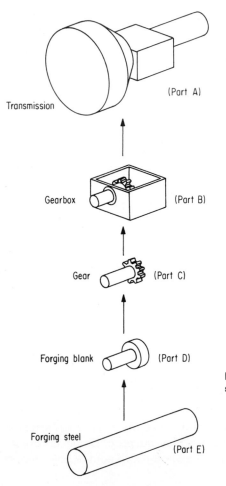

Transmission   (Part A)

Gearbox   (Part B)

Gear   (Part C)

Forging blank   (Part D)

Forging steel

(Part E)

FIGURE 3   Material conversion stages.

individual forecast errors of a group of components needed at one time in order to make an assembly.

If the probability of having one item in stock at a time of need is 90 percent, two related items needed simultaneously will have a combined probability of only 81 percent ($0.9 \times 0.9 = 0.81$). At ten such items, the odds against all of them being available have risen to 2:1 (34.8 percent probability). Even with the service level set at 95 percent, the probability of simultaneous availability for ten different component items is less than 60 percent, and at 14 items drops below 50 percent, as shown in Table 3. These combined probabilities make it evident that when an assembly is to be built from twenty or thirty different components (a proposition not unrealistic—it would hold roughly true for the gearbox in the previous example) ordered by an order point system, the *lack* of a shortage (and the lack of a need to expedite) would actually be a fluke. Note that these shortages are not caused by some unforeseen events, but are generated by the *system* itself.

"Lumpy" Demand

Another dimension of demand to be considered is its relative continuity and uniformity. Order point, as already mentioned, assumes more or less uniform usage, in small increments of the replenishment lot size. The underlying assumption of *gradual inventory depletion at a steady rate* will render the technique invalid when this basic premise is grossly unrealistic. In a manufacturing environment, where we deal with components of pro-

TABLE 3 Probabilities of Simultaneous Availability

Number of component items	Service level 90%	Service level 95%
1	0.900	0.950
2	0.810	0.902
3	0.729	0.857
4	0.656	0.814
5	0.590	0.774
6	0.531	0.735
7	0.478	0.698
8	0.430	0.663
9	0.387	0.630
10	0.348	0.599
11	0.313	0.569
12	0.282	0.540
13	0.254	0.513
14	0.228	0.488
15	0.206	0.463
20	0.121	0.358
25	0.071	0.260

ducts, requirements typically are anything but uniform, depletion anything but steady. Inventory depletion tends to occur in discrete "lumps," due to lot sizing for subsequent stages of manufacture.

The example in Figure 4 shows this clearly. Here the end item, its component, and the raw material are all on order point. These could be a simple wrench, the rough forging that it is made of, and the forging steel. Or they could be the transmission (if it were a shippable end product), the gearbox, and the gear from the previous example. Wrenches (or transmissions) are

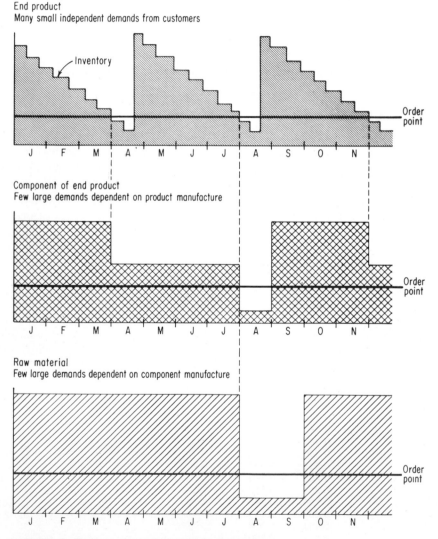

FIGURE 4   Order point and dependent demand.

not made in quantities of 1. When an order is placed on the factory to produce a quantity of the end item (perhaps to replenish its stock), it is necessary to withdraw a corresponding quantity of the component. This will deplete the inventory of the component in one sudden stroke, sometimes driving it below the order point. When it does (as at the end of July in the example), the system will immediately reorder, necessitating a large withdrawal of the raw material. If *its* order point is thereby "tripped," this material is also reordered.

In the example, demand for the inventory items component to the end product shows marked discontinuity. Their average inventory level is considerably higher than the conventional projection of one-half the replenishment lot size plus safety stock. The order point system reorders prematurely, way in advance of actual need, and therefore excess inventory is being carried for long periods of time when there is no actual need for it.

The phenomenon of discontinuous demand illustrates the problem of *timing of requirements*. Inventory management literature largely concerns itself with problems of quantity, while in the real world of manufacturing the question of timing, rather than quantity, is of paramount importance. Order point only implies timing, based as it is on average (past) usage. But average usage data are, for all practical purposes, largely meaningless in an environment of discontinuous, dependent demand.

The example in Figure 4 shows graphically that order point, which essentially assumes continuity of demand subject only to random fluctuation, consequently assumes also that it is desirable to have at least some inventory on hand *at all times*, and a need to replenish inventory *as soon as it is depleted*. When such inventory is subject to discontinuous demand, this is not only unnecessary but undesirable, because it causes inflation of the inventory level.

All three of the inventory items in the Figure 4 example are on order point, but that is not what causes discontinuity of component demand. It occurs even in the absence of order point, because it is caused, as previously mentioned, by lot sizing at the various stages of manufacture. Where a given component item is subject to dependent demand from multiple sources (a "common" component), the demand pattern is not only discontinuous but nonuniform; i.e., the size of the lumps tends to be irregular. This is illustrated in the next example (Figure 5).

Here no order points are involved, and short lead times allow production to be closely geared to demand, but not so closely as to equal it, period by period. Each item is being produced in a different lot quantity, selected for reasons of economy or convenience. In the example, item Z, a unit (pounds, or feet) of steel, is used to produce two different forgings, and each of these forgings, in turn, is used to produce two different finished products, simple wrenches.

In each of the simplified records of Figure 5, the letter D stands for demand, P for production. Each record extends six periods into the future. Because forgings will be needed every time a lot of one or the other of the various wrenches is to be produced, it is possible to construe the demand on the respective forgings by combining the wrench production lot quantities in the corresponding time periods. The forgings are produced in lot quantities of their own, and the demand for the common component material is derived in the same fashion. For simplicity's sake, the unit of measure for the steel is assumed to be equivalent to one forging.

Demand for the finished wrenches in the example is shown to be perfectly steady and level, which is hardly realistic but was chosen to highlight the fact that even with continuous and uniform demand for end products, demand for components will tend to be discontinuous and jagged. Lumpiness of demand is, of course, relative to the period chosen. By increasing the size of the period (from a week to a month, from a month to a quarter, etc.), demand measurements will show more continuity and uniformity. As a matter of fact, in our example even the demand for item Z, the steel, can be completely "stabilized" by increasing the size of the period fiftyfold. Thus if the period in the example represents one week, demand will turn out to be a perfectly uniform 850 units per each 50-week cycle.

Such stabilization, however, has been achieved with the proverbial "mirrors," and the information is not very useful, because the period spanned by the measurement is simply too large. It is the short-range lumpiness of demand that is significant, because manufacturing inventory, and production, must be planned and controlled from day to day and from week to week.

In the Figure 5 example, successive period-demands for item Z are 75-0-25-50-0-25. Note what may not be readily apparent, namely that the *average* demand for item Z equals 17 per period. One unit of steel is consumed in the production of each wrench, and in each period the total demand for the

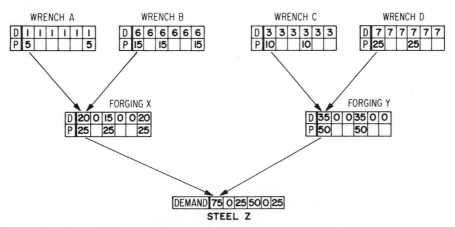

FIGURE 5 Causes of "lumpy" demand.

four wrenches is $1+6+3+7$. The wrenches can be easily forecast, but period-demand for steel does not lend itself to statistical forecasting at all.

The material requirements planning approach does not rely on a forecast of item demand and thus avoids the problems touched upon in the preceding discussion. Its techniques are expressly designed for dealing with dependent, discontinuous, nonuniform demand, which is characteristic for manufacturing environments. The principles on which material requirements planning systems are based are the subject of the next chapter.

REFERENCES

Orlicky, J. A.: "Requirements Planning Systems: Cinderella's Bright Prospects for the Future," Proceedings of the 13th International Conference of APICS, 1970.

Wight, O. W.: "To Order Point or Not to Order Point," *Production & Inventory Management*, vol. 9, no. 3, 1968.

PART TWO

CONCEPTS

The name of the game is timing—MRP's trump card.
R. D. GARWOOD *in* Hot List, *February 1974.*

CHAPTER TWO

PRINCIPLES OF
MATERIAL REQUIREMENTS
PLANNING

As mentioned at the beginning of the preceding chapter, the alternative choice to statistical inventory control is material requirements planning, an approach that recognizes the realities of demand existing in a manufacturing environment. This approach is eminently suitable for the management of inventories subject to dependent demand, as it does not rely on any assumptions regarding patterns of demand and inventory depletion. The material requirements planning approach does, however, assume certain characteristics of the product and of the process used in its manufacture. These and other assumptions, prerequisites, and principles that a material requirements planning system employs are reviewed in the present chapter.

TIME PHASING

Time phasing means adding the dimension of time to inventory status data, by recording and storing the information on either specific dates or planning periods with which the respective quantities are associated. In the older era of inventory control, status of a given item was normally shown, in the system's records, as consisting of only the quantity on hand and the quantity on order. When physical disbursements of the item reduced the sum of these two quantities to some predetermined minimum or reorder point, it was time to place a replenishment order.

This approach was refined around 1950, with the introduction of the *perpetual inventory control* concept. The principal idea behind this concept was to maintain somewhat expanded status information "perpetually" up to date by posting inventory transactions as they took place. This innovation was largely made feasible by the availability of better office equipment, particularly Kardex and punched-card data-processing installations, which streamlined the clerical tasks of posting and calculation.

Inventory status information was expanded by adding data on requirements (demand) and "availability" (the difference between the quantity required and the sum of the on-hand and on-order quantities). The classic inventory status equation was formulated and publicized, as follows:

$$A + B - C = X$$

where $A =$ quantity on hand

$B =$ quantity on order

$C =$ quantity required

$X =$ quantity available (for future requirements)

Thus the status of an inventory item might appear like this:

On hand:	30	or	30
On order:	50		25
Required:	65		65
Available:	15		−10

The quantity required would be derived from customer orders, or a forecast, or a calculation of dependent demand. The quantity available had to be calculated. Negative availability signified lack of coverage and a need to place a new order. The inventory system now could better answer the questions of *what* and *how much*. What remained unanswered under this then advanced approach was the crucial question of *when*. *When* is the quantity on order due to come in, and is it a single order or are there more than one? *When* will the demand actually have to be satisfied, and will it be at one time, or is the requirement a summary figure concealing several demands spaced in time? *When* will the stock run out? *When* should the replenishment order be completed? *When* should it be released? The system was unable to answer these questions, and the inventory planner had to depend on his own estimates and guesses, on rules of thumb, or on physical manifestations of need ("we can ship only thirty against this order for sixty-five").

Time phasing means capturing or developing the information on timing, so as to provide answers to all the foregoing questions. The price of time phasing is the added cost of processing and storage of the time-phased data. The value of the additional information thus made available, however, normally more than offsets the price paid for it. For instance, if the data in the preceding example were time-phased, the status of the item, by week, might appear as follows:

On hand: 30										
Open orders due:	0	0	0	0	25					
Quantities required:	0	20	0	35	0	0	0	0	0	10
Available:	30	10	10	−25	0	0	0	0	0	−10

Answers are now provided to every single *when* question raised previously. There is one open order for 25, due to be received in the fifth week. There are three separate demands for quantities of 20, 35, and 10, which will occur in the second, fourth, and tenth weeks, respectively. The replenishment order need not be completed until the tenth week. This determines the (latest) release date for that order, based on the item's lead time. Time phasing, in this case, yields additional valuable information. In the fourth week the availability is negative, which indicates that while *total* coverage is adequate for the first nine weeks, the timing *within* the nine-week span is out of phase. The inventory planner sees exactly what specific action is called for if a "stockout," or shortage, is to be prevented, and he sees it (in this case) four weeks in *advance*. The open order should be rescheduled to be completed one week earlier.

The difference between a time-phased and a non-time-phased inventory control system, in terms of usefulness and effectiveness, is considerable. The difference in data handling, data manipulation, and data storage requirements is also considerable, as can be seen in the preceding two examples. In the first one, inventory status is expressed through four data elements. In the second example, twenty-six data elements are used.

The data-processing burden in *maintaining* time-phased status data up to date is substantial. This is not only because there are so many more data elements involved, but also due to the fact that with non-time-phased data, only changes in the *quantities* need to be processed, whereas time-phased status information has to reflect changes in both quantity and *timing* (i.e., changes in the timing even when the quantities remain unaffected). Time-phased material requirements planning systems represent a classic computer application in the sense that here the computer is being used to do something heretofore literally impossible—handling and manipulating vast quantities of data at high speed. In a fairly typical situation where status information for 25,000 inventory items is time-phased, by week, over a one-year span, some 5 million data elements may be involved.

INVENTORY SYSTEM CATEGORIES

Material requirements planning (time phasing is implied by the term) evolved from an approach to inventory management in which the following two principles are combined:

1. Calculation (versus forecast) of component item demand
2. Time phasing, i.e., segmenting inventory status data by time

The term *component item* in material requirements planning covers all inventory items other than products or end items. Requirements for end items are stated in the master production schedule, and they are derived from forecasts, customer orders, field warehouse requirements, interplant orders, etc. Requirements for all component items (including raw material), and their timing, are derived from this schedule by the MRP system.

Material requirements planning comprises a set of techniques eminently suitable for the management of inventories subject to dependent demand, and it represents a highly effective inventory control system for manufacturing environments, where the bulk of the inventory is subject to this type of demand. It should be noted that while an MRP system is primarily oriented toward dependent-demand inventory, it also easily accommodates independent-demand items, such as service parts. These can be integrated into the system through the so-called *time-phased order point* technique briefly discussed below, and more fully described in Chapter 4. There are, as previously mentioned, some inventory items that are subject to both dependent and independent demand, such as service parts still used in current production. In an MRP system the service-part demand, which is forecast, is simply added to the dependent demand that has been calculated. The MRP system takes it from there.

With reference to the two above-mentioned principles, demand calculation and time phasing, any manufacturing inventory control system can be assigned to one of four categories based on combinations of these principles. This is illustrated in Figure 6, which shows, in matrix form, the four system categories:

		Component Demand	
		Forecast	Calculated
Maintenance of Status Data	Quantity only	STATISTICAL ORDER POINT	LOT REQUIREMENTS PLANNING
	Quantity and Timing	TIME-PHASED ORDER POINT	MATERIAL REQUIREMENTS PLANNING

FIGURE 6   Inventory system categories.

1. Statistical order point
2. Lot requirements planning
3. Time-phased order point
4. Material requirements planning

Statistical order point, the conventional approach in the past, has already been discussed at some length. It uses forecasting to determine demand and generally ignores the aspect of specific timing. In light of what is possible today thanks to computer technology, this type of system must be considered obsolete for purposes of manufacturing inventory management.

Lot requirements planning was developed and used, by some manufacturing companies, toward the end of the era of punched-card data processing, generally the 1950s and early 1960s. Some companies still use this approach, in which component-item demand is derived from a master production schedule and is correctly calculated as to quantity *per lot* of product or end item, but in which specific timing is disregarded. Requirement and order data are summarized by (product) lot, and it is the position of the lot in the master schedule which implies timing. Specific timing of order releases, due dates, and production schedules is then established—if it is established—through procedures external to the inventory system.

A variation of the lot requirements planning approach is the so-called *single-period requirements planning* system. All product lots scheduled for a given period, usually a month, are combined, in effect, into a superlot which is then treated as an individual lot would be in lot requirements planning. The principal output of systems of this type is an item-by-item listing (by lot or by period) or order action required, without an indication of exactly *when* action is to be taken on each of the items.

Methods of planning by product lot had been in use at a time when the job of detailed time phasing was too big for a punched-card installation, in the sense that millions of card equivalents would have had to be processed (sorted, collated, summary-punched, etc.) at relatively slow card-handling speeds. It would have taken days or weeks to complete the job. Lot requirements planning systems, at one time representing a significant advancement in inventory control state of the art, and superior to the statistical order point approach, became obsolescent when the computer was introduced. At that point, time phasing of inventory status data became feasible and practical.

Time-phased order point is a modern technique of planning and controlling inventory items subject to independent demand. It is eminently suitable for service parts, finished products in factory stock, and field warehouse items. The system processing logic is identical to material requirements planning (see Chapter 4) except for the manner in which item demand is arrived at. Requirements for independent-demand items are forecast (using any forecasting technique the user selects), because they *cannot* be calculated. Any service part that is manufactured has, however, at least one component item (e.g., raw material) which is then treated the same as any other item in an MRP system.

Material requirements planning calculates item demand and time-phases all inventory status data in time increments as fine as the user has specified. Material requirements planning represents the ultimate approach to manufacturing inventory management. Concepts of material requirements planning, the processing logic of an MRP system, and related techniques will be discussed in the balance of this chapter, and in the chapters that follow.

PREREQUISITES AND ASSUMPTIONS OF MATERIAL REQUIREMENTS PLANNING

Unlike the goddess Athena, material requirements planning did not spring into being in full splendor and fully armed. In some rudimentary form, it has no doubt existed as long as manufacturing. It has been evolving gradually, moving onto successively higher plateaus with every enhancement in data-processing capability. Material requirements planning had its origin "on the firing line" of a plant. It has been painstakingly developed into its present stage of relative perfection by practicing inventory managers and inventory planners.

It never made sense to the practitioner to stock thousand-dollar castings, for instance, and to reorder them in economic lot quantities, when he could determine exactly how many of each casting would be required, and when, by consulting the master production schedule. Such expensive manufacturing inventory items have, in most cases, always been treated the way an MRP system treats items under its control. Specific demand for these items has been calculated rather than forecast; existing surplus, if any, has been taken into account to determine net demand; the (usually long) lead time has served to determine order release; the items have been ordered discretely; and detailed status records have been kept. In a sense, the evolution of MRP systems is equivalent to expanding the strict and careful treatment of high-cost, long-lead-time items to items of successively lower cost and shorter lead time (as data-processing capability permitted) until all items have been covered.

Present-day MRP systems, constructed and used in what has become the standard form, imply several prerequisites and reflect certain fundamental assumptions on which these systems are based. The first prerequisite is the *existence of a master production schedule*, i.e., an authoritative statement of how many end items are to be produced and when. An MRP system presupposes that the master production schedule can, in its entirety, be stated *in bill of material terms,* i.e., bill of material (assembly) numbers. The only language an MRP system understands is "part numbers," i.e., inventory item numbers that uniquely identify specific materials, component parts, subassemblies, and end items. An MRP system cannot work with English-language product descriptions, with sales-catalog model numbers, or with bill of material numbers that are ambiguous in the sense that they fail to identify a precise configuration of components for a given assembly. The ability to state a valid and complete master production schedule in bill of material terms is a function of so-called *bill of material structure,* further discussed in Chapter 10.

Another prerequisite is that each inventory item be *unambiguously identified* through a unique code (part number). This requirement extends also to the identification of every manufactured item's component material (what is the item made of?) and to each item's disposition (where used, i.e., what is the item a component of?).

Thus the *existence, at planning time, of a bill of material* containing such information is also prerequisite. The bill of material must not merely list all the components of a given product, but must be so structured as to reflect the way the product is actually made, in steps from raw material to component part to subassembly to assembly to end item.

Another prerequisite to material requirements planning is the *availability of inventory records* for all items under the system's control containing inventory status data and so-called planning factors, as discussed in the next two chapters.

An assumption, or rather precondition for the system's effective operation, is *file data integrity* pertaining to inventory status data and to bill of material data. This is not a system assumption—an MRP system can function with faulty data and still generate outputs that are technically correct *relative* to the data supplied to the system—but an operational assumption. File data must be accurate, complete, and up to date, if the MRP system is to prove successful or even useful. The requirement of file data integrity may seem self-evident, but there are two points to be made in this connection.

First, the fact is that typically the two files in question are chronically in poor shape under any system preceding the installation of material requirements planning. And, second, under a stock replenishment, order point system, it does not overly matter that inventory records are unreliable and that bills of material are inaccurate, incomplete, or out of date. Order point acts merely as an order-launching system (a "push" system), and it must be complemented by an expediting ("pull") system, in order to function at all.

Under an order point system, the bill of material is not even referenced, and the quality of its data is therefore irrelevant for purposes of inventory planning. The *formal* push system uses the inventory status data which may be (and usually are) faulty, but this is compensated for by the *informal* pull system that does not rely on the inventory records at all, but determines specific need for inventory items, and the timing of this need, *physically,* in the stockroom or on the assembly line. It is the expediting action that the whole procurement and manufacturing operation then really depends on.

In contrast, under an MRP system, which provides both the push and pull functions in the formal system, there is no need for the informal system of shortage-list expediting, but this benefit will not be realized if the quantities and timing of orders are incorrect due to lack of file data integrity. This integrity is vital to the MRP system, and the meticulous maintenance of the files involved calls for a special effort on the part of the system user—a novel requirement and cost.

An MRP system presupposes that *lead times for all inventory items are known* and can be supplied to the system, at least as estimates. The lead time used for planning purposes normally must have a fixed value (see Chapter 3 for an exception to this rule). This value can be changed at any time, but more than one value cannot be in simultaneous existence. An MRP system cannot handle indeterminate item lead times.

An MRP system assumes that every inventory item under its control goes *into and out of stock,* i.e., that there will be reportable receipts, following which the item will be (even if only momentarily) in an "on-hand" state and will eventually be disbursed to support an order for an item into which it is dispositioned. This assumption means, in essence, that the progression of the manufacturing process from one stage to the next will be monitored, usually (but not necessarily) by means of a stockroom through which the items pass physically.

In determining the timing of item gross requirements, the (standard) material requirements planning procedure assumes that *all components of an assembly* must be available at the time an order for that assembly is to be released to the factory. Thus the basic assumption is that unit assembly lead time (the time required to produce one unit of the assembly) is short and that the several components are consumed, for all practical purposes, simultaneously. As far as subassemblies are concerned, this assumption almost always holds true. In cases of significant exceptions to this rule (e.g., where it may take several weeks to assemble a unit and expensive components are consumed successively over this period) the regular requirements-computation procedure would have to be modified.

Another assumption under material requirements planning is *discrete disbursement and usage* of component materials. For instance, if fifty units of a component item are required for a given (fabrication or subassembly) order, the material requirements planning logic expects that exactly fifty units can be disbursed and that fifty units will be consumed. Materials that come in continuous form (rolls of sheet metal, coils of wire, etc.) do not meet this expectation cleanly and therefore require that standard planning procedures be modified and the system adapted to handle such inventory items properly.

An assumption implied under material requirements planning is *process independence*. This means that a manufacturing order for any given inventory item can be started and completed on its own and not be contingent on the existence, or progress, of some other order for purposes of completing the process. Thus, so-called "mating part" relationships (item A, at operation 30, must meet item B at operation 50, for the machining of a common surface) and setup dependencies (order for item Y should be set up only when a setup for item X precedes it) do not fit the scheme of things under material requirements planning. This does not mean that material requirements planning is inapplicable, only that it is inapplicable in its standard form. Here the system would have to be adapted to the process environment, again by means of modification and special procedures.

To recap, the principal prerequisites and assumptions implied by a standard MRP system are as follows:

- A master production schedule exists and can be stated in bill of material terms.
- All inventory items are uniquely identified.
- A bill of material exists at planning time.
- Inventory records containing data on the status of every item are available.
- Integrity of file data.
- Individual item lead times are known.
- Every inventory item goes into and out of stock.
- All of the components of an assembly are needed at the time of the assembly order release.
- Discrete disbursement and usage of component materials.
- Process independence of manufactured items.

APPLICABILITY OF MATERIAL REQUIREMENTS PLANNING METHODS

The preceding discussion of prerequisites and assumptions raises the question of material requirements planning applicability to a given type of manufacturing business. Actually, all the prerequisites and assumptions listed, as such, do not represent good criteria of applicability because, even where some of the required conditions do not exist, management can generally create them in order to be able to use material requirements planning methods. Inventory items *can* be uniquely identified, a bill of material *can* be created, integrity of file data *can* be maintained, and so forth. Whether most of the preconditions for material requirements planning do or do not exist in a given case is usually a matter of management practice rather than an attribute of the type of business in question.

It is clear that the application of material requirements planning methods is generally limited to discrete (as against continuous-process) manufacturing. In the past, it was thought that the use of these methods is warranted only in manufacturing operations involving relatively complex assembled products, but developments have disproved that. Companies that manufacture some very simple products, including one-piece products, can (and now do) use MRP systems.

It is true that the first companies to develop and use MRP systems were manufacturers of highly engineered assembled products in the metalworking industries, typically operating machine shops (job shops) in which large numbers of orders were simultaneously in process. This type of environment represents the most severe inventory management and production planning problems, and it was to alleviate these problems that the companies in question reached for material requirements planning methods as soon as it became feasible (with computers) actually to implement them.

Since the pioneer days of material requirements planning, companies in so many diverse manufacturing businesses (including cable and wire, furniture, and packaged spices) have adopted this approach that applicability criteria have been obscured. What is common to all these companies (or plants), and what, in the author's view, represents the principal criterion of material requirements planning applicability, is the *existence of a master production schedule* (not to be confused with a final assembly schedule) to which raw material procurement, fabrication, and subassembly activities are geared.

The master production schedule (more fully discussed in Chapter 11) governs *component* production activities. The final assembly schedule responds to external (customer, field warehouse, etc.) demand for *end products*, is usually stated in different terms (product models, configurations, etc.), involves a shorter lead time, and is made up later in time. In responding to the demand for end products, the final assembly schedule is constrained by the availability of components provided by the master production schedule. In some types of business the two schedules may be identical (such as in cases of small simple products, or products engineered and manufactured to order), but that is a coincidence caused by the nature of the product in question.

Material requirements planning is therefore applicable to manufacturing environments that are oriented toward fabrication (the term here also covers subassembly where subassembly applies) of components. Final assembly operations are normally outside the scope of the MRP system, as we know it in its present standard form. Material requirements planning can be said to be primarily a *component fabrication planning system.* An MRP system can be used by any plant that has, or *can* have, a master production schedule.

The preceding discussion dealt with applicability by type of business. The criterion of applicability by type of inventory item (in a plant using an MRP system) is simple and straightforward: Material requirements planning is applicable to any discrete item, purchased or manufactured, that is subject to dependent demand. Other attributes of the item, such as cost, volume of usage, or continuity of demand, are irrelevant to material requirements planning applicability. Low-cost, high-volume parts do not seem to deserve elaborate treatment, and it is a natural tendency for the first-time MRP system user to exclude such items from his new system. Experience has shown, however, that after several months of operation under material requirements planning, even the lowest-cost, highest-volume items are typically incorporated into the system.

The basic reason for this is simply that it becomes evident that better results can be had under the material requirements planning treatment. The user, at this point, normally has also overcome his initial emotional reaction to the elaborateness of material requirements planning procedures (which, after all, are being performed by a machine with no apparent difficulty or loss of time), and the cost argument is seen for what it is—the expense of processing some additional items by an existing MRP system is trivial.

REFERENCES

Everdell, Romeyn: "Time Phasing: The Most Potent Tool Yet for Slashing Inventories!" *Modern Materials Handling,* November 1968.
Wight, O. W.: "Time Phasing," *Modern Materials Handling,* October 1971.

CHAPTER THREE

THE MATERIAL REQUIREMENTS PLANNING SYSTEM

The absence of an order point approach does not an MRP system make. The term *material requirements planning* implies certain definite system attributes such as time-phased inventory status data, the computation of net requirements, a maximum length of a planning period, a minimum planning horizon span relative to lead time, and the development of so-called planned orders.

The reader should understand that there are genuine MRP systems and pseudo-MRP systems in industry use. There are companies (or rather, plants) that do *some form of* material requirements planning without having a full-blown, or "real" MRP system. This subject is discussed in Chapter 8. In the current chapter, we are concerned with genuine MRP systems in one or the other of their standard forms.

There are a limited number of alternative MRP system approaches (reviewed in Chapter 7) but a variety of specific techniques and special procedural features tailored to meet unusual requirements of a given system user. In the discussion that follows, the author will attempt to isolate concepts and characteristics of (genuine) MRP systems that are common to such systems regardless of approach or specific technique used.

OBJECTIVES OF THE SYSTEM

All MRP systems have a common objective, which is to determine (gross and net) *requirements,* i.e., discrete period-demands for each item of inventory, so as to be able to generate information needed for correct inventory order action. This action pertains to procurement (purchase orders) and to production (shop orders). It is either *new* action or a revision of *previous* action. New action consists in the placing (release) of an order for a quantity of an item, due on some future date. The essential data elements accompanying this action are:

- Item identity (part number)
- Order quantity
- Date of order release
- Date of order completion (due date)

Order action relative to purchased items takes place in two steps: a requisition placed on Purchasing by Inventory Control, and a subsequent order placed on a vendor selected by Purchasing. The types of order action that effect a revision of action taken previously are limited to the following:

- Increase in order quantity
- Decrease in order quantity
- Order cancellation
- Advancement of order due date
- Deferment of order due date
- Order suspension (indefinite deferment)

To generate information for correct order action is not the only objective of an MRP system, which also serves other functions (discussed in Chapter 7), but it is the primary one. It is not much different from the objective of other (non-MRP) inventory systems in *intent.* The difference lies in the respective systems' ability to *realize* this intent. Order point systems, in particular, have difficulty in ordering the right quantity of an item (see previous discussion of the EOQ) at the right time (see Figure 4 in Chapter 1), and their ability to order with a valid order due date is even more questionable. As to the ability of such systems to revise previous order action, they have virtually none.

MRP systems meet their objective by computing *net requirements* for each inventory item, time-phasing them, and determining their proper *coverage.* The basic function of material requirements planning is the conversion of gross requirements into net requirements, so that the latter may be covered by (correctly timed) shop orders and purchase orders.

The "netting" process consists of a calculation of gross requirements and of allocating existing inventories (quantities on hand and on order) against these gross requirements. For example:

Gross requirements:		120
On hand:	25	
On order:	50	75
Net requirements:		45

If safety stock is planned for the item in question—this is not usual under material requirements planning, but the system presents no obstacle—the net requirements would be increased by the quantity of the safety stock, as follows:

Gross requirements:		120
On hand:	25	
On order:	50	
	75	
Safety stock:	−20	55
Net requirements:		65

In an MRP system, the net requirement quantities are always related to time, i.e., to some date or period. The net requirements are then covered by *planned orders,* and the order quantities either match net requirements or are calculated by employing one of several lot-sizing techniques designed to take into account the economics of ordering. The timing of planned-order releases is also determined by the MRP system, and the information is stored (or merely printed out) for purposes of future order action.

The function of providing coverage of net requirements is served only in part through *planned* (i.e., future) orders. The MRP system also reevaluates the timing of *open* orders relative to (possibly changed) net requirements in the near future, and it signals the need for rescheduling these orders, forward or backward in time, as required, in order to realign coverage with net requirements.

THE PURPOSE OF THE SYSTEM

A material requirements planning system is *capacity-insensitive* in that it will call for the production of items for which capacity may not, in fact, exist. This might appear to be a shortcoming of material requirements planning but, on a moment's reflection, it can be seen that this is not so. A system can be designed to answer either the question of what *can* be produced with a given capacity (i.e., what the master production schedule should be) or the question of what *need* be produced (i.e., what capacity is required) to meet a given master production schedule, but not both. An MRP system is designed to answer the latter question.

It assumes that capacity considerations have entered into the makeup of the master production schedule. An MRP system "believes" the master production schedule, and the validity of its outputs is always *relative to the contents of that schedule.* Another way of stating this is to say that the master production schedule can be invalid (vis-à-vis available capacity) but the outputs of an MRP system (assuming valid file data and correct procedures) cannot.

The output of an MRP system is not necessarily always realistic in terms of lead time, capacity, and availability of materials, particularly when the system plans requirements for an unrealistic master production schedule. It is then merely saying: "This is what you would have to be able to do in order to implement the schedule." Why the schedule is unrealistic is thus revealed, in specific terms.

In any manufacturing operation, the questions of what materials and components are needed, in what quantities, and when — and the answers to these questions — are vital. An MRP system is designed to provide just these answers.

MRP systems are a highly effective tool of manufacturing inventory management for the following reasons:

- Inventory investment can be held to a minimum.
- An MRP system is change-sensitive, reactive.
- The system provides a look into the future, on an item-by-item basis.
- Under material requirements planning, inventory control is action-oriented rather than clerical bookkeeping–oriented.
- Order quantities are related to requirements.
- The *timing* of requirements, coverage, and order actions is emphasized.

Because of its focus on timing, an MRP system (and only an MRP system) can generate outputs that serve as valid inputs to other systems in the area of manufacturing logistics, such as purchasing systems, shop scheduling systems, dispatching systems, shop floor control systems, and capacity requirements planning systems. A sound MRP system constitutes a solid basis, a gateway, for other computer applications in production and inventory control.

The position of an inventory planning system, relative to other manufacturing logistics functions or systems, is shown in Figure 7. The relationships depicted in this chart exist in any manufacturing company or plant. A manufacturing operation, in essence, consists of the procurement of materials and the conversion of these materials into a shippable product. The principal outputs of the inventory system, whatever this system may be, are purchase requisitions and shop orders, each one of these calling for a specific quantity of some inventory item. Any procurement or manufacturing activity takes place only *after* the inventory system has generated a call for the item. The inventory system triggers all such activities. In terms of information flow, it is the *upstream* system.

Any and all systems along the two streams (procurement and manufacturing) of inventory system output are designed merely to execute the plan that is represented by this output. These *downstream* systems cannot com-

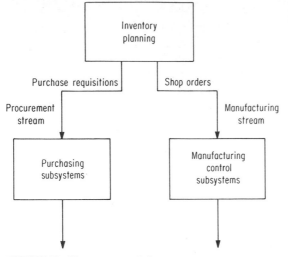

FIGURE 7   Upstream and downstream systems.

pensate for, or improve, the possibly low quality (validity, accuracy, completeness, timeliness) of the information they receive as input. Regardless of how well implemented the downstream systems themselves may be, their real effectiveness still depends on the quality of the inputs they process. "Pollution" of the information originating upstream, in the inventory system, permeates all downstream functions and activities. It therefore follows that within the framework of the overall logistics system, the role of the inventory subsystem is of first importance.

When the function labeled "inventory planning" in Figure 7 is exercised by a material requirements planning system, a reliable quarterback is directing the plays. An MRP system has the ability to generate calls for the right items in the right quantities at the right time, with the right date of need for every order. The system issues its action calls according to a detailed, time-phased plan that it develops. It maintains this plan constantly up to date by reevaluating and revising it in light of ongoing changes in the environment. It also continuously monitors the validity of all open-order due dates relative to such changes. With an MRP system making the calls, the execution systems downstream *can* function effectively. Without it they cannot.

SYSTEM INPUTS AND OUTPUTS

A material requirements planning system, properly designed and used, can provide a number of desirable outputs containing valid and timely information. The primary outputs of an MRP system are the following:

- Order-release notices, calling for the placement of planned orders
- Rescheduling notices, calling for changes in open-order due dates

■ Cancellation notices, calling for cancellation or suspension of open orders
■ Item status analysis backup data
■ Planned orders scheduled for release in the future

Secondary or byproduct outputs come in a great variety and are being generated by the MRP system at the user's option. These outputs, further discussed in Chapter 7, include:

■ Exception notices reporting errors, incongruities, and out-of-bounds situations
■ Inventory-level projections (inventory forecasts)
■ Purchase commitment reports
■ Traces to demand sources (so-called pegged requirements reports)
■ Performance reports

All MRP system outputs are produced by processing inputs (relating data) from the following sources, illustrated in Figure 8:

1. The master production schedule
2. Orders for components originating from sources external to the plant using the system
3. Forecasts for items subject to independent demand
4. The inventory record (item master) file
5. The bill of material (product-structure) file

The master production schedule expresses the overall plan of production. It is stated in terms of end items, which may be either (shippable) products or highest-level assemblies from which these products are eventually built in various configurations, according to a final assembly schedule. The span of time the master production schedule covers, termed the *planning horizon,* is related to the cumulative procurement and manufacturing lead time for components of the products in question. The planning horizon normally equals or exceeds this cumulative lead time.

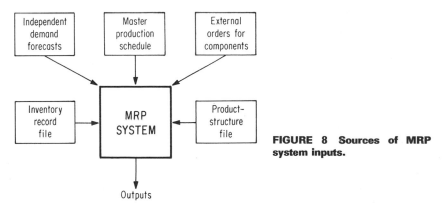

FIGURE 8   Sources of MRP system inputs.

The master production schedule serves as the main input to an MRP system, in the sense that the essential purpose of this system is to translate the schedule into individual component requirements, and other inputs merely supply reference data that are required to achieve this end. In concept, the master production schedule defines the entire manufacturing program of a plant and therefore contains not only the products the plant will produce, but also *orders* for components that originate from sources external to the plant, as well as *forecasts* for items subject to independent demand. In practice, however, such orders and forecasts are normally not incorporated into the master production schedule document, but are fed directly to the MRP system as separate inputs.

Externally originating orders for components include service-part orders, interplant orders, original equipment manufacturer (OEM) orders by other manufacturers who use these components in *their* products, and any other special-purpose orders not related to the regular production plan. Components may be ordered for purposes of experimentation, destructive testing, promotion, equipment maintenance, etc. The MRP system treats orders of this category as additions to the gross requirements for the respective component items. Beyond this, regular material requirements planning treatment applies.

Forecasts of independent demand for component items subject to this type of demand can be made outside of the MRP system, or the system can be programmed to perform this function, by means of applying some statistical forecasting technique. The forecast quantities are treated as item gross requirements by the MRP system. Items subject only to independent demand (such as service parts no longer used in regular production) should be under "time-phased order point" control (described in Chapter 4). Items subject to both dependent and independent demand have the forecast quantities simply added to the (computed) gross requirements. Note that service-part demand is either forecast, or *recorded* upon receipt of orders (placed by a service-part organization operating its own system), but as a rule not both.

The inventory record file, also called *item master file,* comprises the individual item inventory records containing the status data required for the determination of net requirements. This file is kept up to date by the posting of *inventory transactions* which reflect the various inventory events taking place. Each transaction (stock receipt, disbursement, scrap, etc.) changes the status of the respective inventory item. The reporting of transactions therefore constitutes an indirect input to the MRP system. Transactions update item status, which is then consulted and modified in the course of computing requirements.

In addition to status data, the inventory records also contain so-called *planning factors* used principally for the determination of the size and timing of planned orders. Planning factors include item lead time, safety stock (if any), scrap allowances, lot-sizing algorithms, etc. Planning-factor values are subject to change at the system user's discretion. A change in one or more planning factors normally changes inventory status.

   The bill of material file, also known as the product-structure file, contains information on the relationships of components and assemblies, which are essential to the correct development of gross and net requirements. The bill of material plays a passive role in the requirements computation process. In this process, the function of the bill of material is akin to that of a city directory which the MRP program consults when it needs to "visit" the inventory records of the components of an assembly. All assembled items carry the storage addresses (called *pointers*) of the respective bills of material in their inventory records. The inventory file and the bill of material file are thus cross-referenced or *chained* for purposes of requirements computation. More information on chained files will be found in Chapter 9.
   All the inputs reviewed above enter into the material requirements planning process, the principal purpose of which is to establish (reestablish) correct inventory status of each item under its control. The factors involved in establishing this status are the following:

1. Requirements
2. Coverage of requirements
3. Product structure
4. Planning factors

What sets the material requirements planning process in motion varies, depending on system implementation and system use. With so-called *regenerative* MRP systems which employ batch-processing techniques, the replanning process is carried out periodically, typically in one-week intervals. Here passage of time triggers the process. With so-called *net change* MRP systems, it is the inventory events (transactions) that cause replanning to take place, more or less continuously. (Regenerative and net change MRP systems are discussed in Chapter 5).
   Changes in requirements, coverage, product structure (engineering changes), or planning factors affect inventory status and must therefore be reflected in the replanning. Regenerative MRP systems, in effect, take a "snapshot" of these factors *as they are* at the time of each periodic requirements computation, on the assumption that any and all changes have been incorporated during the preceding interval. These systems deal periodically with situations that are static at the time. Net change MRP systems, on the other hand, must continuously deal with a dynamic, or fluid, situation. This requires that changes in any of the four factors mentioned be reported to the system as they occur.

FACTORS AFFECTING THE COMPUTATION OF REQUIREMENTS

The computation of requirements is complicated by six factors:

1. The structure of the product, containing several manufacturing *levels* of materials, component parts, and subassemblies

2. *Lot sizing,* i.e., the ordering of inventory items in quantities exceeding net requirements, for reasons of economy or convenience

3. The different *individual lead times* of inventory items that make up the product

4. The timing of end-item requirements (expressed via the master production schedule) across a *planning horizon* of, typically, a year's span or longer, and the recurrence of these requirements within such a time span

5. Multiple requirements for an inventory item due to its so-called *commonality,* i.e., usage in the manufacture of a number of other items

6. Multiple requirements for an inventory item due to its *recurrence* on several levels of a given end item

Product Structure

Product structure imposes the principal constraint on the computation of requirements. This computation, while arithmetically very simple, requires that a rather involved procedure be followed. This is caused by the fact that a given component item can exist in its own right as a uniquely identified physical entity (a unit of raw material, a component part, a subassembly), and it can also exist physically, but as an already-assembled component (or "consumed" material) of another inventory item, in which case it has lost its individual identity. For example, gear C in Figure 3 (Chapter 1) can exist as such, and would be so carried on the inventory record, and it can also exist as part of the (already-assembled) gearbox B or transmission A, without an identity of its own. For purposes of determining net requirements, the physically existing quantities of the item must, in effect, be accounted for irrespective of identity.

Such accounting will be the more laborious the more *levels* of the product are involved. Product "depth" is therefore a factor in the scope and duration of the material requirements planning data-processing job. The concept of product level (or manufacturing level) is related to the way the product is structured, i.e., manufactured. Each stage in the manufacturing process of converting material into product is equivalent to a level of product structure.

The engineering document that defines the product is the *bill of material,* which lists components of each assembly and subassembly. Its conventional graphic representation is shown in Figure 9. The assembly in question is termed the *parent item,* and its *component items* are listed by identity

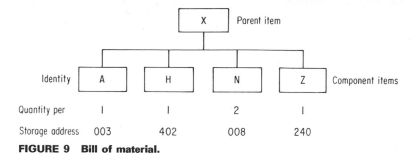

FIGURE 9   Bill of material.

code (part number), with quantity per (one unit of) parent item and storage
address of the respective inventory item record. The term *bill of material*
is used interchangeably for a single-item bill (such as shown in Figure 9).
for all such bills, collectively, pertaining to a given product, and for the entire bill of material file. (Bills of material will be further discussed in Chapter
10.)

When the individual bills defining a product are linked together graphically, as in Figure 10, they form a hierarchical, pyramidlike structure, and
the levels emerge into view. By convention, in the United States the levels
are numbered from top to bottom, beginning with level 0 (sometimes 1)
for the end product. The structure may be likened to a Christmas tree, and
vertical lines of progression (such as X-A-B-C-D-E in Figure 11) are called
branches. In cases of complex products, bills for the products themselves
are usually not maintained and the file contains only bills for major assemblies. The items on the highest level in a product-structure file are termed
end items.

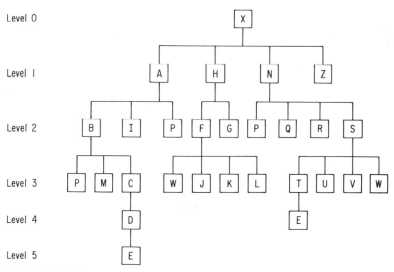

FIGURE 10   Hierarchy of bills of material.

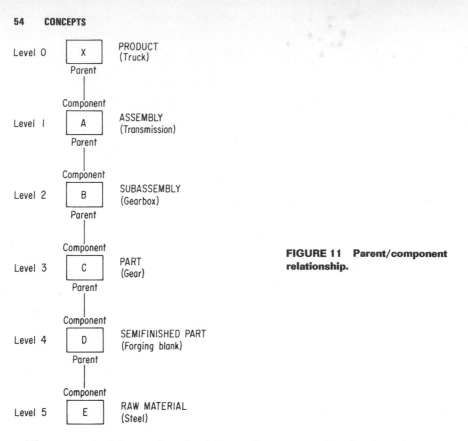

FIGURE 11   Parent/component relationship.

The concept of the product level is usually associated with relatively complex, assembled products, which contain many (typically six to ten) levels. But any manufactured product, no matter how simple, involves at least two, and probably more, levels. A one-piece wrench has at least three levels, i.e., steel, forging blank, and finished wrench. A nuts-and-bolts manufacturer purchases steel rod (one level) which he draws into wire (another level) from which a screw (a third level) is formed. Even the simplest products assembled from manufactured components have *at least* three, and most likely more, levels.

In determining net requirements for a low-level (note that the lowest level carries the highest number) inventory item, the quantity that exists under its own identity, as well as any quantities existing as (consumed) components of parent items, parents of parent items, etc., must be accounted for. The basic logic of "netting" requirements is best demonstrated through an example. Let us assume that 100 trucks X are to be produced and that the following are in inventory (on hand and on order):

Transmission A:	2
Gearbox B:	15
Gear C:	7
Forging blank D:	46

The task is to determine net requirements for these items. When first confronted with this type of problem, most people will apply the following logic:

Item A: $100 - 2 = 98$
Item B: $100 - 15 = 85$
Item C: $100 - 7 = 93$
Item D: $100 - 46 = 54$

This, however, is incorrect. The true net requirement for item D, for instance, is not 54 but 30, and the correct netting logic that leads to it is as follows:

Quantity of trucks to be produced:	100
Transmissions required (gross):	100
Transmissions in inventory:	2
Net requirements, transmission A:	98
Gearboxes required for 98 transmissions (gross):	98
Gearboxes in inventory:	15
Net requirements, gearbox B:	83
Gears required for 83 gearboxes (gross):	83
Gears in inventory:	7
Net requirements, gear C:	76
Forgings required for 76 gears (gross):	76
Forgings in inventory:	46
Net requirements, forging D:	30

The net requirement quantity for item D can be verified as follows:

Quantity of trucks to be produced: 100
Quantity of item D that will be consumed: 100

Inventory of D:	46	
Inventory of C containing D:	7	
Inventory of B containing C:	15	
Inventory of A containing B:	2	
	70	
Net requirements for item D:	30	
Totals:	100	100

The computation of net requirements proceeded in the direction from top to bottom of the product structure, in a level-by-level fashion. This procedure accounts for, or flushes out, component item D in its consumed state "hiding" in higher-level items A, B, and C, which *will be used* in the manufacture of product X. If the computation proceeded in the other direction, the where-used traces might lead into other branches of the bill of material that do not apply to product X. For example, an additional quantity of item D might be found hidden in parent item Y. If it entered into the netting process, the net requirements for item D would be understated, because item Y is not used in the manufacture of truck X.

Net requirements are developed by allocating (reallocating) quantities in inventory to the quantities of gross requirements, in a level-by-level process.

The level-by-level netting procedure is laborious, but it cannot be circumvented or shortcut. The net requirement on the parent level must be determined before the net requirement on the component-item level can be determined.

The downward progression from one product level to another is called an *explosion*. In executing the explosion, the task is to identify the components of a given parent item and to ascertain the location (address) of their inventory records in computer storage so that they may be retrieved and processed.

The bill of material file (or product-structure file) guides the explosion process. Product-structure data are not operated on but merely consulted by the system to determine component identities, quantities "per," and addresses (previously illustrated in Figure 9). The generic name of the computer program (software) that organizes and maintains the product-structure file is the *bill of material processor*. The program also handles the retrieval of individual bills of material, as required during the explosion process.

Lot Sizing

Lot sizing (as defined above) is also a factor in the requirements computation, and it is another reason why the top-to-bottom, level-by-level procedure must be followed. In the preceding example, a tacit assumption was that parent items A, B, and C will be ordered in quantities equal to the respective net requirements for these items. But in reality, lot sizing, where employed, would invalidate this assumption. This is because the gross requirement for a component derives directly from the (planned) *order quantity* of its parent(s).

If we modify the preceding example by stipulating that for gear C, production order quantities must be multiples of 5 (because of some consideration in the gear machining process), the net requirement of 76 will have to be covered by a planned order for 80. This will increase the gross requirement for forging blank D correspondingly, as illustrated in Figure 12. When the planned order for 80 gears (parent item) is released, 80 forging blanks (component item) will have to be issued.

Lot sizing, i.e., the particular technique used to determine order quantities for a given inventory item, therefore affects the requirements for its components. For an MRP system to be able to carry out a complete explosion, lot sizing must be part of the procedure, and the respective lot-sizing rules (algorithms) must be incorporated into the computer program that controls the requirements computation. The subject of lot sizing will be reviewed in Chapter 6.

The general rule of material requirements planning logic can be stated as follows: The mutual parent/component relationship of items on contiguous product levels dictates that the net requirement on the parent level,

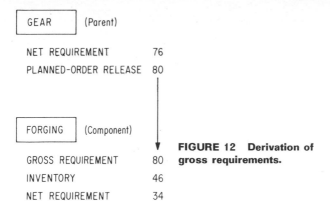

GEAR (Parent)

NET REQUIREMENT   76
PLANNED-ORDER RELEASE 80

FORGING (Component)

FIGURE 12   Derivation of gross requirements.

GROSS REQUIREMENT   80
INVENTORY   46
NET REQUIREMENT   34

as well as its coverage by a planned order, be computed before the gross requirement on the component level can be correctly determined. The *timing* of a gross requirement for a component item coincides with the timing of an order release planned for its parent, as shown in Figure 13.

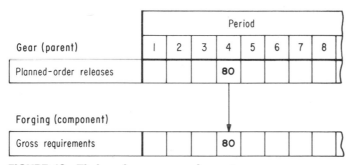

FIGURE 13   Timing of a gross requirement.

Item Lead Times

Lead times of the individual inventory items are a complicating factor in the computation of material requirements. The preceding example of net requirements determination for forgings, gears, etc., was oversimplified in ignoring, among other things, item lead times. It is these lead times that will determine the timing of releases and scheduled completions for the orders in question. Because a component-item order must be completed before the parent-item order that will consume it can be started, the back-to-back lead times of the four items in the example make up the *cumulative lead time*, a sort of critical path that determines the earliest time that the end products could be built, or, given the end-product schedule date, the latest time for the start of the lowest-level item order. Cumulative lead time is graphically represented in Figure 14.

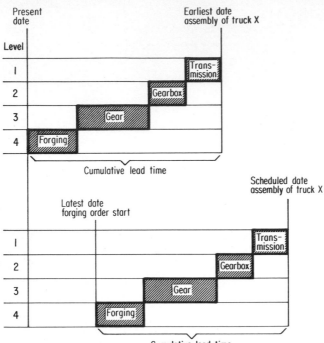

FIGURE 14   Cumulative lead time.

If the manufacturing lead times for the four items in the example were:

Forging blank D:	3 weeks
Gear C:	6 weeks
Gearbox B:	2 weeks
Transmission A:	1 week
	12 weeks (cumulative lead time)

and assembly of the end product, truck X, were scheduled for a date arbitrarily designated as week 50, component-order release dates and completion dates could be calculated by successively subtracting the lead time values from 50.

Complete order for item A:	week 50
Minus lead time of item A:	1
Release order for item A:	49
Complete order for item B:	49
Minus lead time of item B:	2
Release order for item B:	47
Complete order for item C:	47
Minus lead time of item C:	6
Release order for item C:	41
Complete order for item D:	41
Minus lead time of item D:	3
Release order for item D:	week 38

The above release dates of parent orders would establish the timing of gross requirements for the respective component items, as illustrated in Figure 13. Because, in the example, none of the gross requirements can be fully satisfied from inventory, the timing of net requirements for each of the items coincides with that of gross requirements. The timing of the orders providing coverage of net requirements is geared to the latter (for completion dates) and is a function of the respective lead times (for release dates). In the above example, it is assumed that lot sizing does not affect the lead time, i.e., that item lead time does not vary with the quantity being ordered.

Time phasing solves the problem of the effect of item lead time on the timing of requirements. Lead-time values (or procedures for determining these values based on order quantity) must be supplied to the MRP system which stores them for use in establishing a proper alignment of requirements and planned-order data in the course of the requirements explosion. Subtracting the lead time from the date of the net requirement, i.e., positioning the planned-order release forward of the timing of the net requirement it covers is called *offsetting for lead time.*

Recurrence of Requirements within the Planning Horizon

The planning horizon of the master production schedule usually covers a time span large enough to contain multiple (i.e., recurring) requirements for a given end item. This represents another complication in the computation of component requirements. The truck X example assumes that the inventory quantities of all the component items involved are available for netting against the gross requirements generated by the lot of 100 trucks. But there may be another lot (or several) of the same end product (or of a different end product using the same transmission) that precedes the one for 100 in the master production schedule. If that is the case, *its* net requirements must be accounted for before the net requirements for the lot of 100 can be determined.

If we assume that there is a preceding lot of 12 trucks X (lot no 1), the net requirements for the respective lots (retaining the lot-sizing rule for gear C) would be calculated as follows:

	Lot no. 1	Lot no. 2
Transmission A		
Gross requirements:	12	100
Inventory:	2	0
Net requirements:	10	100
Gearbox B		
Gross requirements:	10	100
Inventory:	15	5
Net requirements:	−5	95
	(available for lot no. 2)	

Gear C

Gross requirements:	0	95
Inventory:		7
Net requirements:	0	88
Planned-order quantities:	0	90

Forging blank D

Gross requirements:	0	90
Inventory:		46
Net requirements:	0	44

As can be seen, the existence of a preceding lot of 12 has changed the net requirements for the lot of 100. The net requirements for the forging blank, for instance, have increased from 34 (Figure 12) to 44. Note that this increase of 10 does not match the increase of 12 in the end-product requirements. This difference is caused by the lot-sizing rule (order in multiples of 5) applied at the item C level.

The requirements-calculation procedure followed in the current example is identical to the one used in lot requirements planning, which was briefly discussed in the preceding chapter. Under this approach, requirements are determined for one end-item or product lot at a time, and to the extent that the various end items use common components, the chronological sequence of the lots (for all products) must be strictly observed for the requirements data to be valid. These data, once developed, remain valid *as long as the chronological sequence of the lots in the master production schedule continues unchanged.*

In the development of lot requirements, component inventories have been allocated (applied against gross requirements) according to the sequence of (all) the end-item lots. If this sequence subsequently changes — as it often will in practice — component inventories must be reallocated and requirements redetermined. A change in end-item lot sequence affects not only the timing but also the quantities of requirements. This can be seen in the above example of the forging blank. Had lot no. 2 preceded lot no. 1 (this will become more realistic if we think of the lots as representing two different models of trucks that use the same transmission), the requirements developed in the earlier example would have been correct — the net requirements for forging D would have been:

        34 for lot no. 2
        15 for lot no. 1
    Total: 49

but when the sequence of the lots is reversed, the net requirements for the same item are (as per the latest example):

        0 for lot no. 1
        44 for lot no. 2
    Total: 44

This phenomenon constitutes a severe problem in lot requirements planning. Because the sequence of the lots (of all products in the master production schedule) normally keeps changing, either the individual lot requirements are being repeatedly reprocessed or they are not—the usual case—and the plant operates with invalid requirements information and orders that may be wrong in both quantity and timing.

The sequence of end-item lots affects both the quantities and the timing of requirements in an MRP system also, but because this system computes requirements by product level rather than by lot, and because time phasing follows the correct chronological order of requirements as per the current master production schedule, no distortions occur. For this reason, a changing lot sequence is of little concern under the time-phased material requirements planning approach, and it has virtually no effect on the data-processing burden of the MRP system.

Common Usage of Components

Common usage of a component item by several parent items is another complicating factor in the computation of requirements by an MRP system. In the examples used thus far, all the component items had a single parent, i.e., a single source of demand. In the real situation, many components will be found to have multiple parents. The lower the level of the component item, the more parent items it tends to have. In our example, forging blank D is used to make gear C. But the same blank might very well be used for the manufacture of half a dozen different gears. The lower-level steel, from which this forging is made, would almost certainly be used for a large number of different parts made from that particular grade and diameter of steel bar.

In order to determine the net requirements for such a common-usage item correctly, its gross requirements stemming from all its parent items for which there are planned orders must be determined first. (Note: the mere existence of a parent item is not tantamount to a gross requirement.) In addition to dependent demand generated by its parent items, a component may also be subject to independent demand, if it is used as a service part. Such demands, if any, must also be added to the gross requirements for the item in question. The gross requirements schedule of an inventory item represents a summary of demands originating from one or more sources, and applicable to various points in time. This is illustrated in Figure 15.

The level-by-level (rather than lot-by-lot) approach to the computation of requirements under an MRP system minimizes the problem of multiple parent demands. All the parents of a given component item tend to be on the same, next-higher level. Because that entire level (i.e., all the items on that level) is processed first, all the parent planned orders are developed before the next-lower level is netted. This means that the component's requirements need not subsequently be reprocessed and renetted, due to emergence

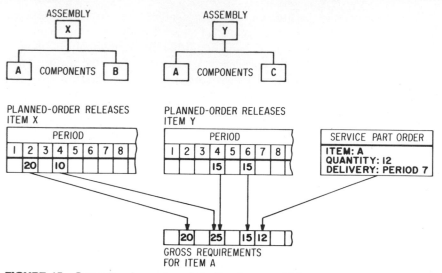

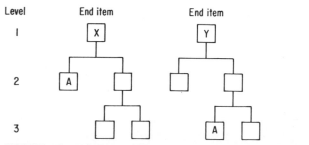

GROSS REQUIREMENTS
FOR ITEM A

FIGURE 15   Gross requirements originating from multiple sources.

of another gross requirement generated by another parent item. The foregoing applies *provided* the component item in question appears on only one
level in the product structure. Some items, however, may appear on two or
more different levels. This leads to the next complicating factor.

Multilevel Items

Recurrence of gross requirements for a given item, during the requirements-computation process, may be caused by the fact that the item's several parents are on different levels. Because a component item, by definition,
is always on the next level below its parent item, this means that whenever
an item's parents appear on more than one level, the item itself has multiple
levels associated with it. There are two cases: An item may exist on different
levels in the structure of different end items which use it in common (Figure
16), or it may exist on different levels in the structure of one end item (Figure 17). In a given case, both of these conditions may exist at the same time.

**FIGURE 16   Existence of common components on different
levels.**

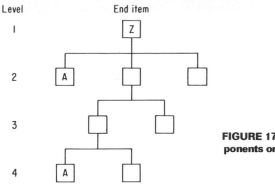

FIGURE 17 An end item's components on multiple levels.

The problem here is one of having to reprocess and re-net at every recurrence of gross requirements stemming from parent items that appear on multiple levels. This would mean multiple retrievals of the component-item record from storage during the requirements explosion, and a reduction in data-processing efficiency.

This problem is solved by employing the so-called *low-level coding* technique. The lowest level at which any inventory item appears is identified through an analysis of the bill of material file, and this information—the low-level code—is added either to the bill of material or to the item's inventory record. In the level-by-level requirements-computation process, the processing of the item is then delayed until the lowest level on which it appears is reached. At that point, all the possible gross requirements stemming from parent items at *any* of the higher levels have been established and the need for multiple retrieval and processing has been forestalled. The concept of low-level coding is illustrated in Figure 18.

The use of the low-level code is advantageous only to the extent that the benefit of higher processing efficiency outweighs the cost of developing and *maintaining* the low-level coding. Most versions of the bill of material

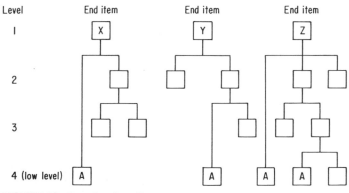

FIGURE 18 Low-level coding.

processor program mentioned previously provide the function of developing and maintaining the low-level code. There is no *logical* requirement for the low-level code in calculating gross and net requirements; i.e., its absence will not prevent the MRP system from arriving at correct results.

All the factors discussed above that affect and complicate the material requirements planning process must be taken into account by the procedural approach used by any MRP system. Different such approaches in the past have gradually been perfected and streamlined, and they are by now largely standardized in what is called the *processing logic* of an MRP system. Processing logic will be the subject of discussion in the next chapter.

PART THREE

MATERIAL REQUIREMENTS PLANNING LOGIC

The logic of MRP is inescapable.
L. J. BURLINGAME *in* APICS News, *February 1973.*

CHAPTER FOUR

PROCESSING LOGIC

The term *logic*, when used in a systems context, pertains to the reasoning behind a procedure, or a system of procedures, rather than to specific procedural steps. The validity of the results a procedure, or system, will yield is a function of the soundness of that reasoning. The intent of the present chapter is to describe the inner workings of a material requirements planning system, at a level of detail required to make this description reasonably comprehensive. The problem in doing so, however, is that there are alternative approaches to MRP system implementation and that the individual systems installed in industry cover a spectrum of special features, functions, and procedures. How an MRP system works must therefore be described largely in terms of processing logic rather than in terms of specific procedure, if it is not to be a case study.

INVENTORY STATUS

The status of an inventory item must be known before it can be determined what, if any, inventory management action is to be taken on that item. Inventory status (or stock status) is expressed by means of data that define an item's current position. Status information is intended either to answer or to help answer (depending on how complete the information is) the essential questions of:

- What do we have?
- What do we need?
- What do we do?

The answer to the last question follows from the evaluation of the status, which can be performed either by an inventory planner or by a computer executing an evaluation procedure.

The most primitive expression of inventory status is limited to data on quantities on hand and on order, and action is then determined by comparing need (demand) to status or upon depletion of inventory to some predetermined minimum, in which case the action taken reflects anticipated future need.

A more elaborate expression of inventory status is provided by the classic "perpetual inventory control" equation previously introduced in Chapter 2 and repeated below, which states the elements of expanded inventory status, and their relationship. This equation, while valid, is still somewhat primitive:

$$A + B - C = X$$

where A = quantity on hand
B = quantity on order
C = quantity required
X = quantity available

If X has a positive value, it indicates the quantity available for future requirements. If it is negative, it is an indication of an impending shortage, i.e., inadequate coverage. The idea behind this venerable approach to inventory control is, of course, for the value of X to equal or exceed zero at all times. This is accomplished by increasing the value of B by placing a new order whenever X approaches zero or turns negative. This policy would appear to preclude shortages, but it does not, because the expression of inventory status is too crude on three counts:

1. Information on timing is lacking.
2. The data on B and C represent summaries.
3. The status formula does not provide for planned (future) coverage.

For example, status might be indicated as follows:

```
On hand:  100
On order: 120       100 + 120 − 200 = 20
Required: 200
```

The technique signals that all is well and no action is called for, but in fact there will be a shortage, as becomes evident when information on timing is associated with the status data:

```
On hand:  100
On order: 120, due June 1
Required: 200, May 15
```

Coverage is adequate in terms of quantity but not in terms of timing. To illustrate the opposite case, let the status be as follows:

    On hand: 20
    On order: 100 $20 + 100 - 200 = -80$
    Required: 200

The technique signals that an order for 80 or more pieces should be placed, to provide coverage. Let us assume that the status is examined by an inventory planner on March 1, and that 80 units of the item, which has a lead time of four weeks, are ordered on that date. This action proves incorrect in light of more detailed information on inventory status, such as:

    On hand: 20
    On order: 100, due March 10
    Required: 110, March 15
             90, June 15

This technique of expressing inventory status does not make the adequacy of coverage sufficiently clear. In both of these examples, the action signals arc false. The message in the first case should have been: "Reschedule the open order to May 15," and in the second: "An order for at least 80 will have to be placed, but not for another ten weeks." The technique in question does not provide for orders planned for future release (as the second of the examples illustrates) and in assessing status, depends on open orders only.

In an MRP system, all the above shortcomings in expressing inventory status are overcome by expanding the number of status elements and by time-phasing status data. The classic equation is, in effect, expanded to
$$A + B + D - C = X$$
where D = quantity planned for future order release.

The MRP system evaluates the status of each inventory item, automatically establishes planned-order coverage, and signals for consistently correct action. Under material requirements planning, the elements of inventory status (all of them associated with timing information) are these:

- Quantity on hand
- Quantities on order
- Gross requirement quantities
- Net requirement quantities
- Planned-order quantities

These status data can be divided into two categories, by type:

1. Inventory data
2. Requirements data

Inventory data consist of on-hand and on-order quantities, and their timing. These data are *reported* to the system and can be verified *by inspection*.

Requirements data consist of the quantities and timing of gross requirements, net requirements, and planned-order releases. These data are *computed* by the system and can be verified only *through recomputing*.

TECHNIQUES OF TIME PHASING

One of the oldest inventions of human civilization is the division of time's continuous flow into increments suitable for measuring its passage, and the construction of calendars to provide a frame of reference. Our Gregorian calendar serves satisfactorily for most purposes, but when inventory-planning and production-scheduling procedures are to be automated (i.e., their execution transferred from a human being to a machine), certain characteristics of this calendar present difficulties. The Gregorian calendar does not employ a decimal base, months have an uneven number of days, and the pattern of holidays is irregular.

Scheduling Calendars

Since these factors would unnecessarily complicate time-related computing procedures, it is common to devise special decimal calendars that are used for this purpose. There are a variety of so-called *scheduling calendars* or *shop calendars,* but what all have in common is the principle of consecutively numbering weeks and/or days. In the typical scheme, weeks are given two-digit designations (weeks 00-99) and working days three-digit designations (days 000-999). This results in a 100-week or 1,000-day scheduling "year," respectively.

Figure 19 shows a numbered-week calendar. In this example, the "year" is divided into four-week "months" designated as *periods*, which can be used as planning time-units of consistent length, in addition to the weeks. Note the simple arithmetic of converting weeks into periods and vice versa:

- $\dfrac{\text{Week}}{4}$ = period, after decimal fraction is rounded up
- Period $\times$ 4 = last week of that period
- (Period $\times$ 4) $-$ 3 = first week of that period

Figure 20 shows a numbered-day calendar. In this case, it is the popular 1,000-day, or *M-day*, shop calendar which counts only working days. In the use of this calendar, one week is normally equated with five working days. Thus if an item had a five-week manufacturing lead time, 25 would be subtracted from its due date to arrive at the order release date. The actual span of time might be more than five weeks, if holidays or a plant vacation happened to intervene.

The features of the two types of calendar can be combined, in various ways. An *M*-day calendar, for instance, can also have its (Gregorian) weeks numbered, either without exception or skipping over plant vacation weeks.

PERIOD	WEEK	MON	TUES	WED	THUR	FRI	SAT	SUN	MONTH
24	93	1	2	3	4	5	6	7	JAN
	94	8	9	10	11	12	13	14	
	95	15	16	17	18	19	20	21	
	96	22	23	24	25	26	27	28	
25	97	29	30	31	1	2	3	4	FEB
	98	5	6	7	8	9	10	11	
	99	12	13	14	15	16	17	18	
	00	19	20	21	22	23	24	25	
1	01	26	27	28	1	2	3	4	MAR
	02	5	6	7	8	9	10	11	
	03	12	13	14	15	16	17	18	
	04	19	20	21	22	23	24	25	

FIGURE 19 A numbered-week scheduling calendar.

A numbered-week calendar can also identify days. This is usually accomplished by adding a third digit to identify a specific day. Thus a date of 952 might be interpreted as the second day of week 95. This, in turn, might mean Tuesday or the second working day, depending on the specific design of the calendar.

Shop calendars are being used so as to make the scheduling arithmetic straightforward, i.e., to allow points in time to be determined, and identified, by means of simple addition or subtraction. Time-phased data, in an automated system, normally bear reference to a shop calendar. The latter is superimposed on the regular (year, month, and day) calendar, which permits unambiguous translation of date designations from one calendar to the other.

MONTH	MON	TUES	WED	THUR	FRI	SAT	SUN
JULY	1 / 989	2 / 990	3 / 991	④	5 / 992	6	7
	8 / 993	9 / 994	10 / 995	11 / 996	12 / 997	13	14
	15 / 998	16 / 999	17 / 000	18 / 001	19 / 002	20	21

FIGURE 20 M-day scheduling calendar.

Dates and Time-Buckets

In a material requirements planning system, inventory status data are time-phased by associating them with either *days* (relatively short time periods) or *planning periods* such as weeks or months (relatively long time periods). While the specific method of time phasing that is being employed will determine the terms in which the internal arithmetic is carried out by the system, the method of *display* of time-phased data (on paper or on a CRT screen) can be selected independently. A given day can be converted to its respective planning period for purposes of display, and a planning period can be expressed in terms of one of its constituent days, usually its starting day. The two alternatives involved here are termed:

1. The *date/quantity* approach
2. The *time-bucket* approach

Under the first, data are normally displayed in vertical arrays; under the second, horizontal arrays are the rule. In material requirements planning, the time-bucket method (a bucket is equivalent to a record field) is the more popular, and it is almost universally used for purposes of time-phased data display, because the bucket format, being more graphic, facilitates visual evaluation. An example contrasting the two forms of display (of the same set of data) appears in Figure 21. It is possible to design an MRP system in such a way that requirements and inventory data can be entered, stored, and internally processed by date/quantity but displayed in time-bucket format.

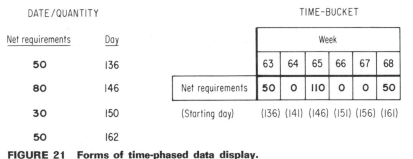

FIGURE 21   Forms of time-phased data display.

Because time-buckets correspond to periods of time normally spanning more than a single day, they represent a rather coarse division of time. For this reason, the precise meaning of the timing of data assigned to time-buckets must be fixed by convention. The logic of the MRP system (and, consequently, its computer program) must therefore incorporate the various time-phasing conventions specified by the system designer. These conventions pertain to the following:

1. The timing of an *event*
2. The representation of an *activity*
3. The *size* of the bucket

An event is associated with a single point in time. When data representing an event, such as a future receipt of material, are assigned to a time-bucket, it is not self-evident *exactly when*, during the period in question, the event is scheduled to occur. One of the following conventions is normally used to fix the day of the event for purposes of planning:

- *First* day of the period
- *Midpoint* of the period
- *Last* day of the period
- Any time during the period but *no later than* its last day

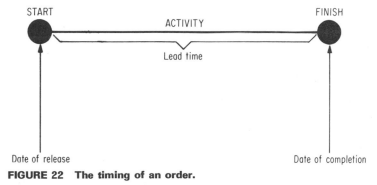

FIGURE 22   The timing of an order.

An activity is connected with two points in time, its beginning and its termination, but one time-bucket can represent only one or the other. What it does represent is fixed by convention. A case in point is an order for a quantity of an inventory item, which involves two events and an activity (Figure 22). If the order data are to be time-phased by assigning them to a single time bucket, the more important of the two events will be so represented, whereas the other will be merely implied, be recorded in some subsidiary record, or go unrecorded.

For example, in the case of an open (previously released) order, its future completion date (due date) is more critical than its date of release, which is past. Thus a row of buckets labeled, for instance, "quantities on order," as in Figure 23, would represent the timing of scheduled order *completions*

	Period							
	I	2	3	4	5	6	7	8
Quantities on order			50			75		

FIGURE 23   The timing of order completions.

—fifty in period 3 and seventy-five in period 6—rather than of order releases. In the case of orders scheduled for future release (so-called planned
orders), on the other hand, the timing of the *releases* would be of first importance, and the buckets would reflect that, rather than the timing of
completions. Figure 24 shows that sixty are planned for release in period 2
and another fifty in period 6. To facilitate the interpretation of such data,

		Period							
	I	2	3	4	5	6	7	8	
Planned-order quantities		60				50			

FIGURE 24   The timing of order releases.

it is customary to name the event in question in the label of the respective
row of buckets. In the preceding two examples, more descriptive labels
might be:

- Scheduled receipts
- Planned-order releases

Bucket size, i.e., the length of the period represented by one time-bucket,
is also fixed by convention. A bucket might represent one week, five working days, ten working days, a four-week period, a month, etc. In most of
today's material requirements planning systems, time-buckets represent
weeks. It is possible, however, to assign different time values to buckets
within one row. In a given system, for example, the first twenty-six buckets
might represent weeks, the next six buckets, months, and the next four,
quarters, as illustrated by Figure 25. In a mixed system of this type, pas-

							Period										
	I	2		23	24	25	26	JUL	AUG	SEP	OCT	NOV	DEC	I	II	III	IV
Gross requirements	10	15		5	20	10	10	40	30	50	50	50	30	120	150	150	100

FIGURE 25   A row of buckets with different time values.

sage of time distorts the pattern somewhat, and this must be compensated
for either by letting the number of weekly buckets fluctuate between twenty-
three and twenty-six, or by overlapping the last weekly buckets with the
first monthly bucket. For example, gross requirements for week 27 might
be shown separately from those of the month of July, although they would
be contained in the total shown for the latter.

GROSS AND NET REQUIREMENTS

The concept of gross versus net requirements has briefly been reviewed in Chapter 3. The gross requirement for an inventory item equals the quantity of demand for that item. Its net requirement is arrived at by allocating the available inventory on hand and on order to (i.e., subtracting from) the gross requirement.

Gross Requirements

The term *gross requirement* has a specific meaning in this context, however. It is the quantity of the item that will have to be disbursed, i.e., issued to support a parent order (or orders), rather than the total quantity that will be consumed by the end product. These two quantities may or may not be identical.

To illustrate: In the Chapter 3 example of truck X and component item D, 100 trucks are to be produced, and each unit of the end product contains one unit of item D. The gross requirement for D could therefore be said to equal 100. This figure, while meaningful in product costing, etc., is quite meaningless for purposes of material requirements planning, where the question is not what quantity of a component will go out the door with the product, but what (minimum) quantity will have to be procured or manufactured (i.e., the net requirement) to allow the product to be built and shipped in the quantity required. In the example mentioned, the gross requirement for item D is computed to be 76, and the net requirement, 30. The gross requirement could have been 100, however, had there been no inventories at higher (gear, gearbox, transmission) levels. In a material requirements planning environment, the gross requirement is equivalent to *demand at item level*, rather than to demand at product or master production schedule level.

There may be multiple sources of demand, and therefore of gross requirements, for a given component item. This has also been brought out previously. An item may be subject to dependent demand from several parent items that use it in common, and it may also be subject to independent demand generating from sources external to the plant. These gross requirements for the item are combined and summarized, by planning period, in the *gross requirements schedule,* i.e., the respective row of time-buckets, as previously illustrated in Chapter 3, Figure 15. These requirements data are reproduced in Figure 26. Using these data to develop sub-

	Period								Total
	1	2	3	4	5	6	7	8	
Gross requirements		20		25		15	12		72

FIGURE 26   Gross requirements schedule.

sequent examples, we must now introduce some inventory data so that net requirements can be correctly determined and time-phased.

Net Requirements

Assume that there are 23 units of this item on hand, and 30 on order due in period 3. This is displayed in time-bucket format in Figure 27.

		Period								Total
		1	2	3	4	5	6	7	8	
Gross requirements			20		25		15	12		72
Scheduled receipts				30						30
On hand	23									

FIGURE 27   Time-phased status before net requirements computation.

The logic of the net requirements computation is simple:

	Gross requirements
minus	Scheduled receipts
minus	On hand
equals	Net requirements

In using this formulation, it is understood that if the result is a negative value, i.e., if the sum of quantities on hand and on order exceeds the gross requirement, the net requirement is zero. With data in time-phased format, the calculation is performed successively for each period, and unapplied inventory is carried forward. This is shown in Table 4.

The correctness of the computation is verified by a check of totals, as follows:

	Total gross requirements:	72
minus	Total scheduled receipts:	−30
minus	On hand:	−23
equals	Total net requirements:	19

TABLE 4   Calculation of Net Requirements

Period	Gross requirements	Scheduled receipts	On hand	Result		Net requirements
1	0	−0	−23	=	−23	0
2	20	−0	−23	=	−3	0
3	0	−30	−3	=	−33	0
4	25	−0	−33	=	−8	0
5	0	−0	−8	=	−8	0
6	15	−0	−8	=	7	7
7	12	−0	−0	=	12	12
8	0	−0	−0	=	0	0
Totals	72	30				19

	Period								Total
	1	2	3	4	5	6	7	8	
Gross requirements		20		25		15	12		72
Scheduled receipts			30						30
On hand	23								
Net requirements							7	12	19

FIGURE 28   Time-phased status after net requirements computation.

This is illustrated in Figure 28 in time-phased record format. Under an alternative method of calculating net requirements, the quantity on hand is time-phased, i.e., projected into the future, period by period, and the first negative value then represents the first net requirement. Differences between successive negative values equal the net requirements in the respective later periods. The logic of the on-hand/net-requirements computation is as follows:

	Balance on hand at the end of a given period
plus	Quantity on order due in the succeeding period
minus	Gross requirements of the succeeding period
equals	Balance on hand at the end of the succeeding period

Under this method, the "negative on hand" is understood to equal a net requirement, recorded cumulatively. The calculation is performed in Table 5.

This method provides a more efficient display in that it combines the projected-on-hand and the net requirements information in a single row of time-buckets, as shown in Figure 29. Although it may appear that the data, when presented this way, are more difficult to interpret, little additional skill is actually required for interpretation. The discrete, period-by-period net requirements need not be mentally calculated from the cumulative figures but can, in fact, be read directly from the record. This is due to the

TABLE 5   Alternative Calculation of Net Requirements

Period	On hand at beginning of period	Scheduled receipts	Gross requirements		On hand at end of period
1	23	+0	−0	=	23
2	23	+0	−20	=	3
3	3	+30	−0	=	33
4	33	+0	−25	=	8
5	8	+0	−0	=	8
6	8	+0	−15	=	−7
7	−7	+0	−12	=	−19
8	−19	+0	−0	=	−19

	Period								Total
	I	2	3	4	5	6	7	8	
Gross requirements		20		25		15	12		72
Scheduled receipts			30						30
On hand	23	23	3	33	8	8	-7	-19	-19	-19

FIGURE 29   Alternative method of net requirements display.

fact that in all periods that have net requirements, these *net requirements equal gross requirements* except for those periods during which inventory either runs out or is added to by a new receipt. Figure 29 provides an example: the first net requirement of 7 in period 6 is shown as such, and the subsequent net requirements equal gross requirements, i.e., 12 and 0. Note also that the last (cumulative) net requirements figure, −19, equals that of the total net requirements for the eight periods covered by the record.

Safety Stock and Net Requirements

Earlier there was mention of the fact that the planning of safety stock on the item level affects the calculation of net requirements. For purposes of this calculation, the quantity of safety stock is either subtracted from the on-hand quantity or added to the gross requirement. Either alternative produces the same effect, namely increasing net requirements correspondingly and sometimes shifting the first net requirement one period forward. In the Figure 29 example, had there been safety stock of two units, the projected-on-hand and net requirements quantities would have been as shown in Figure 30.

When safety stock is planned at the item level, the material requirements planning logic attempts to conserve its quantity and to "protect" it from being used up, so that this quantity might always be on hand. To the extent

Safety stock: 2	Period								Total
	I	2	3	4	5	6	7	8	
Gross requirements		20		25		15	12		72
Scheduled receipts			30						30
On hand	23	23	3	33	8	8	-7	-19	-19	-19
Net requirements							9	12		21

FIGURE 30   Net requirements after safety-stock deduction.

that the system succeeds in thus safeguarding safety stock, it creates "dead" inventory that is carried along but never used — a distinctly undesirable condition. Item safety stock forces the MRP system to *overstate requirements*, which in itself is undesirable. The system either tells the truth or does not. An overstated requirement sometimes leads to distorted timing, when the safety stock causes the net requirement to be pulled forward in time.

Overstated requirements and false timing (order due dates) tend to cause confusion, unnecessary expense, and most important, loss of credibility suffered by the MRP system. Factory personnel will quickly discover whether or not they can rely on the integrity of information being generated by the system. Foremen, using common sense, will almost certainly disregard the due date indicated on a given shop order, and delay its completion, if they know that a quantity of the item is available in stock or that the order is scheduled for completion before actually needed. In time, vendors of purchased items will learn that missing a due date has no serious consequences, and they will tend to miss more due dates thereafter.

Safety stock (at item level) is part of the stock replenishment concept and as such has no legitimate place in an MRP system, despite the fact that it can easily be incorporated into such a system. The primary purpose of safety stock is to compensate for fluctuation in (uncertain) demand, i.e., for forecast error. But in an MRP system, demand for the individual component items is not being forecast and is therefore not subject to forecast error. Component-item demand is certain, relative to the master production schedule.

This schedule may be based on a forecast of demand for products or end items. If any uncertainty exists, it is at the master production schedule level, not at the component-item level. Safety stock, where required, should therefore be provided through the master production schedule; i.e., it should be planned in terms of end items. The MRP system, which explodes the contents of the master production schedule into detailed component-item requirements need not, and should not, duplicate safety-stock inventory at the component-item level.

When safety stock is planned through the master production schedule, it has the added advantage of assuring that the respective components will be provided in matched sets, allowing the safety-stock quantities of end items actually to be built. There is no similar assurance when component-item safety stocks are planned independently of each other. The preceding arguments regarding the proper place of safety stock can be summed up by stating that *safety stock is properly applied only to inventory items subject to independent demand.*

There is an exception to this rule. While the primary function of safety stock is protection against uncertainty of *demand,* a secondary function is to compensate for uncertainty of *supply.* There is justification for carrying some safety stock of an item where the resupply performance is erratic and uncontrollable. Planning and carrying safety stock for the reason mentioned should, as a rule, be limited to purchased items, on an exception basis. The resupply (completion) of manufactured items need not be erratic, as performance to schedule is controllable, particularly in a material re-requirements planning environment (see Chapter 7).

COVERAGE OF NET REQUIREMENTS

The quantities and timing of net requirements for a given inventory item can be thought of as indicating impending shortages, caused by lack of coverage. Assuming an adequate planning horizon, an MRP system detects such shortages sufficiently in advance to allow their coverage to be planned in an orderly manner. An MRP system detects future *potential* shortages and plans their coverage so that *actual* shortages will not occur.

Planned Orders

In an MRP system, net requirements are covered by *planned orders,* i.e., new orders for the respective items scheduled for release in the future. Depending on the planning horizon, the level of the item in the product structure, and the applicable lot-sizing rule, an item with net requirements will have one or more planned orders indicated. The timing of the first (earliest) planned order is governed by the timing of the first net requirement. The order quantity must equal or exceed that of the net requirement. If this quantity exceeds it, the timing of the next (second) planned order may be affected. A planned order may cover net requirements occurring in one or more planning periods.

To generate a planned order correctly, the system must determine the following:

1. The timing of required order completion (due date)
2. The timing of order release
3. The order quantity

The timing of order completion derives, of course, from the timing of the net requirement being covered. Because the net requirement will usually be related to a time-bucket, i.e., a period rather than a point in time, the exact timing of the net requirement has to be fixed by convention, as pointed out previously. This convention, even though it may never have been explicitly stated, is implicit in the logic used to determine the timing of the planned-order release by any given MRP system.

In the previous example represented by Figure 29, the first net requirement is 7 in period 6. The question is whether the planned order that will cover this net requirement should be scheduled for completion in period 5 or in period 6. This question is resolved by the net requirement timing convention, which will usually be one of the following:

- The net requirement will arise at the *beginning* of the period.
- The net requirement will arise at the *midpoint* of the period.
  └─ *Convention*

In the first case, the point in time fixed is the same as the end of the preceding period, and the order completion would be planned for (i.e., no later than the end of) period 5. In the second case, order completion would be planned for period 6. The point of order completion will, of course, determine the point of order release, and the latter will be planned for one of two contiguous earlier periods, depending on the convention used.

Offsetting for Lead Time

As previously mentioned, the timing of the planned-order release is arrived at by offsetting for lead time, i.e., by subtracting the value of the lead time (expressed in shop calendar units) from the shop calendar date of order completion. For example:

Order completion:	week	6
Lead time (weeks):		−4
Order release:	week	2

Order completion:	day	328
Lead time (days):		−20
Order release:	day	308

As this example shows, the lead time must be stated in terms of the planning period being used. When, as is the usual case, the planning period equals a week or longer, some minor distortions may occur. When the quoted lead time is 10 days (eight working days), the system treats it as two weeks. When the lead time is one day, the system treats it as one week. Sometimes the distortion could become extreme, such as when subassembly A is made in one day, the next day is consumed in making subassembly B, which in turn goes into assembly C, built on the third day. In cases like this, to prevent the MRP system from planning these items one week apart (and inflating the cumulative lead time), their lead times may be specified as zero. The system will then order all three for the same week.

We can now complete our previous example (Figure 29) by adding a row of time-buckets for planned-order releases, and by recording a planned order (arbitrarily lot-sized to cover both net requirements) offset for an assumed lead time of four periods. Figure 31A reflects the midpoint convention, Figure 31B the start-of-period convention. Depending on the convention used, the planned-order release would be scheduled for either period 1 or period 2. When the *planned* order is eventually released, it will become an *open* order and will be recorded in the "scheduled receipts" row of the record. The convention that determines the timing of the planned-order release will then also determine the timing of the scheduled receipt, which will be recorded either in bucket 5 or bucket 6.

Figure 32 shows how the record would appear following the release of the

Lead time: 4		Period								Total
		I	2	3	4	5	6	7	8	
Gross requirements			20		25		15	12		72
Scheduled receipts				30						30
On hand	23	23	3	33	8	8	-7	-19	-19	-19
Planned-order releases			19							19

A   Lead time offset

Planned-order releases	19									19

B   Lead time offset

FIGURE 31   Alternatives of offsetting for lead time.

planned order, in period 2. In this example, as well as in all subsequent examples and discussions, the assumption is that the midpoint convention applies. The individual item lead times used by the MRP system in determining planned-order releases are, by necessity, estimates in most cases. The lead-time value of four periods used in the previous example represents the amount of time that could be expected to elapse between order release and order completion—if everything else went according to plan. This is the *planned lead time,* not to be confused with the *actual lead time.* The latter can generally be determined only in retrospect, because it is the amount of

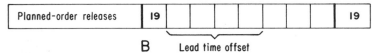

		Period							Total
		2	3	4	5	6	7	8	9	
Gross requirements		20		25		15	12			72
Scheduled receipts			30			19				49
On hand	23	3	33	8	8	12				0
Planned-order releases										0

Total gross requirements   **72**

Coverage

On hand   **23**

Total receipts   **49**   **72**

Surplus   **0**

FIGURE 32   Status following release of planned order.

time it actually took to complete the order, in light of possibly changed requirements and unplanned events. The actual lead time of a given item may, and often does, vary widely from order to order.

Lead-Time Contents

Planned, or normal, lead times must be used by the MRP system for purposes of planning, but their "accuracy" is not crucial. These lead times are, after all, used merely to determine order *release* dates, which are considerably less important than the *completion* dates related to actual lead times. The lead time of a manufactured item is made up of a number of elements, listed here in descending order of significance:

- Queue (waiting to be worked on) time
- Running (machining, fabrication, assembly, etc.) time
- Setup time
- Waiting (for transportation) time
- Inspection time
- Move time
- Other elements

In a general machine shop (job shop) environment, the first of the elements listed normally accounts for roughly 90 percent of average total elapsed time. In an individual case, queue time is a function of a job's relative priority, as it finds itself in contention for a given productive facility with other jobs. The queue time, and consequently, the actual lead time of the respective order, will increase or decrease as its priority is changed—the "hottest" orders spend little time in queue. An actual lead time is usually quite flexible, and in emergency situations can be compressed to a small fraction of the planned lead time.

An MRP system has an inherent ability, discussed in Chapter 7, to reevaluate all open order due dates and to indicate changes in work priorities that are required for the orders to finish on the dates of actual need, irrespective of the originally assigned due dates. The disparity between planned and actual lead times is therefore of no concern. Planned lead times serve to time order releases, and no more than that.

In establishing planned lead-time values, it is possible to compute them through more-or-less elaborate procedures and formulas based on work standards, in-plant travel distances, average or planned queue times, etc., but the precision thus achieved is spurious. Lead-time "accuracy" is indeterminate—the concept is elusive and devoid of meaning. That is why an empirically derived manufacturing lead time, or any reasonable estimate, will do for purposes of material requirements planning.

In a job shop environment, lead time of run-of-the-mill parts tends to vary with the number of operations (and therefore, the moves and waits in queue) involved. An empirical formula sometimes used to arrive at planned lead times for purposes of material requirements planning takes the form of a linear equation, such as the one that follows:

$$L = 2N + 6$$

where L = lead time, in working days
N = number of operations

Thus a fabricated item requiring ten operations would have a planned lead time of twenty six working days, using the above formula. In a specific application, the number of days allowed per operation may be larger or smaller, and a different value of the constant may be chosen, to suit the particular conditions.

Note that the above method (and other methods that may be used, including straight estimates) yields a fixed lead time that will not vary with the quantity of the order. In cases where machining time per operation per piece is significant (turning large shafts, planing and milling heavy castings, etc.), a lead-time-computation procedure can be devised that takes lot size into account.

Planned lead time is sometimes artificially inflated by the inclusion of an element called *safety lead time* or safety time. This element is inserted at the end of the normal lead time, for the purpose of completing an order in advance of its real date of need. Where safety lead times are used, the MRP system, in offsetting for lead time, will plan both order release and order completion for earlier dates than it would otherwise. Order due dates will be advanced from dates of real need by the amount of safety lead time. In the example of Figure 32, if safety lead time of one period were used, the order for nineteen pieces would have been released one period earlier and the scheduled receipt would appear in the period-5 bucket.

The concept of safety lead time is actually quite similar to that of safety stock. The primary purpose of both is to compensate for the vagaries of item demand. The effect of safety lead time is to create an inventory excess, which then can be used to meet unanticipated demand. In practice, however, this inventory tends to remain in work-in-process, and the extra time serves to facilitate expediting the completion of the order by the date of *real* need, i.e., the date that would have been the order due date in the absence of safety lead time.

The Timing and Size of Planned Orders

The ability to generate planned orders, i.e., to plan for coverage of all future net requirements, is one of the most significant characteristics of an MRP system. For every inventory item with net requirements, the system develops a *planned-order schedule* consisting of quantities and timing of as many planned-order releases as may be required to cover net requirements throughout the planning horizon. This schedule details inventory order action that will have to be taken in the future.

Planned-order schedules constitute one of the most valuable outputs of an

MRP system, despite the fact that the bulk of the planned-order data is not related to current order action. The main value of planned orders lies in providing the basis for a correct determination of their component-item requirements (a component gross requirement derives directly from a parent planned order, as pointed out previously), in terms of both quantity and timing. Planned orders provide "visibility" into the future and form the basis for various projections, including projected on-hand inventory, future purchase commitments, and most importantly, production capacity requirements.

Once the net requirements for a given inventory item are determined and time-phased, the *timing* of any covering planned order can be established in a straightforward manner, as described earlier in this chapter. The answer to the question of planned-order *quantity*, however, is not equally clearcut. At this point in the material requirements planning process, one of a number of possible ordering policies, or *ordering rules*, is applied. Thus the planned-order quantities, or lot sizes, are a function of the lot-sizing rule specified for the item in question. Different lot-sizing rules can—and usually do—apply to different items or item classes within one MRP system.

A number of approaches to lot sizing in an environment of discrete period-demands are possible, and several new techniques (lot-sizing algorithms) have been developed since the late 1950s when the first material requirements planning systems were implemented. Because there are so many different lot-sizing techniques to be described, an entire chapter (Chapter 6) will be devoted to this subject. Examples of planned-order quantities used in other chapters either correspond to net requirements, period by period (one of the lot-sizing techniques that can be used), or arbitrarily larger quantities are shown that represent one of the techniques designed to cover more than one period's net requirements.

EXPLOSION OF REQUIREMENTS

The key to the entire material requirements planning (replanning) process is the linkage between parent- and component-item records. There is only one logical link between items on contiguous levels of the product structure, and that is the parent planned-order release and the component gross requirement. These coincide in time, because the component item(s) must be planned to be available at the time the parent order is released for production, at which time the component item(s) will be consumed. The linkage of parent and component inventory records is depicted in Figure 33.

The material requirements planning process, i.e., the so-called *explosion* of requirements from the master production schedule down into the various component-material levels, is guided by the logical linkage of inventory records. Gross requirements for the high-level items are processed against (on-hand and on-order) inventory to determine net requirements, which are

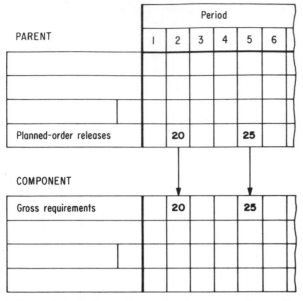

FIGURE 33 **Linkage of parent and component records.**

then covered by planned orders. The quantity and timing of planned-order releases determine, in turn, the quantity and timing of component gross requirements. This procedure is repetitively carried out for items on successively lower levels until a purchased item is reached, at which point the explosion progression terminates. The requirements planning process stops when all the explosion paths that follow the branches of the bill of material have reached purchased (component-part or raw-material) items. The results of a requirements explosion for three items on contiguous levels are illustrated in Figure 34.

In this example, component items B and C do not have multiple parents; i.e., they are not common-usage items. In the real situation, however, multiple parents can be expected to exist, particularly for low-level items. If the explosion progressed in the manner shown in Figure 34, i.e., straight down from item A to its immediate components, and from those to *their* components, the results would have to be recomputed as subsequent explosions of high-level items revealed common usage of items B and C (and other components of A). While the final result would be the same, the data-processing efficiency would be unnecessarily low.

The standard technique for maximizing processing efficiency is to process *all* the items on a given level before addressing their components on the next lower level. This is known as *level-by-level processing.* Under this approach, planned orders are developed for all the items on level 1, so that they may be consolidated for purposes of determining gross requirements for any common components on level 2. This means that each item inventory record is retrieved and processed only once. When a given item appears on more than one level of the product structure, low-level coding (discussed in Chapter 3) will cause the processing of its record to be delayed until the lowest level on which the item finds itself is processed. The level-by-level approach to material requirements planning is illustrated in Figure 35. For accuracy's sake, it must be mentioned here that under so-called net change MRP systems described in Chapter 5, this approach is somewhat modified.

The previously mentioned link between item inventory records is standard, but the link between the hierarchy of records and the master production schedule, the so-called *master schedule interface,* is susceptible to optional treatment. There are three options to choose from, and for any given MRP system the option chosen must be clearly defined if the system is to function satisfactorily. Figure 36 represents a sample master produc-

Item A – level 1

		Period								
		1	2	3	4	5	6	7	8	9
Gross requirements		10		15	10	20	5		10	15
Scheduled receipts				14						
On hand	12	2	2	1	-9	-29	-34	-34	-44	-59
Planned-order releases			9	20	5		10	15		

Item B – level 2

		Period								
Gross requirements			9	20	5		10	15		
Scheduled receipts										
On hand	28	28	19	-1	-6	-6	-16	-31	-31	-31
Planned-order releases		1	5		10	15				

Item C – level 3

		Period								
Gross requirements			1	5		10	15			
Scheduled receipts										
On hand	8	7	2	2	-8	-23	-23	-23	-23	-23
Planned-order releases			8	15						

FIGURE 34 Explosion of requirements.

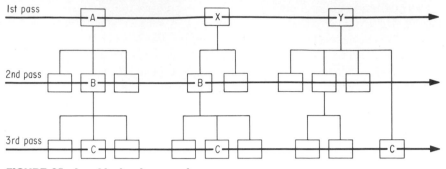

FIGURE 35   Level-by-level processing.

tion schedule, in the usual matrix format. This would be the key input to the MRP system, but the question remains as to the *meaning* of the data contained in this schedule. Does the quantity of 100 of end item A in period 1 represent a gross requirement, a production requirement, or a planned order? Its treatment by the MRP system will vary depending on the answer to this question.

If the master production schedule represents gross requirements, its contents would simply be entered into the gross requirements schedules of the respective end-item records and the processing would be standard (Figure 37). The MRP system will net against both on-hand and on-order quantities, with the result that only an additional 120 sets of item-A components would need to be produced in the first five periods. Under this option, the master production schedule does not reflect a *production plan* but a *requirements plan*. This is not a recommended treatment—confusion will arise if management views the schedule as a plan of production, but the MRP system does not treat it that way.

The second alternative treats the master production schedule as reflecting *production* requirements; i.e., 300 units of item A are to be finished in the first five periods. In this case, the system must be programmed to exclude any on-hand quantities (but not on-order quantities) from the netting process for highest-level items. This means a modification of the regular processing logic, applicable to these items only. This procedure is sound, and it

End item	Period				
	1	2	3	4	5
A	100		100		100
B	15	20	25	20	15
C	50	60		60	

FIGURE 36   A master production schedule.

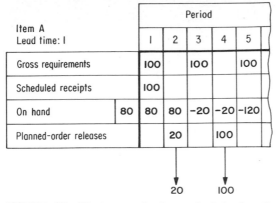

Item A Lead time: 1		Period				
		1	2	3	4	5
Gross requirements		100		100		100
Scheduled receipts		100				
On hand	80	80	80	-20	-20	-120
Planned-order releases			20		100	

20   100

FIGURE 37 Master production schedule interface: gross requirements.

presupposes that end-item demand has been netted against on-hand inventories during the preparation of the master production schedule. An example of this alternative is shown in Figure 38.

Under each of the two alternative treatments discussed above, the master production schedule, in conjunction with the MRP system, will "produce" item A in the quantities indicated—the system will order correct quantities to be assembled or completed, and barring some difficulty, item A will be available according to what the schedule calls for.

The third option treats the master production schedule as a schedule of planned-order releases, which means that the schedule will not "produce" the end items but only their components (Figure 39). The assembly of end items would then have to be ordered apart from the MRP system, most likely via a final assembly schedule. This may or may not be desirable, depending

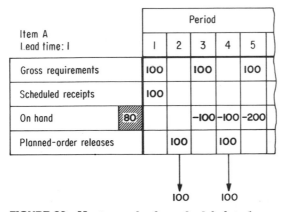

Item A Lead time: 1		Period				
		1	2	3	4	5
Gross requirements		100		100		100
Scheduled receipts		100				
On hand	80			-100	-100	-200
Planned-order releases			100		100	

100   100

FIGURE 38 Master production schedule interface: production requirements.

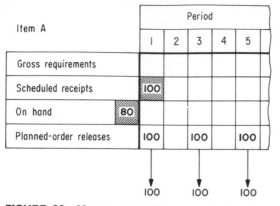

FIGURE 39   Master production schedule interface: planned-order releases.

on the type of product being manufactured. If the end items in the master production schedule are not shippable products but merely major assemblies of products, this treatment will prove suitable only for items that are actually produced *in conjunction with* the final assembly of the product, rather than in advance of final assembly.

A variation of this treatment of the master schedule interface uses *firm planned orders* (described in Chapter 8) for the quantities in question, forcing the MRP system to "produce" the end items by releasing each such order in due time and scheduling its completion. In a "make to stock" manufacturing operation, where the time-phased order point approach is used to control finished-goods inventory, the planned-order schedules of the stocked items constitute, collectively, the master production schedule. Here the firm-planned-order technique would be used to space the planned orders so as to level the load on the plant. The time-phased order point and its uses will be reviewed in the next section.

TIME-PHASED ORDER POINT

Time-phased order point is an approach that allows time-phasing techniques to be used for the planning and control of independent-demand items. The demand for such items has to be forecast, and their supply would normally be controlled by means of order points.

Conventional versus Time-phased Order Point

For an example, a service part supplied from factory stock might have the following planning factors:

Lead time $(L) = 2$
Safety stock $(S) = 100$
Period-demand forecast $(F) = 17$
Order quantity $(Q) = 50$

The order point would then be determined as follows:

$$S + (F \times L) = 100 + (17 \times 2) = 134$$

The same example, in time-phased format, is shown in Figure 40. The forecast is projected over the entire planning horizon and represents gross requirements. The current quantity on hand of 170 will have dropped below safety stock of 100 in period 5, and a replenishment order of 50 is planned to arrive at that time. Offsetting for lead time, the planned-order release is scheduled for period 3. In period 8, the quantity on hand (34 + 50) will once again be less than 100, and another planned order, scheduled for release in period 6, will cover this. The results are identical to those obtained under statistical order point (note that the previously computed order point of 134 is reached some time in period 3, at which time the replenishment order is planned to be released), except that under time-phased order point an entire schedule of planned replenishment orders is developed, instead of one order at a time, as is done under the conventional statistical order point approach.

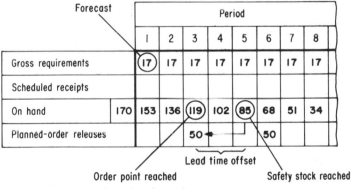

Forecast

Lead time offset

Order point reached   Safety stock reached

FIGURE 40   Time-phased order point.

Actually, the term *time-phased order point* is a misnomer as no order point as such is used for any purpose, and its value (134 in our case) is not even computed by the system. The material requirements planning logic takes over and provides for ordering at the right time. The value of the order point need not be known, as the replenishment order is not being triggered by it, but rather by the on-hand quantity dropping down to the safety-stock level, and the lead-time offset times the order correctly.

The MRP system requires no modification for purposes of implementing time-phased order point. The system treats the independent-demand item exactly the same way it handles any item for which safety stock is specified (see Figure 30). The time-phased order point does everything its conventional counterpart does, and in addition it provides the capabilities to:

1. Keep open-order due dates valid
2. Furnish the capacity system with a planned-order schedule
3. Plan gross requirements for the item's component material(s)

This means that both dependent- and independent-demand manufactured items can be covered by the same priority-planning system, and the relative priorities of *all* shop orders can be kept valid. The material requirements planning logic keeps reevaluating the validity of open-order due dates, and such orders are rescheduled in accordance with the dates of actual need. This is especially significant for items under time-phased order point control, because their gross and net requirements are *expected* to keep changing due to forecast error.

When the time-phased order point is properly used, open orders for items under its control are being continually rescheduled, backward and forward, so as to make their due dates coincide with dates of (projected) actual need, and to keep their relative priorities valid. If this is done, it can be seen that the system will maintain the correct inventory status, and correct coverage, irrespective of the vagaries of actual demand. A close monitoring of the efficacy of the forecasting model, tracking signals, etc., therefore lose their importance. The time-phased order point works well even when forecasting is poor, as will be further explored in Chapter 12.

There is one more advantage to planning and controlling independent-demand items by means of the time-phased order point. In a manufacturing environment, when such items are under the control of this technique, the capacity requirements report can reflect a complete load with good "visibility," as planned-order schedules spanning the planning horizon are available to the capacity requirements planning system for *all* items. This will be reviewed in more detail in Chapter 7.

Known Future Demand

Time-phased order point allows a known future lump requirement to be correctly entered and processed, in contrast to the conventional order point, which is quite unequipped to handle a situation of this type. For example, a service part that is forecast, based on past usage, at 25 units per period, may be ordered by a customer in a quantity of 200, to be delivered at some specified future date. With the conventional order point, the question is whether an order for 200 should be released immediately even though the lead time is less than the delivery time, or whether it should be released at the proper, later time. In the latter case, the problem is what special procedure to institute so as not to miss the (future) order release date.

The statistical order point technique itself will, of course, reorder when the inventory drops down to the order point quantity, *whenever* that may happen. Moreover, once the order for 200 is released, it will increase the (on-hand plus on-order) inventory correspondingly, and this will tend to act to prevent another replenishment order from being released until the order in question is shipped. By then, it may be impossible to meet regular service-part demand if stock on hand has been depleted.

With time-phased order point, none of these problems arises. The order for 200 is simply entered as a gross requirement in the appropriate bucket of the inventory record and is added to whatever quantity has been forecast for that period to cover regular demand. No more need be done, as the system will automatically order correctly, at the proper time, to cover both forecast and known future demand.

Effect on Management of Parts Service

The time-phased order point is an outgrowth and extension of the MRP system, and it is interesting to note what effect on the service-part function such a system tends to have. Historically, this function in a manufacturing company has been evolving toward organizational separation and independence from the manufacturing function in general, and production-and-inventory control in particular. This has been caused primarily by the marketing nature of a service-part inventory and by the marketing orientation of the people in charge of this inventory. In this evolutionary process, service-part stock is first segregated from production-part stock physically, to prevent manufacturing personnel from borrowing service parts for purposes of production. Such borrowing is done to cover shortages caused primarily by deficiencies in the inventory control system. Next comes a separate service-part department, independent of the production control manager. A separate, different inventory control system evolves for service parts. Finally, the service-part organization operates its own warehousing and distribution facilities geographically remote from the plant which manufactures the parts.

The installation of an MRP system by the plant tends to reverse this trend. First, the service-part organization comes under pressure to adopt the time-phased order point approach, so that the plant might have a better visibility into future service-part requirements. The two previously disparate inventory systems become compatible and then, in effect, two parts of one (MRP) system. With good planning and control of inventories, the former justification for physically segregating the inventories no longer exists. A consolidation of these inventories results in a lower level of total inventory investment. Stock is freely "borrowed" between production and part service, but under control by the MRP system, which simply (and impartially) allocates existing stock to production and service-part requirements in time sequence of actual need. The result is improved customer parts service and fewer production shortages.

ENTRY OF EXTERNAL ITEM-DEMAND

In the typical manufacturing environment in which an MRP system would be used, the bulk of the component-item demand derives from the master production schedule and is generated internally through the requirements planning (explosion) process. At least some of the demand for components, however, normally also comes from sources external to the plant (e.g., service-part and interplant requirements) or nonproduction sources within the plant (e.g., experimental, quality-control, and plant-maintenance requirements). The demand, if any, in the latter category is usually minimal and sporadic, not warranting separate planning or forecasting. Service-part and interplant demand, on the other hand, may be both significant and recurring. This demand is conveyed to the MRP system in one or more of the following forms:

1. Entry of orders placed by a service warehouse
2. Entry of orders placed by another plant
3. Forecasting of service-part demand
4. Processing of planned-order schedules of a service warehouse time-phased order point system
5. Processing of planned-order schedules of another plant's MRP system

The Entry of Orders

Service-part and/or interplant orders are entered into a plant's MRP system by means of transactions that increase gross requirements of the item in question, in the time-bucket corresponding to the order due date. Gross requirements stemming from parent planned orders and those generated by external demand-sources are thus consolidated, and the requirements planning process proceeds in regular fashion. Orders for service parts may be generated by a service warehouse or by an organizationally autonomous service-part department that maintains an inventory control system of its own.

When external (this term also covers business units of the company other than the plant using the MRP system under discussion) component-item demand is expressed in the form of orders, the supplying plant specifies delivery lead times, which means that the organization requesting the parts must normally make commitments well in advance of actual need. Under this arrangement, there tend to be never-ending complaints about orders being received with less than the agreed-upon lead time. The supplying plant typically regards these orders as firm and noncancellable. Generally speaking, this method of treating component-item demand between different organizations of a company is never entirely satisfactory, and delivery service tends to be poor.

Forecasting of Service-Part Demand

In those cases where a plant using an MRP system has a service-part responsibility (rather than a separate service-part organization ordering from it), the logical way, and the most effective, of treating service-part demand is to use the time-phased order point approach. This permits service parts to be integrated into the MRP system, without any need to modify its processing logic.

As mentioned earlier, service-part demand for items in current production has to be (explicitly or implicitly) forecast, and the forecast quantities, by period, are added to the gross requirements of the items in question. The time-phased order point simply extends this principle to cover parts no longer used in current production. The forecast quantities are recorded in the gross requirements buckets of the inventory records of the respective items, even though there are no other (parent planned-order) requirements. The particular statistical techniques used in the past to determine safety stock and to forecast demand for these items can be retained when they are put under time-phased order point.

The time-phased order point provides the way for smoothly integrating independent-demand items into an MRP system. The processing logic of this system profitably applies to service parts that are no longer used in current production, despite the fact that the system is primarily intended to plan production items. Note that many service parts are subassemblies and that *manufactured* service parts entail at least one lower (raw-material) level. Time-phased order point permits, as no other technique does, requirements for component items of service parts to be correctly determined and timed.

Planned-Order Schedules of "Customer" Systems

Demand for component items that comes from sources external to the plant (other units of the company are viewed as "customers" for these components) can be entered into the plant's MRP system by means of planned-order schedules generated by the "customer's" system. This presupposes that a service-part warehouse uses the time-phased order point. Instead of conveying their requirements by means of *actual orders,* the "customer" organizations simply submit schedules of *planned orders* for processing by the supplying plant's MRP system. This represents the most desirable way, and the most effective method, of registering external demand with the supplying plant, because it provides maximum visibility of future requirements.

The principle of feeding the output of a "customer" system directly to the supplying plant's MRP system extends also to the company's *product* warehouses or distributorships, and to actual customers who operate MRP systems of their own. In both cases, the precondition for thus interfacing the systems is a product that appears as an end item in the supplying plant's master production schedule and has an item inventory record in the plant's system. The use of this method of conveying demand can be expected to increase dramatically in the future, because of its many advantages to both trading partners.

When a warehouse's time-phased order point system, or another plant's MRP system, directly interfaces with the supplying plant's system, two time-phased inventory records of the same item are logically linked in a pseudo-parent/component relationship. Let us take an imaginary service part X which has a record in a time-phased order point system and another record in the supplying plant's MRP system, as illustrated in Figure 41.

At the warehouse-system level, item X acts as a pseudoparent item, linked by its planned-order release schedule to the gross requirements schedule of pseudocomponent item X at the plant-system level. The two records of item X are, as it were, put one on top of another. When this is done, *independent* demand for the item at the warehouse level is translated, by the system's processing logic, into *dependent* demand at the plant level.

Because the item in question has two time-phased inventory records, its normal lead time must not be duplicated but rather *divided* between the records. At the parent level, planned lead time should equal the transportation or delivery-time portion of the total, e.g., one week; at the component level, planned lead time should equal the manufacturing portion of the total, e.g., several weeks or months. In Figure 41, these lead times are shown as one week and four weeks, respectively.

This concludes the discussion of those aspects of an MRP system's processing logic that all such systems have in common. There are two alternative implementations of the material requirements planning approach, however, each of which embodies a different requirements planning procedure. The alternative implementations, known as *regenerative MRP systems* and *net change MRP systems,* are geared to different frequencies of replanning. Their description and comparison constitutes the subject of the next chapter.

Item X
Safety stock: 20
Lead time: 1

		Period						"Customer" system
		1	2	3	4	5	6	
Gross requirements		10	10	10	10	10	10	
Scheduled receipts								
On hand	48	38	28	18	8	−2	−12	
Planned-order releases			30			30		

Item X
Lead time: 4

								Supplying plant system
Gross requirements			30			30		
Scheduled receipts			30					
On hand	5	5	5	5	5	−25	−25	
Planned-order releases		25						

FIGURE 41   Pseudoparent/component relationship.

REFERENCES

Inventory Management, Chapter 5 of Communications Oriented Production Information and Control System (COPICS), vol. 4, form no. G320-1977, International Business Machines Corp., 1972.

Material Requirements Planning by Computer, American Production and Inventory Control Society, 1971.

Plossl, G. W. and O. W. Wight: "Designing and Implementing a Material Requirements Planning System," Proceedings of the 13th International Conference of APICS, 1970.

CHAPTER FIVE

REGENERATIVE SYSTEMS AND NET CHANGE SYSTEMS

There are two basic alternatives of MRP system implementation:

1. Schedule regeneration
2. Net change

The first of these affords high data-processing efficiency but limits the frequency of replanning, as a practical matter, to a weekly or longer cycle. The second is designed for high-frequency (or continuous) replanning, at the expense of overall processing efficiency. The principal outputs of these two MRP system varieties are identical in content—everything else being the same, there is only one correct solution—and the inputs are nearly identical, the exception being a different treatment of item inventory status maintenance. The main difference between regenerative and net change systems lies in the frequency of replanning and in what sets off the replanning process. In the first instance, it is the submission of a master production schedule for processing. In the second, it is inventory transactions that initiate replanning.

These and other differences between schedule regeneration and net change will be described and cataloged later in this chapter. Any given MRP system is either regenerative or net change—there can be no hybrids—but the difficulty in endeavoring to describe the difference between these system alternatives lies in the fact that in industry there is found a whole spectrum of implementations. A given regenerative system may have "borrowed" some features of a net change system; conversely, a net change system may be used the way a regenerative system is intended to be used. This sometimes creates confusion in trying to classify a particular MRP system that, on the surface, looks like the other kind of system.

To avoid such confusion in this chapter, the author will describe "pure," or "classic," versions of schedule regeneration and net change. In practice, one version may adopt some features of the other. This may be done for purposes of convenience, economy, etc., but is not *essential* for the system's operation.

SCHEDULE REGENERATION

The conventional, and traditional, approach to material requirements planning is based on what is called *schedule regeneration*. Under this approach, the entire master production schedule, which constitutes the prime input to an MRP system, is broken down into detailed time-phased requirements for every individual item.

Characteristics of the Regenerative Approach

Under the regenerative approach,

■ Every end-item requirement stated in the master production schedule must be exploded.
■ Every (active) bill of material must be retrieved.
■ The status of every (active) inventory item must be recomputed.
■ Voluminous output is generated.

In regenerative material requirements planning, all requirements are exploded in one batch-processing run, as the master production schedule is periodically being "regenerated." During this run, the gross and net requirements for each inventory item are recomputed and its planned-order schedule is re-created. The entire process is carried out in level-by-level fashion, starting with the highest (end-item) product level and progressing down to the lowest (purchased-material) level. All items on a given level arc processed (low-level code, as noted in Chapter 4, determines exceptions) before the next-lower level is addressed.

Schedule regeneration relies mostly on sequential data-processing techniques, and it is a batch-processing method that entails an inherent massive data-handling task. As a batch approach it must be, by definition, tied to some *periodic* frequency. Each regeneration (explosion) represents a replanning of requirements and an updating of inventory status for all items covered by the MRP system. Intervening changes, if any, in the master production schedule, in product structure, and in planning factors, are accumulated for processing in the next regeneration. A weekly or biweekly replanning cycle is typical of regenerative MRP systems installed in industry.

The operation of such systems consists of two distinct, alternating phases:

1. Requirements planning (explosion) run
2. Intracycle file updating

The latter consists of the reporting of inventory transactions to the system and of posting to the individual inventory records. This brings these records up to date for purposes of inquiry as well as for the next requirements re-planning run. (File maintenance for changes in both product structure and planning factors, such as lead times and scrap allowances, is assumed. It does not constitute a separate phase of operation.)

It was pointed out in Chapter 4 that two types of data constitute the status of any given inventory item in a material requirements planning environ-ment, i.e., inventory data (on hand and on order) and requirements data (gross requirements, net requirements, and planned-order releases). Under the regenerative approach to material requirements planning, the require-ments data are not a *logically integral* part of the item inventory record. This means that item inventory status is actually being established and displayed in two versions, namely:

1. Inventory status in its *narrower sense* (partial status)
2. Inventory status in its *broader sense* (full status)

The first, consisting of inventory data and, in some implementations, allo-cated-on-hand data, is being maintained via the file-update process, at a relatively high frequency, e.g., daily. The second, which also includes re-quirements data, is, strictly speaking, not *maintained* but rather recon-structed or *reestablished*, at a different, lower frequency, e.g., weekly. The output of the requirements planning run which reestablishes this status is typically printed as a report rather than stored. When it is stored, it is for purposes of inquiry rather than for maintaining it up to date.

Note that in the file-update phase a given transaction updates only the one item record that it affects *directly*. Because of the parent/component rela-tionship between items, and because of the logical link between the parent's planned order and the component's gross requirement, certain transactions (such as scrap) may upset the status of the item in a way that, *in fact*, affects items on another (lower) level also. In a regenerative MRP system, however, the file-update program is oblivious of interitem relationships, which are designed to be reestablished by the regeneration program during a require-ments planning run. Thus an inventory transaction, under a regenerative system, never triggers an explosion into a lower product level. This allows a gradual deterioration in the validity of requirements data to take place following each requirements planning run.

The two points just made are of utmost significance, and they are hereby repeated for emphasis:

1. *A transaction may change the status of an item in a way that, in fact, also affects the status of its components.*

2. *If component-item status is not modified as a result of such a transaction, the validity of requirements data within the system gradually deteriorates.*

Frequency of Replanning

Inherent to schedule regeneration, always a big job, is the task of massive data handling which entails a delay in obtaining the results of the requirements planning run and dictates that the job be done periodically, i.e., at economically reasonable intervals. This causes the system to be out of date, in some degree, *at all times.*

How serious a disadvantage this represents in a given case depends on:

- The *environment* in which the MRP system must operate
- The *uses* to which it is being put

In a dynamic, or volatile, environment the situation is in a continuous state of change. There are frequent changes in the master production schedule. Customer demand fluctuates and orders are being changed, perhaps day by day. Interplant orders arrive erratically. There are rush service-part orders. There is scrap. There is a constant stream of engineering changes. All this means that requirements for individual inventory items, and their timing, are subject to rapid change.

In an environment of this kind there is a strong need for timeliness of response to change, but a regenerative MRP system can replan only periodically—at best, probably once a week. Its reflexes are relatively sluggish, because it is not really geared to the rhythm of the operation it is intended to support.

In a more stable environment, a regenerative MRP system may function satisfactorily, as far as *material requirements* are concerned. But material requirements planning is more than just an inventory control system, and its capability to maintain open-order due dates up to date, and thus valid, is of vital importance. This function of an MRP system, the planning of open-order priorities, will be more fully discussed in Chapter 7. Open-order due dates form the basis of any sound method of establishing relative priorities of shop orders, and of operation sequencing. If these priorities are to be kept valid, however, the shop-order due dates on which they are based must obviously be up to date. If shop priorities are to be valid at all times, order due dates must be up to date at all times. An MRP system that replans in weekly (or longer) cycles, however, can obviously do no better than to generate order due dates that are only periodically up to date.

The frequency of replanning is a critical variable in the *use* of an MRP system. It is also a critical parameter in the *design* of the system, because the regenerative approach makes it impractical to replan at a frequency higher than about once per week. To make it feasible to replan requirements more often, a solution to the problem of data-processing economics (the scope of the replanning job, its duration, the volume of its output) must be found, and the delay inherent in any massive batch-processing run must be avoided. An MRP system designed on the nonregenerative, or net change, concept provides the solution.

NET CHANGE MATERIAL REQUIREMENTS PLANNING

The function that the requirements planning run provides is essential. The explosion cannot be eliminated or circumvented, but it can be stretched out. Net change material requirements planning manifests itself through consecutive, *partial explosions* performed with high frequency, in substitution for a full explosion performed periodically at relatively long intervals.

The partial explosion is the key to the practicability of the net change approach, as it minimizes the scope of the requirements planning job at any one time and thus permits frequent replanning. Because the explosion is only partial, it automatically limits the volume of the resulting output. Under the net change approach, the explosion is partial in two senses:

1. Only part of the master production schedule is subject to explosion at any one time.

2. The effect of transaction-triggered explosions is limited to lower-level components of the item providing the stimulus for the explosion.

In the discussion that follows, these two aspects of a net change MRP system will be reviewed separately.

Master Production Schedule Continuity

The net change concept views the master production schedule as one plan in continuous existence, rather than as successive versions or issues of the plan. The master production schedule can be updated at any time, by adding or subtracting the net difference from its previous status. Periodic issues of a new schedule are treated in the same way, in effect as a special case of updating for change.

This concept is illustrated in Figure 42. The schedule is envisioned as resembling a Chinese scroll unwinding with passage of time. Each bucket in the master production schedule grid contains either a zero or some positive value. The schedule extends indefinitely into the future, with all buckets beyond the planning horizon having zero contents. Passage of time brings segments of the future within the planning horizon, at which time the buckets' contents are normally changed (via the issue of a new schedule) from zero to a positive value.

Updating and changing the master production schedule are equivalent

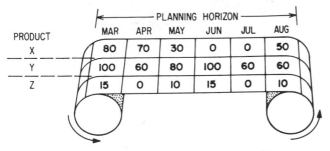

FIGURE 42   Master production schedule continuity.

under the net change concept. Because either is effected by means of addition or subtraction of the net difference relative to its previous status, the task of replanning is minimized. This treatment of the master production schedule was pioneered by American Bosch of Springfield, Massachusetts, in a biweekly batch MRP system implemented in 1959.[1]

Figure 43 illustrates this approach. If a six-month schedule appeared in March as in Figure 43A and in April as in Figure 43B, the difference from previous status would net out as shown in Figure 43C. This is the *net change* that is processed (exploded) by the MRP system on whatever day the new schedule goes into effect.

[1] See list of references at the end of this chapter.

A

PRODUCT	MAR	APR	MAY	JUN	JUL	AUG	SEP
X	80	70	30	0	0	50	0
Y	100	60	80	100	60	60	0
Z	15	0	10	15	0	10	0

B

PRODUCT		APR	MAY	JUN	JUL	AUG	SEP
X		70	30	0	0	35	40
Y		60	80	100	60	60	0
Z		0	10	15	0	10	15

C

PRODUCT		APR	MAY	JUN	JUL	AUG	SEP
X						−15	+40
Y							
Z							+15

FIGURE 43   Net change between consecutive master production schedules.

In the example, out of a total of eighteen master production schedule buckets within the planning horizon, fifteen remain unaffected. The schedule for product Y continues unchanged. In this case, the data-processing job on a net change basis is only a fraction of the job that a regenerative MRP system would have to perform. Under the schedule-regeneration approach, the contents of all eighteen buckets would be input into the system, and all inventory records as well as bills of material related to products X, Y, and Z would have to be accessed and processed.

An additional important point is represented by the fact that if the need to reduce the August quantity of product X had been recognized at some time in March, it could have been processed by a net change system at that time, without waiting for the next (April) issue of the schedule. In that case, the net impact of the April schedule, as far as product X is concerned, would be limited to the addition of forty for September.

Updating of Item Status

The principle of net change—the processing of only the difference from previous status—extends also to item status updating. This makes it feasible to maintain inventory status in its broader sense (as defined previously) up to date for all items covered by the system, without regenerating any of the data. Gross requirements and net requirements data are not reconstituted but merely modified, updated. Under the net change approach, these data are updated in the process of posting inventory transactions to item records. The function of file updating, limited under the regenerative approach to on-hand and on-order data, is expanded to cover all the status data in the item record.

This requires that time-phased requirements data be logically integrated with the traditional (on-hand and on-order) inventory status data and that a permanent requirements file be created within the system. In contrast to the regenerative method, this file is stored for the purpose of being maintained up to date by the net change MRP system. Because the gross requirements for a given item derive from the quantities and timing of planned-order releases of its parent items, the planned-order release data are also stored, either separately or as part of this file.

Two concepts related to inventory status characterize a net change MRP system:

1. Record balance
2. Interlevel equilibrium

An inventory item record is said to be in balance when the projected on-hand quantities correspond to existing gross requirements and scheduled receipts and when the planned orders are correctly determined as to both quantity and timing. The next inventory transaction will change the status and may disturb this balance. In a net change material requirements planning environment the record is rebalanced; i.e., the projected on-hand/ net-requirement quantities are recomputed, and the planned-order releases are realigned or changed, as required, before the record is returned to file. All inventory records on file are in individual balance at all times.

In the Figure 44 example, if the open order for twenty-three is reduced to twenty following the scrapping of three pieces, the net requirements will both increase and move forward in time. To restore balance, the planned-order release will have to be rescheduled. The rebalanced record is shown in Figure 45.

Lead time: 3 Order quantity: 25		Period							
		1	2	3	4	5	6	7	8
Gross requirements		10	2		10	13		20	4
Scheduled receipts				23					
On hand	14	4	2	25	15	2	2	-18	-22
Planned-order releases					25				

FIGURE 44   Status before scrap.

Lead time: 3 Order quantity: 25		Period							
		1	2	3	4	5	6	7	8
Gross requirements		10	2		10	13		20	4
Scheduled receipts				20					
On hand	14	4	2	22	12	-1	-1	-21	-25
Planned-order releases			25←—						

FIGURE 45   Status rebalanced following scrap.

The concept of interlevel or file equilibrium extends the principle of balance to sets of records that are logically related. This means that gross requirements for every item must correspond *at all times* to the quantities and timing of planned-order releases of its parent items.

Because the timing of the planned-order release in the example has changed (from period 4 in Figure 44 to period 2 in Figure 45), the gross requirements of component items have also changed and the former equilib- rium between parent- and component-item records has been upset. To re- store equilibrium, the system immediately processes the net change in the components' gross requirements. Figure 46 represents this net change.

The restoration of interlevel equilibrium necessitates a (partial) explo- sion of requirements. Lower-level item records are identified via the pro- duct-structure file and are retrieved. They are then reprocessed so as to re-

Component items	Period							
	1	2	3	4	5	6	7	8
CHANGE IN GROSS REQUIREMENTS		+25		-25				

FIGURE 46   Net change in component gross requirements.

align their logical linkage to the parent item and to reestablish a balance in the status of the individual items. To the extent that this reprocessing changes the planned-order release schedules of the component items, the explosion progresses further down the product structure, through as many levels as required.

This is illustrated in Figure 47. The item-record file depicted in Figure 47A is in equilibrium. Assuming that the next transaction was a customer return of four units of assembly X (Figure 47B), this upset the equilibrium between records X and Y. Following its restoration, the equilibrium between Y and Z was upset in turn, was restored, and so on. In this example, a single transaction has caused an explosion into three lower levels.

The Role of Transactions

The processing logic illustrated here is the same as that used in the regenerative approach. *Transaction-triggered explosions*, however, are a unique characteristic of a net change MRP system. This characteristic cannot be "borrowed" or adopted by a regenerative system. It is the prime attribute of a net change system and its key identification mark. It cannot be grafted onto a regenerative MRP system without it *becoming* a net change system.

The principle of interlevel equilibrium demands that inventory transactions, when presented to the system, be fully processed. The updating process triggered by a given transaction is completely carried out down the product structure, as required. Note that this modifies the procedure of level-by-level processing discussed in Chapter 4. Compare Figure 35 in that chapter with Figure 48, illustrating the explosion path in a net change system. Whenever a change in status of one item (caused by a single transaction entry) affects other related items on lower levels, all the respective records (regardless of their number) are updated as a result of this entry. This means that transactions may be entered in *random sequence*, and at *random times*. (If they are not so entered but rather batched for, say, daily processing, it would be inefficient to follow the explosion path illustrated in Figure 48. It would normally be modified to proceed in level-by-level fashion: A,Y,B,B,C,C,C.)

A net change MRP system is transaction-oriented and can be transaction-driven when inventory transactions are entered through remote on-line terminals. Because the system updates inventory status in its broader sense, including requirements data, any entry (input) posted to an item

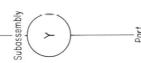
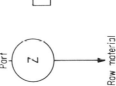
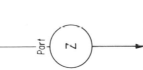

FIGURE 47 Restoration of interlevel equilibrium.

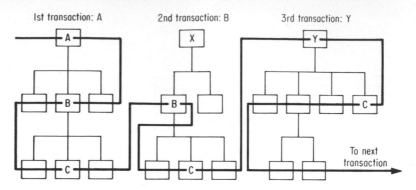

FIGURE 48   Modified level-by-level processing.

record that affects the time-phased status data acts as a transaction. All such entries, encompassing the following, are viewed and treated as inventory transactions by the system:

- Inputs from the master production schedule
- Gross requirements alterations resulting from changes in planned-order release schedules on the parent level (internally generated transactions)
- Gross requirements alterations resulting from external, direct entry to a lower-level item record (e.g., a service-part order for a component)
- Traditional inventory transactions

In a net change MRP system there is *no distinction between the file-updating and requirements-planning phases.* Under the net change approach, inventory control (or inventory accounting) and requirements planning are fused into a single inventory management function. In existing industry implementations of net change MRP systems, neither changes in product structure nor changes in planning factors are normally treated as transactions; that is to say, their entry in the course of item-record file maintenance does not set off the replanning process. These types of change are reflected in the inventory status only following the next transaction entry against the item affected, unless special procedures (extraneous to the MRP system) are devised to change the status at the time of maintenance.

Allocation of Quantities on Hand

The requirement of interlevel equilibrium in a net change environment creates one special demand on the system's processing logic. When a planned order for a manufactured item is released (transformed from a planned-order release to a scheduled receipt), the required quantities of its components *must be allocated* in the respective component records, as will be explained below.

Order-release action takes place when a planned order becomes mature, i.e., when the timing of its planned release coincides with the current period. Passage of time (or rebalancing of the record) brings the planned-order quantity into the first bucket (*action bucket:* see also Figure 72 and the section "Releasing a Planned Order" in Chapter 8).   The example in Figure 49 shows how the record previously presented in Figure 45 would appear at the beginning of period 2.   Because the first planned-order bucket is full, the system will signal the need for order-release action.   After the trans-action reporting this action has been posted, the record appears as shown in Figure 50.   Because the contents of the first bucket have been reduced by 25, the principle of interlevel equilibrium demands that gross requirements at the next-lower level be reduced accordingly.

Lead time: 3 Order quantity: 25		Period								
		2	3	4	5	6	7	8	9	
Gross requirements		2		10	13		20	4		
Scheduled receipts			20							
On hand	4	2	22	12	-1	-1	-21	-25	-25	
Planned-order releases		25								

FIGURE 49   A mature planned order.

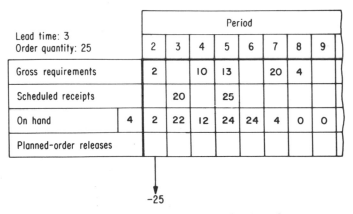

Lead time: 3 Order quantity: 25		Period								
		2	3	4	5	6	7	8	9	
Gross requirements		2		10	13		20	4		
Scheduled receipts			20		25					
On hand	4	2	22	12	24	24	4	0	0	
Planned-order releases										

−25

FIGURE 50   Status following the posting of order release.

This reduction would, however, distort the status of the lower-level com-ponents because, at the time of parent-order release, the component gross requirements have not yet been satisfied physically.   The corresponding quantities of these components (intended for disbursement in support of the parent order) are still on hand at the moment.   Due to the time lag be-tween order release and the filling of the respective material requisition

A

	Period			
PARENT	2	3	4	5
Planned-order releases	25			

COMPONENT

ORIGINAL STATUS OF COMPONENT ITEM (NET REQ. = 20)

Gross requirements		25			60
Scheduled receipts					
On hand	65	40	40	40	-20
Planned-order releases			20		

B

PARENT					
Planned-order releases		0			

−25

COMPONENT

STATUS DISTORTED FOLLOWING RELEASE OF PLANNED ORDER (NET REQ. = 0)

Gross requirements		0			60
Scheduled receipts					
On hand	65	65	65	65	5
Planned-order releases			0		

FIGURE 51   Distortion of status following order release.

(component disbursement), a distortion of component-item status would occur.   This is illustrated in Figure 51.

In Figure 52A the problem is solved by adding an allocation field to the item record, and by incrementing it by the quantity of gross requirement reduction at parent-order release time.   The quantity of stock on hand allocated (to released parent orders), sometimes called *uncashed requisitions*, serves as a substitute gross requirement added to the first period for purposes of calculating the projected on-hand quantities.   Following the physical disbursement of the item, the respective transaction reduces the content of both the on-hand and the allocated fields, by the same amount.   This is shown in Figure 52B.

The *logical requirement* for allocating on-hand quantities is yet another distinguishing characteristic of a net change MRP system.   Under the regenerative approach, the allocation procedure is optional.   The allocated on-hand quantity must be reflected by the record (i.e., the uncashed requisi-

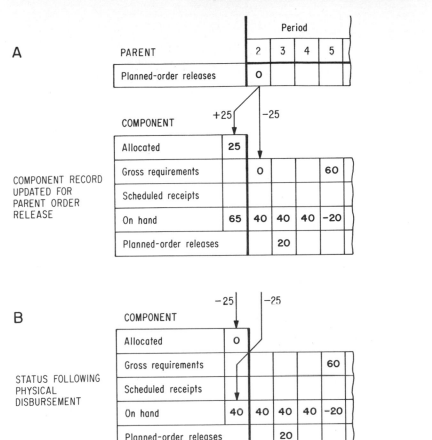

FIGURE 52   Function of allocation field.

tions must be accounted for) only where the parent order is recorded (posted) as a scheduled receipt immediately upon order release.   The release then constitutes a transaction that acts to reduce the planned-order quantity and to increase the on-order quantity in the parent's status.   If component material were not allocated, the MRP system, when replanning requirements, would have no way of knowing that the respective quantities are not, in fact, available to be applied against gross requirements for these component materials.   The result would be understated net requirements for these materials, as has been illustrated in Figure 51B.   If the posting of the order-release transaction is deferred, however, until after the requisition has been filled, the allocated on-hand field is not required as no distortion would occur.

The Function of Control-Balance Fields

An interesting, and useful, feature of a net change MRP system are the "control-balance" fields in the time-phased inventory record shown in Fig-

Lead time: 3 Order quantity: 25	Control balance	Period							
Allocated	I	3	4	5	6	7	8	9	10
Gross requirements	I		10	13		20	4		
Scheduled receipts		20							
On hand	3	22	12	-1	-1	-21	-25	-25	-25
Planned-order releases	25	25							

FIGURE 53   Delinquent performance.

ure 53. Through the use of these fields the system is able to monitor performance to plan and to generate management information for control of this performance. As the system updates the item-record file for passage of time (normally, once a week with one-week time buckets), the contents, if any, of the buckets representing the period just passed are "shifted" into the control-balance fields, except for the on-hand data.

The control balances then represent delinquent performance. The previous example in Figure 49 indicates that performance planned for period 2 calls for two units to be consumed (disbursed, shipped) and twenty-five units to be ordered. If actual performance had turned out to be one unit (assuming that the parent order for two units was released but only one unit of this component was disbursed) and zero, respectively, the record would appear as in Figure 53. In this case, the delinquent planned-order release quantity has also been added to the contents of the period-3 bucket, for greater ease of evaluation by the inventory planner.

Negative quantities are recorded in the control-balance fields whenever a transaction indicates premature (or excessive) performance. For example, if, following the status shown in Figure 49, three units had been consumed,

Lead time: 3 Order quantity: 25	Control balance	Period							
Allocated		2	3	4	5	6	7	8	9
Gross requirements	-1			10	13		20	4	
Scheduled receipts	-20			40					
On hand	21	21	21	51	38	38	18	14	14
Planned-order releases	-15								

-40

FIGURE 54   Premature or excessive performance.

twenty units (prematurely) received, and forty units placed on order during period 2, the record, following the transactions, would appear as in Figure 54.

Releasing an order for forty units, instead of the planned twenty-five, may cause a problem on the component level (no problem if the record in Figure 54 pertains to a purchased item), because only twenty-five have previously been reserved (i.e., a gross requirement for twenty-five was recorded and coverage planned accordingly) on that level. If the component item(s) have multiple parents with planned-order releases in period 2, the total gross requirements for the component(s) may equal or exceed the forty that the parent item (Figure 54) claims. This means that the system will not immediately detect that the equilibrium between parent- and component-item records has been upset.

The transaction will be processed, the material requisition will be filled by the stockroom, and the order will be released to the shop. When another parent order is released, however, the common-component records will not contain the corresponding gross requirements, and the discrepancy will be recorded as a negative quantity in the (gross requirements) control balance of these records. What is worse, there may not be enough of the component material(s) in stock to allow the order to be released to the shop, because the fifteen units earmarked for it have been disbursed against the previous transaction.

The control balances represent *deviations from plan* that can be printed out, at the end of each period, in the form of a special performance-control report used for purposes of follow-up and corrective action. Such reports can easily be generated as a byproduct of a net change MRP system. A regenerative MRP system, by its very nature, is unequipped to yield this type of management information.

This completes the review of the differences between the two alternative implementations of MRP systems. The essential distinguishing characteristics of regenerative versus net change MRP systems are summarized in Table 6.

Requirements Alteration

A special feature of some regenerative programs called *requirements alteration* is sometimes confused with net change. Requirements alteration is designed to process intervening changes in the master production schedule, between the regular requirements-planning runs. The purpose here is to avoid complete schedule regeneration or full explosion. Inputs to the system are the new values (new bucket contents) in the master production schedule for the respective end items, rather than net changes from the previous status of this schedule. The system then carries out a *partial regeneration* of requirements, limiting the explosion to the changed end items and their components.

TABLE 6 Characteristics of MRP Systems

	Regenerative	Net change
Master production schedule		
Viewed as	Consecutive issues	Continuum
Input to MRP system	Entire contents	Net difference from previous status
Explosion	Full, periodic	Partial, continuous
Requirements data		
Logically integral to item record	No	Yes
Up-to-date maintenance	No	Yes
Method of generation	Reconstituted	Modified, updated
Item inventory status		
File update	Limited to inventory data	Includes inventory and requirements data
Status in narrower sense	Maintained continuously	Not separately maintained
Status in broader sense	Reestablished periodically	Maintained continuously
Records in balance	Only at explosion time	At all times
Interlevel equilibrium		
Establishment	Reestablished only at explosion time	Maintained continuously
Effect of transaction entry	Only updates record directly affected	Transaction-triggered partial explosions
Logical requirement for allocation	No	Yes
Operating phases		
Requirements planning	Periodic, long intervals	No distinction
File updating	Intracycle, short intervals	
Performance control reporting	No	Yes

Requirements alteration is designed to respond only to changes in the master production schedule and not to transaction-caused changes in lower-level item status. It is intended as an intracycle program, to be followed by a regular requirements regeneration. Because requirements alteration updates the status (in its broader sense) of only those lower-level items affected by a given change in the master production schedule, the status of the rest continues deteriorating, as pointed out earlier. If the MRP system is to keep from degenerating, it must not be operated in a constant requirements alteration mode. (An exception to this rule would be the use of the requirements alteration program to reprocess the unchanged portion —normally the bulk—of the master production schedule at regular regeneration time.)

Modes of Use

A net change MRP system can be implemented for either of two modes of use:

1. High-frequency replanning (on, typically, a *daily batch* basis)
2. *Continuous,* or on-line, replanning

Typical practice, in manufacturing companies that have implemented net change systems, is daily batch for transaction processing (and consequently, replanning) with continuous on-line inquiry into the inventory-item file. Under this approach, transactions are accumulated throughout the day and are sorted prior to the updating run. For reasons of data-processing efficiency, other sequential processing techniques may be used, including low-level coding. The transaction-processing run updates the respective inventory-item records and carries out partial explosions, as required to maintain interlevel equilibrium.

Even though it may be used for daily batch processing, the system's design allows it to become on-line transaction-driven whenever the user deems this mode desirable. On-line transaction entry is a matter of terminal and software arrangements external to the logic of the net change MRP system proper, which is independent of these arrangements. The system, in any case, is up to date as of the last transaction processed. The less delay there is in bringing transactions to it, the more up to date it can be.

A net change MRP system lends itself quite naturally to being operated in a continuous replanning mode, because of its ability to fully process a single transaction at the time of its (random) entry. Net change material requirements planning can function as an on-line program as soon as the other, technical conditions for on-line operation are met. Transactions will then be processed in a random stream, with partial explosions taking place as required. In this environment, low-level coding, as well as other batch-processing techniques, has no utility.

EVALUATING NET CHANGE

In comparison with regenerative material requirements planning, the net change approach enables the system to:

- Minimize the requirements-planning job at master production schedule release time
- Process schedule changes occurring between releases as a matter of course, without need for special (requirements alteration) programming
- Be independent of the *timing* of both releases and changes
- Be continually up to date
- Generate nondelay outputs, thus communicating the need for user action at the earliest time possible

From the user's point of view, the most valuable feature of a net change system is its *reactiveness,* its unique capability of timely response to change.

Negative aspects of net change material requirements planning can be categorized as follows:

1. Reduced self-purging capability, and the consequent need for stricter disciplines in external operating procedure
2. The relative processing inefficiency of a net change program
3. The "nervousness" of a net change system

Need for Stricter Discipline

From a practical point of view, any need for stricter discipline on the part of the user is indeed a disadvantage, but the argument that tight discipline must be maintained with net change is misleading to the extent that it implies a "permissive" environment under the regenerative approach. The fact is that loose practices and lack of data integrity will cause the outputs of *any* MRP system to be invalid. Errors in a regenerative system do not hurt any less than those in a net change system, but the latter tends to make them more readily apparent—actually an advantage.

The characteristic of self-purging, sometimes attributed to regenerative systems, is seen as deriving from the fact that every time a new version of the master production schedule is processed, the old material requirements plan is literally thrown away. The job of exploding and planning requirements then proceeds from scratch. This appears to have the advantage of throwing away old errors along with the old plan. The old errors will reappear, however, unless their cause has been removed following the previous processing run.

The argument that stricter discipline is necessary when using a net change system has validity only to the extent that it may be less demanding to *reconstitute* valid system input and reference data periodically rather than to *maintain* them continuously. Companies that use net change material requirements planning maintain a standby program for requirements regeneration, to be substituted for the net change program if and when the system accumulates too many errors. The standby program is then run once, to purge the system by regenerating all requirements data. In actual practice, net change systems are being thus purged about once per year.

Data-processing Inefficiency

As to the aspect of data-processing inefficiency, it is a fact that net change is less efficient, and therefore more costly, primarily due to multiple access to inventory records in transaction posting, as well as in exploding requirements. But this cannot be considered a valid argument against net change because any data-processing method that does not utilize sequential processing techniques is, by definition, relatively inefficient. In net change material requirements planning, the emphasis is on *inventory management and production planning efficiency*, not on *data-processing efficiency*. In the development of MRP systems, as in other business computer applications, there is a tradeoff between data-processing efficiency and the efficacy of the business function the system is intended to support. In these cases, the objective of data-processing efficiency should always be subordinated to the larger goal of improving the effectiveness of the *business*.

System "Nervousness"

The most interesting attribute of net change material requirements planning is the system's apparent hypersensitivity or "nervousness." Since file updating, under the net change approach, is equivalent to replanning, it may appear that the system calls for continual revision of user action taken previously. This is of concern especially where due dates of open purchase orders are concerned, when it is not considered practical to subject these due dates to constant revision. In evaluating this aspect of a net change system, it is important to draw a distinction between:

- The system being informed, up to the minute
- The frequency of action taken on the basis of the information

The latter can obviously be decided upon (based on practical considerations), independently of the former. A deliberate withholding of user action in the full knowledge of current facts is preferable to a lack of action caused by ignorance of these facts. The critic of a "nervous" system argues, in effect, that it is better for an inventory and production planning system to be out of date. Such an argument cannot be seriously considered. "Nervousness" *on the level of planning* is a virtue, not a drawback, of a net change MRP system. Hypersensitivity *on the level of reaction* can, and should, be dampened.

Not every change in inventory status calls for reaction. Many minor changes of the type that would otherwise require action are absorbed by inventory surpluses that exist as a result of previous changes and/or inventory management decisions. These surpluses are created by safety stock, scrap allowances, and temporary excesses in inventory due to lot sizing, engineering changes, reduced requirements, overshipments, overruns, and premature deliveries by suppliers. The system constantly strives to use up such temporarily excessive inventories as early as possible, through the net requirements planning process. Inventory excesses are thus automatically prevented from accumulating, but under normal conditions they exist, in some measure, at any point in time.

Prompt reaction to changes in requirements or other elements of inventory status is generally called for when requirements increase or when the timing of planned performance advances. For the opposite type of change, a delay in reaction can be tolerated. Changes can occur every minute of the day. Inventory status is not significantly affected by most of the updating entries, but certain transactions, e.g., unscheduled stock disbursements, scrap, physical inventory adjustments (short counts), miscellaneous demand exceeding forecast, do cause replanning/rebalancing of inventory status.

Action Cycles

Many changes may occur in the same inventory record on the same day, in which case the timing of open orders appears to require revision several times that day, even though the changes may have a mutually cancelling effect. The inventory planner's reaction to change can, however, be decoupled from the rate at which individual changes occur and are processed by the system. The most common method of dampening reaction to change is simply to delay such reaction. In practice, this takes the form of periodic *action cycles* on the part of the inventory planner. He need not react to the continuous stream of individual changes, but can let them accumulate for some period of time.

The system can provide output of action requests on a cyclical basis. Some action messages would typically be generated, in a batch, once a day. Most requests for normal order action (release of shop orders and purchase requisitions) belong in this category. Different action cycles apply to various types of action, depending on their *purpose*. Thus due dates for all open shop orders may be reevaluated once per shift, so as to maintain the validity of shop priorities. For certain types of messages (premature supplier deliveries, for example), a weekly cycle would be sufficient.

Other types of messages, however, should be generated without any delay, because corrective-action time is critical. For example, an open purchase order may become a candidate for cancellation as a result of changed requirements. A 24-hour delay in reacting to the new situation can make the difference between being or not being able to cancel. Other examples of situations that call for reaction without delay are excessive scrap and a significant downward adjustment of on-hand inventory following a physical count.

When major changes in the master production schedule are being processed, or following regular periodic issues of the schedule, all action-request output should be suppressed until the entire net change has been completely processed by the system. That type of change may affect thousands of records, and the status of an inventory item may change several times during the processing of such a change.

Planning cycles and action cycles are established on a more or less arbitrary basis. Delaying action on available information does dampen reaction to change, but delay obviously cannot be prolonged indefinitely. Under any action cycle, once delay is terminated, subsequent changes can still invalidate the action taken. As a general rule, it is better to act with less delay under a system capable of frequent—or continuous—replanning, reevaluation, and revision of previous action, than to tolerate unresponsiveness by operating on long planning and action cycles.

A net change MRP system offers a range of responses, from zero-delay to weekly and monthly cycles. The relative promptness of reaction to change should be a function of the type of change in question. The net change approach provides many choices of use and implementation. While it can be implemented in any one of several degrees of sophistication in input-output flow arrangements, the system's central architecture remains unaffected by any of these (external) arrangements, and by the technology of input-output devices used. This means that it can be transformed, whenever its user is ready, into an on-line, communications-oriented inventory management system without a change in approach, reeducation, and fundamental system overhaul.

HISTORICAL NOTE

In 1961, at the J. I. Case Company tractor plant in Racine, Wisconsin, a project group under the author's direction designed and installed the first *continuous* net change material requirements planning system. The original system was implemented on an IBM 305 RAMAC with 15 million characters of disk file capacity. This prototype version of a net change system was relatively crude. Inventory records of 500 character positions corresponded to one RAMAC disk track sector. Each such record contained three 1-week buckets plus seven 4-week buckets. There were only two types of output: an action ticket which included the image of the entire record (generated automatically or in response to inquiry), and a weekly performance control report. The system covered about 20,000 active part numbers, including 4,000 assemblies with up to seven assembly levels.

At that time, no programming support was available for a material requirements planning application. The J. I. Case programmer team wrote their own equivalent of a bill of material processor, in addition to the application programs. The development and programming effort took ten months following a two-month feasibility study. The project team expended approximately six man-years in the development and programming phase. This is exclusive of system-related work performed by user personnel. The prototype system was implemented on a stand-alone basis, with the computer fully dedicated to the net change material requirements planning application. The system was subsequently reimplemented on an IBM 1410 System with an IBM 1301 disk file unit, and still later converted to an IBM System/360 Model 50.

The author's closest collaborators on the project were: A. R. Brani (Case), J. A. Chobanian (Case), H. D. Jones (Case), T. L. Musial (IBM), and E. F. Roeseler (Case). Company affiliations are as of that time. The author held overall responsibility for the system in his capacity, at that time, of Director of Production Control for the J. I. Case Company.

REFERENCES

Manufacturing Control at American Bosch Division on the IBM RAMAC 305, application manual form no. E20-2053, International Business Machines Corp., 1960.

Orlicky, J. A.: "Net Change Material Requirements Planning," *Production & Inventory Management,* vol. 13, no. 1, 1972.

————: "Net Change Material Requirements Planning," *IBM Systems Journal,* vol. 12, no. 1, 1973.

————————————————————————

CHAPTER SIX

LOT SIZING

In recent years, the traditional interest in the classic problem of the economic order quantity (EOQ) has shifted to lot sizing in an environment of discrete period-demands. This development has been stimulated by the emergence of MRP systems, which express demand for inventory items in discrete time-series fashion, by computing time-phased gross and net requirements. As this book is being written, the largest portion of the scant literature related to material requirements planning, including virtually all of the scientifically oriented writing on the subject (see list of references at the end of this chapter), is devoted to discrete-demand, time-series lot sizing. This is, without a doubt, the best-researched aspect of material requirements planning. A number of distinct new techniques have been developed, the most important of which are described and evaluated in this chapter, along with the more traditional approaches to lot sizing.

LOT-SIZING TECHNIQUES

The most widely recognized approaches to lot sizing are as follows:

1. Fixed order quantity
2. Economic order quantity (EOQ)
3. Lot for lot
4. Fixed period requirements
5. Period order quantity (POQ)

6. Least unit cost (LUC)
7. Least total cost (LTC)
8. Part-period balancing (PPB)
9. Wagner-Whitin algorithm

The first two of the above are demand-rate oriented; the others are called *discrete lot-sizing techniques,* because they generate order quantities that equal the net requirements in an integral number of consecutive planning periods. Discrete lot sizing does not create "remnants," i.e., quantities that would be carried in inventory for some length of time without being sufficient to cover a future period's requirements in full.

Lot-sizing techniques can be categorized into those that generate fixed, i.e., repetitively ordered quantities, and those that generate varying order quantities. This distinction between *fixed* and *variable* is not to be confused with that between *static* and *dynamic* order quantities. A static order quantity is defined as one that, once computed, continues unchanged in the planned-order schedule. A dynamic order quantity is subject to continuous recomputation, as and if required by changes in net-requirement data. A given lot-sizing technique can generate either static or dynamic order quantities, depending on how it is being used.

Of the nine techniques listed above, only the first one is always static, and the third one is, by definition, dynamic. The rest, including the EOQ, can be used for dynamic replanning at the user's option. The last four are expressly intended for such replanning. It must be pointed out that dynamic order quantities are a mixed blessing in a material requirements planning environment. While they always reflect the most up-to-date version of the materials plan, they affect the requirements (and thus also the planned coverage) for their component items. A recomputation of a parent planned-order quantity will often mean that component-item *open orders* have to be rescheduled, in addition to recomputing and/or retiming *planned orders.*

Upsetting previous plans on component-item levels can sometimes cause severe problems, and while such problems inevitably arise in the course of operations, some of them could be avoided, to the extent that they are caused internally, by the system recomputing previously planned orders. There is merit in the recommendation made by some users of MRP systems that a planned order, once established, be "frozen" as to its quantity (if at all possible) and that only its timing be subsequently changed, as required by changing net requirements. This practice is especially recommended for planned orders that are timed within the span of the cumulative product lead time (as against orders planned for the longer-term future), because only these orders create gross requirements on lower levels that are likely to be covered by open orders.

A review of the nine lot-sizing techniques enumerated above follows. These techniques are usually discussed in connection with *manufactured* inventory items and the term *setup* covers all (fixed) costs of ordering. The reader should understand, however, that the logic on which these techniques are based is not limited to manufactured items. Where the cost of ordering purchased items is significant and/or where quantity discounts apply, any of the economics-oriented lot-sizing techniques can be used, after appropriate modification.[1]

Fixed Order Quantity

A fixed order quantity policy may be specified for any item under an MRP system, but in practice it would be limited to selected items only, if used at all. This policy would be applicable to items with ordering cost sufficiently high to rule out ordering in net requirement quantities, period by period. The fixed order quantity specified for a given inventory item may be determined arbitrarily, or it can be based on intuitive/empirical factors.

The quantity may reflect extraneous considerations, i.e., facts not taken into account by any of the available lot-sizing algorithms. Such facts may be related to the capacities of certain facilities or processes, die life, packaging, storage, etc. It is understood (and the MRP system would be programmed accordingly) that when using this lot-sizing rule, the order quantity will be increased if necessary, to equal an unexpectedly high net requirement in the period the order is intended to cover. For example, if the fixed order quantity were 60 and the earliest net requirement 75, the planned-order quantity would normally be increased to 75, because it would make little sense to generate two orders of 60 each for the same period. Note that this also applies to the EOQ, particularly where it is used as a fixed quantity, repetitively ordered over a period of time (typically one year). An example of a fixed order quantity of 60 is provided in Figure 55. Note that in this and subsequent examples the order quantities are not offset for lead time; i.e., each quantity is shown under (keyed to) the earliest period it is intended to cover.

Period	1	2	3	4	5	6	7	8	9	Total
Net requirements	35	10		40		20	5	10	30	150
Planned-order coverage	60			60					60	180

FIGURE 55   Fixed order quantity (60).

Economic Order Quantity

The EOQ policy, although never intended for a material requirements planning environment, can easily be incorporated into an MRP system if the user so wishes. Figure 56 shows EOQ coverage of the same net require-

[1] *Purchasing,* general information manual form no. GH20-1149-1, International Business Machines Corp., 1973, pp. 140–164.

Period		1	2	3	4	5	6	7	8	9	Total
Net requirements		35	10		40		20	5	10	30	150
Planned-order coverage	58				58				58		174

FIGURE 56   Economic order quantity.

ments as used in the previous example.   These net requirements data will be carried over into subsequent examples of lot sizing, to point up the differences in the performance of the various techniques. The periods will be assumed to represent months, and the following cost data will be used throughout:

Setup (S)	$100
Unit cost (C)	$50
Carrying cost (I)	0.24 per annum
(I_p)	0.02 per period

These cost data will facilitate calculations required in the use of some of the discrete lot-sizing techniques, as the cost of carrying one unit of the inventory item for one period costs one dollar. The EOQ calculation is as follows:

$$Q = \sqrt{\frac{2US}{IC}} = \sqrt{\frac{2 \times 200 \times 100}{0.24 \times 50}} = \sqrt{3{,}333} = 58$$

where Q = economic order quantity
U = annual usage (in units)

The value of U in the above calculation was obtained by annualizing the nine-month demand (net requirements) of 150:

$$9 : 150 = 12 : X$$

$$X = \frac{150 \times 12}{9} = 200$$

In this case, the known future demand, rather than historical demand, was used as a basis for estimating annual usage. The example illustrates a problem all forward-looking lot-sizing techniques face, namely a finite, or limited, planning horizon. In our example, an EOQ based on future demand would require a year's demand data, but the system provides only nine months' visibility. Most of the discrete lot-sizing techniques are not based on annual usage, but they assume a certain minimum visibility for each lot in the planned-order schedule, including the *last one*. In most cases, however, the quantity of the last lot is truncated by the proximity of the far edge of the planning horizon, as will be seen in subsequent examples.

As to the effectiveness of the EOQ in a discrete-demand environment, a look at the Figure 56 example reveals that the first order quantity of 58 includes a "remnant" of 13 pieces that are carried in inventory in periods 1 through 3 to no purpose. Similarly, 6 pieces are carried unnecessarily in periods 4 through 7 due to the size of the second lot. The ordering "strategy" provided by the EOQ approach (of ordering three times in quantities of 58) will be seen to be relatively poor, in comparison with some of the other examples that follow.

The EOQ is based on an assumption of continuous, steady-rate demand, and it will perform well only where the actual demand approximates this assumption. In our example, the demand is both discontinuous and nonuniform. The more discontinuous and nonuniform the demand, the less effective the EOQ will prove to be.

Lot-for-Lot Ordering

This technique, sometimes also referred to as *discrete ordering*, is the simplest and most straightforward of all. It provides period-by-period coverage of net requirements, and the planned-order quantity always equals the quantity of the net requirements being covered. These order quantities are, by necessity, dynamic; i.e., they must be recomputed whenever the respective net requirements change. The use of this technique minimizes inventory carrying cost. It is often used for expensive purchased items, and for any items, purchased or manufactured, that have highly discontinuous demand. Conversely, items in high-volume production and items that pass through specialized facilities geared to continuous production (equivalent to permanent setup) are normally also ordered lot for lot. Figure 57 provides an example of this method of ordering.

Period	I	2	3	4	5	6	7	8	9	Total
Net requirements	35	10		40		20	5	10	30	150
Planned-order coverage	35	10		40		20	5	10	30	150

FIGURE 57   Lot-for-lot approach.

Fixed Period Requirements

This technique is equivalent to the primitive rule of ordering "X months' supply," used in some stock replenishment systems, except that here the supply is determined not by forecasting but by adding up discrete future net requirements. In its rationale, it is similar to the fixed order quantity approach—the span of coverage may be determined arbitrarily or intuitively.

Under this technique, the user specifies how many periods of coverage every planned order should provide. Whereas under the fixed order quantity approach the quantity is constant and the ordering intervals vary, under fixed period requirements the ordering interval is constant and the quantities are allowed to vary. For example, if two periods' requirements were

Period	I	2	3	4	5	6	7	8	9	Total
Net requirements	35	10		40		20	5	10	30	150
Planned-order coverage	45			40		25		40		150

FIGURE 58   Fixed period requirements.

specified, this technique would order every other period, except when zero requirements in a given period would extend the ordering interval. This method is illustrated in Figure 58.

Period Order Quantity

This technique, popularly known as POQ, is based on the logic of the classic EOQ, modified for use in an environment of discrete period-demand. Using known future demand as represented by the net requirements schedule of a given inventory item, the EOQ is computed through the standard formula, to determine the number of orders per year that should be placed. The number of planning periods constituting a year is then divided by this quantity to determine the ordering interval. The POQ technique is identical to the one just discussed, except that the ordering interval is *computed*. Both of these fixed-interval techniques avoid "remnants," in an effort to reduce inventory carrying cost. For this reason, the POQ is more effective than the EOQ, as setup cost per year is the same but carrying cost will tend to be lower under POQ.

A potential difficulty with this approach, however, lies in the possibility that discontinuous net requirements will be distributed in such a way that the predetermined ordering interval will prove inoperative. This will happen when several of the periods coinciding with the ordering interval show zero requirements, thus forcing the POQ technique to order fewer times per year than intended.

Using the previous EOQ example and the annualized demand data, the POQ is determined as follows:

EOQ $= 58$

Number of periods in a year $= 12$

Annual demand $= 200$

$$\frac{200}{58} = 3.4 \text{ (orders per year)}$$

$$\frac{12}{3.4} = 3.5 \text{ (ordering interval)}$$

The application of these results (assuming the interval alternates between 4 and 3) appears in Figure 59. Note that the third order covers only one period's requirements because of insufficient horizon, and would have to be recomputed (probably three times) in the future. In comparison with some

Period	1	2	3	4	5	6	7	8	9	Total
Net requirements	35	10		40		20	5	10	30	150
Planned-order coverage	85					35			30	150

FIGURE 59   Period order quantity.

of the other discrete lot-sizing techniques described below, the effectiveness of POQ — like that of the classic EOQ from which it springs — proves relatively low in the face of discontinuous, nonuniform demand.

Least Unit Cost

This technique and the three that follow have certain things in common. All of them allow both the lot size and the ordering interval to vary. They share a common assumption of discrete inventory depletions *at the beginning* of each period, which means that a portion of each order, equal to the quantity of net requirements in the first period covered by the order, is consumed immediately upon arrival in stock and thus incurs no inventory carrying charge. Inventory carrying cost, under all four of these lot-sizing methods, is computed on the basis of this assumption rather than on *average* inventories in each period.

All four of the techniques share the EOQ objective of minimizing the sum of setup and inventory carrying costs, but each of them employs a somewhat different attack. The least unit cost (LUC) technique is best explained in terms of trial and error, and this approach is used here although less primitive methods of computation do exist. In determining the order quantity, the LUC technique asks, in effect, whether this quantity should equal the first period's net requirements or whether it should be increased also to cover the next period's requirements, or the one after that, etc. The decision is based on the "unit cost" (i.e., setup plus inventory carrying cost per unit) computed for each of the successive order quantities. The one with the least unit cost is chosen to be the lot size. Table 7 contains the computation of the first lot. The next one is computed in identical fashion, starting with period 4. The least unit cost is found at lot quantity of 45, which will cover

TABLE 7   Computation of Least Unit Cost

Setup: $100
Inventory carrying cost: $1 per unit per period

Period	Net requirements	Carried in inventory (periods)	Prospective lot size	Carrying cost, $ For lot	Carrying cost, $ Per unit	Setup per unit, $	Unit cost, $
1	35	0	35	0	0	2.86	2.86
2	10	1	45	10.00	.22	2.22	2.44
3	0	2					
4	40	3	85	130.00	1.53	1.18	2.71

Period	I	2	3	4	5	6	7	8	9	Total
Net requirements	35	10		40		20	5	10	30	150
Planned-order coverage	45			60			45			150

FIGURE 60   Least unit cost.

periods 1 and 2. The next order of 60 will cover periods 4 through 6, and the third order of 45, periods 7 through 9 (Figure 60). The limitation of the LUC approach lies in the fact that the technique considers only one lot at a time. The unit cost varies, sometimes widely, from one lot to the next. Tradeoffs between consecutive lots could sometimes be made that would reduce the *total* cost of two or more lots. Our example contains such a situation: if the requirement in period 7 were added to the quantity of the second lot, its inventory carrying cost would increase by $15, but that of the next lot would decrease by $40. The lot-sizing technique described next attempts to overcome this flaw in LUC logic.

Least Total Cost

The least total cost technique (LTC) is based on the rationale that the sum of setup and inventory carrying costs (total cost) for *all* lots within the planning horizon will be minimized if these costs are as nearly equal as possible, the same as under the classic EOQ approach. The LTC technique attempts to reach this objective by ordering in quantities at which the setup cost per unit and the carrying cost per unit are most nearly equal. A second look at Table 7 will reveal that the LUC technique chose a quantity at which setup cost per unit ($2.22) significantly exceeds carrying cost per unit (22 cents).

Because it seeks the equality of these costs, the LTC technique is able to avoid the relatively laborious computation procedure of LUC· and can proceed toward its goal in a more direct fashion. The vehicle for this is the computation of the so-callled *economic part-period* factor, or EPP. The measure part-period is analogous to a man-year or a passenger-mile. It is one unit of the item carried in inventory for one period. The part-period is a convenient expression of inventory carrying cost for purposes of comparison and tradeoff; i.e., it can be said that to carry a quantity of an item in inventory for a certain period of time will "cost" X part-periods. The EPP is defined as that quantity of the inventory item which, if carried in inventory for one period, would result in a carrying cost equal to the cost of setup. It is computed simply by dividing the inventory carrying charge per unit per period (I_pC) into setup cost (S). In our example, this is

$$\text{EPP} = \frac{S}{I_pC} = \frac{100}{.02 \times 50} = 100$$

The LTC technique selects that order quantity at which the part-period cost most nearly equals the EPP. An example of least total cost computation appears in Table 8. The quantity chosen for the first lot would be 85, because the 130 part-periods that it would cost most nearly approximate the EPP of 100. This order would cover requirements of periods 1 through 5, and the second order of 65 would cover requirements of periods 6 through 9. This is shown in Figure 61.

TABLE 8   Computation of Least Total Cost

Period	Net Requirements	Carried in inventory (periods)	Prospective lot size	Part-periods (cumulative)
1	35	0	35	0
2	10	1	45	10
3	0	2		
4	40	3	85	130

Period	1	2	3	4	5	6	7	8	9	Total
Net requirements	35	10		40		20	5	10	30	150
Planned-order coverage	85					65				150

FIGURE 61   Least total cost.

The LTC approach to lot sizing is generally favored over the LUC, but the arguments its advocates put forward, as well as results of limited simulations, are not entirely convincing. The LTC logic has a flaw of its own in the premise that "the least total cost is at the point where the inventory (carrying) cost and setup cost are equal".[2] This holds true for the EOQ but not for the discrete lot-sizing approach which assumes that inventory depletions occur at the beginning of each period, as pointed out previously.

In the graphic model of the general relationship between setup and carrying costs, the total cost is at a minimum at the point of intersection of the carrying-cost line and the setup curve *only when the line passes through origin* (point zero on the X and Y axes). In the discrete lot-sizing model, however, if a line were fitted to the carrying-cost points, it would have a negative intercept, caused by the assumption that the quantity equal to the demand in the first period incurs no carrying cost. This point can best be illustrated on a model of a series of uniform discrete demands, such as:

Period:	1	2	3	4	5	6	7
Demand:	20	0	20	0	20	0	20

Figure 62 shows a graph of cost relationships, with setup of $100, for such a series. In a graph of nonuniform demand there would, of course, be not one

[2]T. Gorham, "Dynamic Order Quantitites," *Production & Inventory Management,* vol 9, no. 1, 1968.

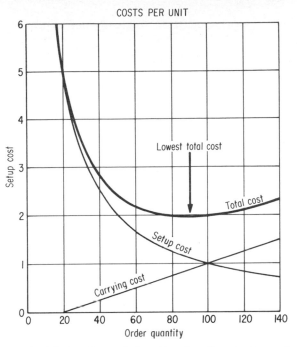

FIGURE 62   Cost relationships for discrete-demand series.

line but several connected shorter lines, each with a different slope. This is why simulations of LUC reveal that the ratio of the setup and carrying-cost elements in the least unit cost is lopsided sometimes one way and sometimes the other. In most cases, however, the setup cost element of least unit cost will be larger than the carrying-cost element. The LTC technique, which seeks to equalize these elements, is therefore biased toward larger order quantities.

Part-Period Balancing

This technique (PPB) employs the same logic as LTC, and its computation of order quantities is identical except for an adjustment routine called *look-ahead/look-back*.[3] This feature is intended to prevent stock covering peak requirements from being carried for long periods of time, and to avoid orders being keyed to (i.e., starting coverage with) periods with low requirements. The adjustments are made only when the condition exists that the look-ahead/look-back corrects. In many cases, therefore, PPB and LTC will yield identical results. This would be the case with the demand data used in the previous examples, and in order to demonstrate look-ahead/look-back, it is necessary to use different series of net requirements. The

[3] J. J. DeMatteis, "An Economic Lot-Sizing Technique: The Part-Period Algorithms," *IBM Systems Journal*, vol. 7, no. 1, 1968, pp. 30–38.

look-ahead adjustment would be operative with the following net requirements schedule:

Period:	1	2	3	4	5	6	7	8	9
Net requirements:	20	40	30	10	40	30	35	20	40
Planned orders:		X			X $\longrightarrow$				

With an EPP of 100, the first lot of 90 would cover periods 1 through 3 and the next lot would be keyed to period 4. But before this is firmed up, a look-ahead to period 5 is made. The 40 units in period 5 would have to be carried in inventory for one period, which would cost 40 part-periods. If the 10 units in period 4 were added to the first lot, they would be carried for three periods at a cost of 30 part-periods. It appears that it would be more economical to key the second lot to period 5. The complete planned-order schedule, adjusted for look-ahead, is shown in Figure 63.

Period		1	2	3	4	5	6	7	8	9	Total
Net requirements		20	40	30	10	40	30	35	20	40	265
Coverage	without look-ahead	90			80			95			265
	with look-ahead	100				105			60		265

FIGURE 63   Part-period balancing with look-ahead.

The look-ahead test is repeated for successive pairs of period-demands until it fails. In our example, the second test (for periods 5 and 6) fails in that it would be more costly to carry 40 for four periods than 30 for one period. If that were not so, the lot would be keyed to period 6. To prevent the look-ahead feature from trying to overcome a steep upward trend in the demand (this would create very large order quantities and defeat the logic of least total cost), an additional test is made. The part-period cost of the last period-demand covered by the prospective lot is compared with the EPP, and the look-ahead process is stopped if the cost equals or exceeds the EPP.

The look-ahead test is always made first. If it fails (i.e., if the possibility of covering an additional period is ruled out), the look-back test is made. Now what is being checked is the possibility of adding the quantity of requirements in the last period covered by the order in question to the next lot, i.e., decreasing the size of the first lot. The look-back can be demonstrated on the following net requirements schedule:

Period:	1	2	3	4	5	6	7	8	9
Net requirements:	20	40	30	15	30	25	50	20	40
Planned orders:	X		$\longleftarrow$ X						

With an EPP of 100, the first lot of 90 would cover periods 1 through 3 and the next lot would be keyed to period 4. A look-back to period 3 indicates that it would cost 60 part-periods to carry stock covering this requirement, whereas it would cost only 15 part-periods to carry the period-4 requirement if the second lot were keyed to period 3. A tradeoff is therefore indicated, the second lot is keyed to period 3, and the first lot is reduced to 60 units. The complete planned-order schedule after look-back appears in Figure 64.

Period		1	2	3	4	5	6	7	8	9	Total
Net requirements		20	40	30	15	30	25	50	20	40	270
Coverage	without look-back	90			70			110			270
	with look-back	60		75			95			40	270

FIGURE 64   Part-period balancing with look-back.

On first reading, it seems that the special features of part-period balancing improve on the effectiveness of the LTC approach. On reflection, however, the look-ahead/look-back proposition proves dubious, and its logic murky. Let us return to the example of look-ahead:

Period:	1	2	3	4	5	6	7	8	9
Net requirements:	20	40	30	10	40	30	35	20	40
Planned orders:	X			X $\longrightarrow$					

It is obviously true that it is cheaper to carry 10 units for three periods than 40 units for one period, but that is not the only consequence of the look-ahead adjustment. The 30 in period 6 will also be carried for one period less. The 35 in period 7, however, would not have incurred any carrying cost had the look-ahead not been employed, but now it will cost 70 part-periods. The look-ahead feature of part-period balancing simply does not look ahead far enough. When the adjustment is made, it tends to change the timing (and coverage) of all subsequent planned orders in the schedule, with results that the technique is oblivious of.

In our example the look-ahead adjustment saves a total of 130 part-periods and incurs a new cost of 100 part-periods. The last lot of 60, however, entails only 40 part-periods due to lack of horizon. It will eventually have to be recomputed and increased so as to pick up an additional 60 part-periods. This will more than offset the net saving of 30 part-periods in periods 1 through 9. But the first three lots will then have covered a larger time span than had they not been adjusted. At this point, the basis has been lost for making a valid comparison of the alternative strategies.

The look-back proposition appears, if anything, even more dubious than look-ahead. It suffers from the same shortcoming as look-ahead in that it fails to examine the consequences of the adjustment throughout the planning horizon. In our example, the look-back produces a net saving of 75 part-periods but adds a fourth setup which is worth 100 part-periods (Figure 64). If setup were larger relative to unit cost, the EPP would be higher and the lots spaced further apart. The last period-demand covered by any prospective lot would then almost always entail more part-periods than the first period of the subsequent lot. Look-back would then be more consistently operative, resulting in more and smaller orders, which would subvert the logic of the least total cost technique on which the look-back is grafted.

Wagner-Whitin Algorithm

This technique embodies an optimizing procedure based on a dynamic programming model.[4] The procedure is too mathematically involved to be suitable for a detailed description here. Basically, it evaluates all possible ways of ordering to cover net requirements in each period of the planning horizon. Its objective is to arrive at the optimum ordering strategy for the entire net requirements schedule. The Wagner-Whitin algorithm is "elegant" in that it reaches this objective without actually having to consider, specifically, each of the strategies that are possible. The Wagner-Whitin solution to the net requirements schedule used in all previous examples, except for part-period balancing, is shown in Figure 65.

Period	1	2	3	4	5	6	7	8	9	Total
Net requirements	35	10		40		20	5	10	30	150
Planned-order coverage	45			65				40		150

FIGURE 65   Wagner-Whitin algorithm.

The Wagner-Whitin algorithm does minimize the combined (total) cost of setup and of carrying inventory, and it is used as a standard for measuring the relative effectiveness of the other discrete lot-sizing techniques. Its disadvantages, usually mentioned in the literature, are a high computational burden and the near impossibility of explaining it to the average MRP system user.

The first of these two arguments is somewhat exaggerated. While it is true that there are typically tens of thousands of inventory items in an MRP system for which planned orders have to be computed and that requirements for a given item tend to change and cause constant recomputations, computational *time*, once a record is in the computer's main memory, is not significant. It is becoming even less so as computer technology progresses—only microseconds are involved here.

The second argument, however, is entirely valid. The complexity of the

[4]H. M. Wagner and T. M. Whitin, "Dynamic Version of the Economic Lot Size Model," *Management Science*, vol. 5, no. 1, 1958.

procedure inhibits understanding by the layman and acts as an obstacle to its adoption in practice.[5] An inherent weakness of the Wagner-Whitin algorithm lies in its assumption that requirements beyond the planning horizon are zero. The technique is designed for a stationary horizon. It would work well, for instance, in the case of custom-designed parts in a limited number of situations, such as a one-time contract for a quantity of special machinery with a firm, staggered-delivery schedule. But in most cases, the planning horizon is not stationary, the life of the typical inventory item is quite long, and additional requirements are constantly being brought within the planning horizon by the passage of time.

Whenever a new requirement appears at the far end of the planning horizon, the Wagner-Whitin ordering strategy (which, by definition, pertains to the entire planning horizon) may have to be revised. At least one lot at the far end of the series is subject to recomputation even if the specific requirements it covers remain unchanged. The validity of a given planned-order quantity computed under this approach may prove ephemeral— lasting no longer than one planning period. This, of course, is true with some of the other algorithms also.

In practice, the Wagner-Whitin optimum strategy proves to be "wrong" if it has to be changed subsequently. From the material requirements planning point of view, instability in the planned-order schedule is undesirable. To the extent that Wagner-Whitin is more sensitive than other lot-sizing techniques to additions of requirements caused by the extension of the horizon—due to its optimum strategy objective—it loses its practical appeal.

LOT SIZE ADJUSTMENTS

The planned-order quantity determined by any of the lot-sizing techniques is subject to certain adjustments dictated by practical considerations. Among these are the following:

- Floors and ceilings
- Scrap allowances
- Multiples
- Raw materials cutting factors

Any of the lot-sizing algorithms discussed previously can be constrained by the imposition of *floors* and/or *ceilings* on the quantity of the item to be ordered. One type of floor has already been mentioned; i.e., the computed quantity, if lower than the net requirements in the period to which the order is keyed, will be increased to at least equal the net requirements. Floors and ceilings may be stated in absolute numbers, e.g., "no less than 50 and no more than 400 units," pertaining to individual inventory items. Alternatively, the limits on quantity may be stated in terms of period coverage, e.g.,

[5] G. W. Plossl and O. W. Wight, *Material Requirements Planning by Computer*, American Production and Inventory Control Society, Washington, D.C., 1971, p. 9.

"no less than 4 weeks' and no more than 12 weeks' requirements," or "not to exceed one year's supply." Floors and ceilings on lot sizes are frequently imposed by management, in view of the fact that the lot-sizing algorithm is blind to a number of practical operating considerations.

A *scrap allowance,* or shrinkage factor, is a quantity added to the computed lot size which is intended to compensate for anticipated scrap or loss in process, and to ensure that the required quantity of "good" pieces is received. This is important only in instances of discrete lot sizing, because the order quantity covers net requirements in an integral number of periods (no "remnants"). The scrap allowance will normally vary from item to item, according to past incidence of scrap.

The scrap allowance may be stated either in terms of pieces or as a percentage of the order quantity. Where the latter approach is used, a fixed percentage is generally undesirable if the planned-order quantities vary significantly from lot to lot. In a machine shop environment, scrap tends to be a function of the number of different setups that are required to complete the part, rather than the quantity being run. In view of this fact, a "declining percentage" formula can be used, such as the following:

$$Q = L + a \sqrt{L}$$

where Q = order quantity
$\quad L$ = lot size computed by the algorithm
$\quad a$ = multiplier reflecting scrap incidence

For example, the lot-sizing technique being used might yield a quantity of 400. This would be adjusted for scrap by adding the square root of 400, that is, 20, for a final order quantity of 420. In this case, the multiplier was assumed to be 1—the value usually used unless the responsible inventory planner specifies a different one. The multiplier, acting to reflect incidence of past scrap of the inventory item in question, may be set to vary from zero (no scrap allowance) to a decimal fraction of 1 to a multiple of 1. With a multiplier of 1, the scrap allowances for various lot quantities would be as shown in Table 9.

In an MRP system, the proper way to handle scrap allowances in the time-phased inventory record is simply to add them to (include them in) the

TABLE 9   "Declining Percentage" Scrap Allowance

Computed lot size	Scrap allowance	Order quantity	Percentage allowed
1	1	2	100
4	2	6	50
9	3	12	33
16	4	20	25
25	5	30	20
100	10	110	10
400	20	420	5
10,000	100	10,100	1

planned-order quantities. When the planned orders are eventually released, the full quantity, including the scrap allowance, should be shown as on order. This quantity would then be reduced as and if scrap transactions are posted to the record. The practice of including scrap allowance quantities in the item's gross requirements (in order to display the projected on-hand quantities as they are expected to be *after* scrap) is unsound, as it distorts the fundamental relationship of parent planned-order quantity to the component item's gross requirements quantity. Furthermore, whether scrap will actually occur is uncertain. Until it does occur, the MRP system should project the item's status as though it will not occur.

Another constraint that can be imposed on the lot-sizing algorithm is the requirement that a given item be ordered in multiples of some number. This may be dictated by considerations of process (so many pieces constitute a Blanchard grinder load, or so many bars of steel are fed to a bar lathe simultaneously), packaging (twelve pieces in a carton), etc. The lot size yielded by the lot-sizing algorithm is, in these cases, increased to the nearest multiple specified.

Raw material cutting factors represent another adjustment to the lot size that it is desirable to make in certain instances. The lot-sizing algorithm, unaware of the form in which raw material (from which the item in question will be made) comes, may generate a quantity that would create problems in cutting this material. For example, if a certain size of sheet metal is cut into nine pieces in the manufacture of a given inventory item, a lot size of 30 will result in either an odd size of raw material being left over or, more likely, the shear operator cutting the four sheets into thirty-six pieces. This will then become the *actual* quantity on order, as against the 30 on order shown by the system.

In cases where more than one type of adjustment is to be made to the order quantity for a given item, the several adjustments are made consecutively in a logical sequence. For example, if the lot-sizing technique yields a quantity of, say, 173 which is equivalent to five periods' requirements, and the item is subject to a three-period ceiling, scrap allowance, and cutting constraint (20 pieces per unit of raw material), the "raw" quantity of 173 would be adjusted as follows:

Raw order quantity:	173
Reduce to three periods' requirements:	121
Add scrap allowance:	11
	132
Increase to nearest multiple of 20:	8
Adjusted order quantity:	140

Scrap allowances, multiples, and cutting factors tend to create an inventory excess. This excess, however, is subsequently applied by the MRP system against later gross requirements. At any point in time, there exists a slight inventory excess, but it does not accumulate.

EVALUATING LOT-SIZING TECHNIQUES

Every one of the lot-sizing techniques reviewed above is imperfect—each suffers from some deficiency, as has been seen. In evaluating the relative effectiveness of these techniques, the difficulty lies in the fact that the performance of the algorithms varies, depending on the net requirements data used and on the ratio of setup and unit costs. Furthermore, some of the techniques assume gradual, steady-rate inventory depletion, whereas others assume discrete depletion, which affects the way inventory carrying cost would have to be computed for purposes of comparison. Ignoring this distinction and basing all inventory carrying costs on discrete depletion at the beginning of each period, the performance of the economics-oriented lot-sizing algorithms for which the same data set was used in the previous examples compares as follows (details in Table 10):

	Total cost
Wagner-Whitin	$395
Least unit cost	420
Least total cost	445
Period order quantity	455
Economic order quantity	506

TABLE 10   Comparison of Lot-Sizing Algorithm Performance

Algorithm	Number of setups	Setup cost, $	Part-periods	Carrying cost, $	Total cost, $
W-W	3	300	95	95	395
LUC	3	300	120	120	420
LTC	2	200	245	245	445
POQ	3	300	155	155	455
EOQ	3	300	206	206	506

The author wishes to stress the fact that these figures are meaningful only in relation to the net requirements schedule, the setup cost ($100), and the unit cost ($50) used in the examples. A change in these data will produce a different sequence. For example, if setup were $300, the POQ would outperform LTC and match LUC in effectiveness. If the requirements data are changed, *the example can be rigged so as to produce practically any results desired,* including the EOQ equal in performance to Wagner-Whitin.[6] The factors that affect the relative effectiveness of the individual lot-sizing techniques are the following:

1. The variability of demand
2. The length of the planning horizon
3. The size of the planning period
4. The ratio of setup and unit costs

The variability of demand consists in nonuniformity (varying magnitude of period-demand) and discontinuity (gaps of no period-demand). The

[6] W. L. Berry, "Lot Sizing Procedures for Requirements Planning Systems: A Framework for Analysis," *Production & Inventory Management,* vol. 13, no. 2, 1972.

length of the planning horizon, i.e., demand visibility, obviously affects the comparative performance of the various algorithms. Shorter planning periods (e.g., weeks instead of months) result in smaller requirements per period, enabling the lot-sizing technique to get closer to the best balance between setup and carrying costs. The setup/unit-cost ratio directly affects the frequency of ordering and thus the lot size.

There does not appear to be one "best" lot-sizing algorithm that could be selected for a given manufacturing environment, for a class of items, and in most cases even for a single specific item. For purposes of material requirements planning, the lot-for-lot approach should be used wherever feasible, and in cases of significant setup cost (typical in the fabrication of component parts), LUC, LTC, PPB, or even POQ should provide satisfactory results. When it comes to selecting a lot-sizing technique (or techniques) to be incorporated in an MRP system, it is the author's opinion that neither detailed studies nor exhaustive debates are warranted—in practice, one discrete lot-sizing algorithm is about as good as another.

Apart from the inherent weaknesses and the difficulty of meaningful comparison between algorithms, the one fact of life that renders, and always will render, any lot-sizing technique vulnerable is the possibility that future requirements will change. After the planned order is released, the order quantity may prove to be wrong in light of change in the magnitude and/or timing of net requirements.

When this happens, it does not matter how elaborately and with what precision the lot size had been computed. All the discrete lot-sizing algorithms are based on the implicit assumption of *certainty of demand*. This is the true Achilles' heel of lot sizing, because, in most cases, the pattern of future demand is never certain. A more realistic assumption would be that the requirements schedule against which the lot size is being computed *will* change.

In comparing the relative effectiveness of one discrete lot-sizing algorithm with that of another, it is possible to determine which of the two is better vis-à-vis a given schedule of net requirements. When the period of time spanned by this schedule has passed into history, however, it might develop that the algorithm originally judged less effective would, in fact, have had the better performance in light of how the requirements actually turned out. The spurious precision of lot-sizing technique is invalidated by what actually happens, as against what had been planned to happen. The relative *actual* effectiveness of a lot-sizing algorithm can be determined only in retrospect.

REFERENCES

Berry, W. L.: "Lot Sizing Procedures for Requirements Planning Systems: A Framework for Analysis," *Production & Inventory Management*, vol. 13, no. 2, 1972.

DeMatteis, J. J.: "An Economic Lot Sizing Technique: The Part-Period Algorithm," *IBM Systems Journal*, vol. 7, no. 1, 1968, pp. 30-38.

Diegel, A.: "Seven Alternatives to Dynamic Programming for Dynamic Lots," paper presented at the 39th National Meeting of the Operations Research Society of America, May 1971.

Gleason, J.M.: "A Computational Variation of the Wagner-Whitin Algorithm: An Alternative to the EOQ," *Production & Inventory Management*, vol. 12, no. 1, 1971.

Gorenstein, S.: "Some Remarks on EOQ vs. Wagner-Whitin," *Production & Inventory Management*, vol. 11, no. 2, 1970.

Gorham, T.: "Dynamic Order Quantities," *Production & Inventory Management*, vol. 9, no. 1, 1968.

———: "Determining Economic Purchase Quantities for Parts with Price Breaks," *Production & Inventory Management*, vol. 11 no. 1, 1970.

Kaimann, R. A.: "A Fallacy of EOQ'ing," *Production & Inventory Management*, vol. 9 no. 1, 1969.

———: "Revisiting a Fallacy of EOQ'ing," *Production & Inventory Management*, vol. 9, no. 4, 1968.

———: "EOQ vs. Dynamic Programming—Which One to Use for Inventory Ordering," *Production & Inventory Management*, vol. 10, no. 4, 1969.

Lippman, S.A.: "Optimal Inventory Policy with Multiple Set Up Costs," *Management Science*, vol. 16, no. 1, 1969.

Peterson, R., and E. A. Silver: *Decision Systems for Inventory Management and Production Planning*, John Wiley & Sons, in preparation.

Plossl, G. W., and O. W. Wight: *Material Requirements Planning by Computer*, American Production and Inventory Control Society, 1971, pp. 6–9 and 30–31.

Purchasing, general information manual form no. GH20-1149-1, International Business Machines Corp. 1973, pp. 140–164.

Rinehard, J. R.: "Economic Purchase Quantity Calculations," *Management Accounting*, September 1970.

Silver, E. A., and H. C. Meal: "A Simple Modification of the *EOQ* for the Case of Varying Demand Rate," *Production & Inventory Management*, vol. 10, no. 4, 1969.

———and———: "A Heuristic for Selecting Lot Size Quantities for the Case of a Deterministic Time-Varying Demand Rate and Discrete Opportunities for Replenishment," *Production & Inventory Management*, vol. 14, no. 2, 1973.

System/360 Requirements Planning, application description manual form no. GH20-0487-3. International Business Machines Corp., 1970, pp. 24–32.

Thomopoulos, N. T., and M. Lehman: "Effects of Inventory Obsolescence and Uneven Demand on the EOQ Formula," *Production & Inventory Management*, vol. 12, no. 4, 1971.

Tuite, M. F., and W. A. Anderson: "A Comparison of Lot Size Algorithms Under Fluctuating Demand Conditions," *Production & Inventory Management*, vol. 9, no. 4, 1968.

Wagner, H. M., and T. M. Whitin: "Dynamic Version of the Economic Lot Size Model," *Management Science*, vol. 5, no. 1, 1958.

Woolsey, R. E. D., E. A. Silver, and H. S. Swanson: "Effect of Forecast Errors on an Inventory Model with Variations in the Demand Rate," *Production & Inventory Management*, vol. 14, no. 2, 1973.

PART FOUR

USING THE SYSTEM

*For those of us who live in a constantly
changing marketing environment and have
to live with the realities of scrap, rework,
absenteeism, and tooling problems, schedules
are in a constant state of ferment. MRP is a
practical way to handle this so that you can
have a genuine schedule that people will follow.*

F. S. MACCOMBIE *in* APICS News, *July 1973.*

CHAPTER SEVEN

MORE THAN
AN INVENTORY CONTROL
SYSTEM

The early material requirements planning systems were conceived and used as replacements for their predecessor inventory control systems which were relatively primitive and/or ineffective. In the use of the new systems, the emphasis was almost exclusively on order-release action. As the systems were further developed and refined, and as the users gained experience in using them, it became apparent that an MRP system yields information that can be of value for several purposes other than just inventory control. Moreover, users discovered that with some minor additional programming, the system can provide outputs in a number of functional categories and thus can serve as a planning system in areas well beyond the boundaries of traditional inventory control.

An MRP system that is properly designed, implemented, and used actually functions on three separate levels:

1. It plans and controls inventories.
2. It plans open-order priorities.
3. It provides input to the capacity requirements planning system.

These are the three principal functions, and principal uses, of an MRP system. Optionally, the system can also serve certain other functions, briefly described below. The three principal functions of the system will later be reviewed in more depth, in separate sections of the present chapter.

THE USE OF SYSTEM OUTPUTS

An MRP system can provide a great number of outputs in a variety of formats, at the user's option. It is not practical to list and describe all the specific outputs and formats generated by MRP systems found in industry, because outputs represent an aspect of the system that lends itself to tailoring, individualization, and infinite modification. An MRP system's files (*data base*) in general, and the inventory status records in particular, contain a wealth of information that provides an opportunity for extracting or further *processing* the data for a whole spectrum of possible outputs.

In the discussion that follows, outputs of an MRP system, which take the form of reports, individual messages (notices), and displays on CRT devices, will be reviewed by functional category rather than individually. Six such categories may be recognized, as follows:

1. Outputs for inventory order action
2. Outputs for replanning order priorities
3. Outputs to help safeguard priority integrity
4. Outputs for purposes of capacity requirements planning
5. Outputs aiding in performance control
6. Outputs reporting errors, incongruities, and out-of-bounds situations within the system

Outputs for inventory order action are based primarily on planned orders becoming mature for release. The MRP system detects such orders by examining the contents of planned-order release buckets in the time-phased inventory records. Other types of inventory order action are increases, reductions, and cancellations of order quantities. These types of output are self-explanatory, and the category should be the one most easily understood in light of the contents of several preceding chapters.

Outputs for replanning order priorities serve to alert the inventory planner to cases of divergence between open-order due dates and dates of actual need, as indicated by the timing of net requirements. Examples of data on which outputs in this category would be based will be presented later in this chapter. In generating these outputs, the MRP system has the capability to indicate precisely by how many periods (or days) each item affected should be rescheduled, and in what direction. Under its standard implementation, the system does not change open-order due dates automatically (although it can easily be programmed to do so) but depends on the inventory planner to take rescheduling action.

Outputs to help safeguard priority integrity, i.e., to keep order priorities not only valid but honest, relate problems of item inventory status to the master production schedule. The concept of priority integrity will be further discussed later in this chapter. To keep priorities honest, the master production schedule must reflect the realities of production; i.e., it must not contain end-item requirements that it will be impossible to meet for lack of· capacity, material, or lead time. Some companies use reports in this category to provide guidance in accepting customer orders for guaranteed delivery. Such reports are generated by "trial fit" (Chapter 11) of the order into the master production schedule, and by letting the MRP system determine component-material and lead-time availability. If the order does not fit, the report indicates a best delivery date alternative.

Outputs for purposes of capacity requirements planning are based on quantities and due dates of both open and planned shop orders, which serve as input to the capacity requirements planning (loading) system. This function will be further discussed later in this chapter. The MRP system makes it possible for the load report to be complete, valid, and extending far enough into the future to allow capacity-adjustment action to be taken in time. To keep the load projection up to date and valid, it must repeatedly be recomputed as the order schedules in the MRP system change.

Outputs aiding in performance control are byproduct outputs of an MRP system that enable management to monitor the performance of inventory planners, buyers, the shop, and vendors, as well as financial or cost performance. A net change MRP system, through the control-balance fields it maintains in the item inventory records (Chapter 5), has an outstanding ability to generate performance-control reports by listing deviations from plan. Special reports on item inactivity, inventory investment projections, and purchase commitment reports also belong in this category of outputs.

When the inventory record contains standard cost, the quantities on hand projected by period (supplemented by planned-order receipts) are simply costed out and summarized by item group to obtain a highly accurate forecast of the inventory investment level. The same is true for open purchase orders—provided they are recorded by valid due date—which can be converted into a purchase commitment report. The product-structure file, with its explosion and implosion chaining (Chapter 9), serves as a basis of product costing. The entire data base, usually also including the routing file, permits management to obtain profit and loss statements, if desired, by individual customer order, by customer, by market, by product, and by product family.

Outputs reporting errors, incongruities, and out-of-bounds situations are called *exception reports* and would cover the following:

■ Date of gross requirement input is outside of the planning horizon.

■ Quantity of gross requirement input (i.e., the number of digits) exceeds size of the field (bucket).

■ Planned order offset into a past period but placed into current period.

■ Number of digits of quantity of component-item gross requirements (perhaps combined from multiple-parent planned orders) exceeds size of the field.

■ Number of digits of quantity of open order exceeds size of the field.

■ Number of digits of quantity of net requirement exceeds size of the field.

■ Number of digits of quantity of planned order exceeds size of the field.

■ Quantity of receipt overflows size of the "quantity on hand" field.

■ Due date of open order outside of planning horizon.

■ Allocated on-hand quantity exceeds current quantity on hand.

■ Past-due gross requirement has been included in the current period.

In addition to exception reports, individual exception messages can be generated at the time of inventory transaction entry, listing reasons for transaction rejections. Such messages would include the following:

■ Part number is nonexistent.

■ Transaction code is nonexistent.

■ Part number is incorrect (rejection based on self-checking digit).

■ Actual receipt exceeds quantity of scheduled receipt by X percent (test of reasonableness).

■ Quantity of scrap in stock exceeds (previous) quantity on hand.

■ Quantity of disbursement exceeds (previous) quantity on hand.

■ Order being released exceeds quantity of planned-order release.

These and similar exception messages are generated as a result of employing diagnostic routines and other system checks discussed in Chapter 9.

AN INVENTORY PLANNING AND CONTROL SYSTEM

This function of an MRP system has been described and discussed, in some detail, in the preceding chapters. We have seen how an MRP system answers the fundamental questions of:

■ What to order
■ How much to order
■ When to order
■ When to schedule delivery

An MRP system can also furnish several types of additional inventory management information, including, as mentioned above, a forecast (more precisely, a projection) of future inventory investment, and clues to an indicated write-off of obsolete and/or inactive items.

Assuming proper system implementation and file-data integrity, an MRP system's outputs are always correct and valid relative to the master production schedule that the system translates into material requirements, and the system signals for correct inventory action at all times. The timeliness of the system's inventory control outputs is a function of replanning frequency (discussed in Chapter 5), which is controlled by the system user.

An MRP system is self-adjusting in that it constantly replans and reallocates existing inventories to changing requirements via the netting process. Manufacturing inventories are therefore minimized relative to the management-imposed master production schedule, lot-sizing policy, and safety stock, and the constraining factor of manufacturing lead times.

A PRIORITY PLANNING SYSTEM

The key to priority planning and priority control of work in the factory are valid open-order due dates. The order due date establishes the relative priority of the order in question, which must contend for limited productive capacity with other orders in the shop. Each shop order entails a number of *operations* that must be performed to complete the order. A distinction must therefore be drawn between:

- Order priority
- Operation priority

Shop scheduling, loading, dispatching, and job-assignment techniques are based on operation priorities. These priorities, to be valid, must be derived from valid order priorities, i.e., valid order due dates. An MRP system has the capability to *establish* valid order priorities at the time of order release and to *maintain* them up to date and valid, by revising a due date that has subsequently been invalidated. This capability is inherent in any MRP system, and it exists whether or not the user takes advantage of it.

The Validity and Integrity of Priorities

An MRP system keeps reevaluating all open-order due dates (for purchase and shop orders both) automatically, as a routine step in its netting process. The system "knows" when an open order is not properly aligned with net requirements and, if programmed to do so, can "tell" the user about it. This will be discussed in more detail and illustrated in examples in the next chapter, as part of the section dealing with the role of the inventory planner. Traditional inventory control systems, as mentioned previously, acted as "push" systems or order-launching systems (order the right item at the right time) that had to be supplemented by "pull" or expediting systems (get the right item completed at the time of actual need). An MRP system functions as a push system and pull system rolled into one.

What the MRP system does, in concept, is attempt to make two dates coincide, namely:

- The due date
- The date of need

The *due date* is defined as the date currently associated with the order. It is the date someone put on the order, and it represents what he *planned,* or expected, to be the date of order completion. The *date of need* signifies the time that the order is *actually* needed. These two dates are not necessarily the same. They may coincide at one time, but they tend to get apart. An MRP system makes these dates coincide at the time of order release, and it monitors them afterward whenever a change in status causes a recomputation of net requirements. The MRP system detects any divergence of the due date and the date of need and, by signalling the inventory planner, causes them to be brought back together by rescheduling the order.

Note that when the dates diverge, the date of need may move in either direction—forward or backward in time. The MRP system can accordingly either "expedite" the order or "deexpedite" it, i.e., have it rescheduled to an earlier or later date. It is obviously important to schedule some orders out when other orders must be completed earlier than scheduled originally.

An MRP system is able to keep priorities valid, but priority *validity* is mechanical (i.e., coincidence of due date with indicated date of need), and it is not the same as priority *integrity*. The validity of all data generated by an MRP system is, as pointed out earlier, relative to the contents of the master production schedule. Thus if this schedule does not reflect what actually must, and can, be produced, the order priorities derived from it by the MRP system will be mechanically valid and at the same time untruthful or unrealistic.

The credibility of a priority planning system depends on both priority validity and priority integrity. This credibility is extremely important because the system, to function successfully, requires cooperation and trust by factory personnel. When the formal priority scheme lacks integrity, shop people soon discover this and revert to the traditional expediting/shortage-list approach. This is tantamount to the collapse of the priority system.

Dependent Priority

The integrity of priorities derives from the master production schedule, and there are basically two ways in which this integrity may be compromised. The master production schedule may contain end items that are either not actually needed at the time indicated or cannot be produced as scheduled for lack of material or components (lack of capacity results in lack of components). The effect of this becomes evident when the concept of *dependent priority* is considered. This concept pertains to the *real* priority (what is really needed when?) as against the *formal* priority (what priority did the system assign to the order?) which may not necessarily be the same.

The concept of priority dependence recognizes that the real priority of an order depends on the availability, or lack of availability, of some other inventory item(s) at the time of order completion. For example, the supply of product A, which is shipped from stock, is forecast to run out in week X. The due date of an order for component item B is week $X - 1$, allowing time to assemble a quantity of product A and replenish its stock in week X. If sales lag and the product is still in ample supply as the component order nears completion, the real priority of the order is lower than its due date indicates.

This can be thought of as *vertical* priority dependence, as the real priority in this case is a function of availability of an item (or items) on a higher level in the product structure. This concept was first introduced in 1964, by means of a new technique for the dynamic updating of operation priorities called *critical ratio*.[1] This technique (as originally formulated) does not rely on due dates and establishes relative priorities by computing the value of the critical ratio for the next operation to be performed on every open shop order, as follows:

$$\text{Ratio A} = \frac{\text{Quantity on hand}}{\text{Order point}} \qquad \text{for example, } \frac{50}{100} = 0.50$$

$$\text{Ratio B} = \frac{\text{Lead time for balance of work}}{\text{Total lead time}} \qquad \text{for example, } \frac{14}{25} = 0.56$$

$$\text{Critical ratio} = \frac{\text{Ratio A}}{\text{Ratio B}} = \frac{0.50}{0.56} = 0.89$$

Ratio A, the disparity between the order point quantity and the quantity of stock on hand, is used as a measure of need. Ratio B, the disparity between the amount of time that was scheduled to be available for operations not yet completed, and the total planned lead time, is used as a measure of response to that need. Ratio A represents the percentage of stock depletion, ratio B the percentage of work completion.

A critical-ratio value of 1.00 signifies that work on the order has kept pace with the rate of stock depletion—the order is "on schedule." A value lower than 1.00 indicates that the pace of work completion lags behind the rate of demand (order is "behind schedule"), and a value higher than 1.00 indicates the opposite ("ahead of schedule"). The lower the value of the critical ratio, the higher the priority of the job.

The critical-ratio approach is ingenious, as the technique establishes relative priorities accurately, and with frequent recomputation the priorities of work on all open shop orders could be kept up to date and valid *if*

[1] A. O. Putnam, "How to Prevent Stockouts," *American Machinist,* vol. 108, no. 4, February 1964.

there were gradual stock depletion at a steady rate, which assumption is implicit in the technique. In the case of dependent-demand items, however, depletion tends to be "lumpy," which renders ratio A meaningless.

The critical-ratio technique described above is strictly geared to an order point, and it therefore fails to the extent that order point fails in an environment of discontinuous, nonuniform item demand. Nevertheless, critical ratio has made a contribution to the state of the art of inventory and production management. This contribution consists not in the practicality of application but in highlighting the fact of vertically dependent priorities. (Since the introduction of the critical ratio, due-date–oriented priority ratios have been developed and are being used successfully with MRP systems; their description, however, is outside the scope of this book.)

In the case of assembled products, there may or may not be a vertical priority dependence, but there is always a *horizontal* dependence. A component is not really needed when a co-component is not available for the assembly of their common parent item. This principle can best be illustrated in an example (Figure 66). The orders for the three manufactured components have different lead times but an identical due date, which coincides with the scheduled assembly of parent item X. If the order for component item A, for instance, is scrapped at a date too late for on-schedule recovery, parent item X will, in fact, not be assembled on the date planned. The real priority of orders B and C has therefore dropped, as they will not be needed on the original order due date.

The MRP system is oblivious of this fact, of course, as the indicated requirements for items B and C have not changed. They have not changed because the parent planned order (for item X) has not been rescheduled and the master production schedule has not changed. The system will therefore continue the original due dates which, while technically correct, are in fact false. It is the responsibility of the system user to reestablish priority

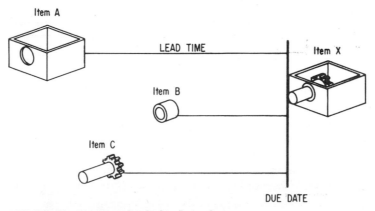

FIGURE 66   Horizontal priority dependence.

integrity. This can be done by rescheduling the parent planned order (using the so-called *firm planned order* techniques described in Chapter 8) and by letting the MRP system replan requirements and dates of need for the component orders in question. If the parent planned order cannot be rescheduled (by compressing its planned lead time) without also rescheduling *its* parent's planned order(s) and other related planned orders on higher levels, the master production schedule may have to be changed. This can and should be done so as to reflect the reality of assembly X (and consequently, higher-level items of which it may be a component) having to be completed at some later date.

Once the master production schedule is once again in harmony with the realities of production, the MRP system will explode it, recompute the respective requirements, and call for a rescheduling of orders B and C according to their new dates of need. Note that the MRP system, in this case, will *automatically* identify *all* open orders affected by the scrapping of the order for item A, will update their priorities, and will determine exactly by how many periods each individual order should be rescheduled. This is an outstanding capability of an MRP system, the full implications of which may not be immediately evident. The example in Figure 66 is extremely simple. In a real case, hundreds of orders (among thousands outstanding in the shop) may be involved. While the inventory planner realizes that the scrapping of the order will delay assembly of the parent item, he does not necessarily know:

- Which parent item
- How many component orders are affected
- The identity of affected orders
- Exactly how each of these orders should be rescheduled

Unless he has a tool—an MRP system—to establish these facts quickly and accurately, he will not even try to solve the problem. The complexity of the problem is compounded by the fact that the scrapped item may have multiple parents, some of which may not figure in the current production plan at all, by the fact that several orders (in different stages of completion) for the same item may be open, and by the fact that lot sizing plus common usage obscure what rescheduling action, if any, should be taken for a given order.

This is a formidable problem that seems to defy solution, particularly when one considers that such minor catastrophes as scrapping an order, equipment breakdown, inability of a vendor to deliver, etc., occur all the time. Such events, when preventing completion of a component order, have an identical effect on priority integrity. An MRP system can solve this type of problem quickly, automatically, and with complete accuracy. Without an MRP system available, it is impractical even to attempt to solve the problem, and there is no hope of maintaining the integrity of order priorities. Order priorities and operation priorities constitute a classic, chronic problem in the manufacturing industry. This problem has proven intractable, and it has defied solution by even the most sophisticated techniques, until the advent of the computer and time-phased material requirements planning.

Severity of Priority Problem

To recap the subject of dependent priorities and to bring it into focus, a classification of priority problems by type of manufacturing business, as suggested by Oliver Wight, will be briefly reviewed.[2] For purposes of this review, manufacturing companies are divided into four categories, as follows:

1. Companies producing a one-piece product made to order
2. Companies producing a one-piece product made to stock
3. Companies producing an assembled product made to order
4. Companies producing an assembled product made to stock

In the first type of manufacturing business (a foundry, a crankshaft manufacturer, etc.), the order-priority problem is the simplest. The customer places an order and requests a delivery date, and when this date is confirmed it represents the priority of the order. Unless the customer changes the order due date, the priority remains fixed. Relative priorities of all open orders derive from their respective due dates.

In the second type of manufacturing business (a nuts and bolts manufacturer, for example), the order-priority problem is a little more complex. To keep these priorities honest, open-order due dates would have to be related to the availability of stock for each of the items in question. In this environment, priorities are vertically dependent on the customer demand that causes stock depletion.

In the third type of manufacturing business (a special machinery manufacturer, for example), the priority problem is quite complex, because the orders for components of the assembled product have horizontally dependent priorities. The availability of *all* the components is prerequisite to the completion of each parent subassembly, and of the end product.

The priority problem is most severe in the fourth type of manufacturing business (for example, a manufacturer of a line of power saws with a single factory warehouse), because here the order priorities are both vertically and horizontally dependent. The real priority of a shop order is a function of the available supply of the parent product, as well as of the availability of co-components required for the assembly of a parent item.

The above classification scheme is somewhat oversimplified, as many types of manufacturing business do not neatly fit into one of the four cate-

[2] O. W. Wight, *Oliver Wight Newsletter No. 10*, September 1971.

gories. Nevertheless, it is useful for purposes of analysis and exposition. From the examples it can be seen that the more severe the priority problem, the more benefits an MRP system will be able to provide.

Priority Control

An MRP system functions (or can function) as a priority *planning* system par excellence. Where it so functions, however, it must be supplemented by a priority *control* system in the factory. The MRP system keeps order priorities up to date by planning and replanning order due dates, but it obviously cannot cause these due dates to be actually met. The priority control system provides the procedural machinery to enforce adherence to plan, and it takes the form of what is variously known as the dispatching system, job-assignment system, shop floor control system, etc.

The instrument of priority control is a *dispatch list* or departmental schedule, typically being generated daily or weekly (the latter is of lower effectiveness), which may be in the form of a printed report, cards, individual work-sequence messages printed via a remote typewriter, or a listing conveyed through a visual-display device. In any of these cases, the essence of the dispatch list is a ranking, by relative priority, of jobs (material that an operation is to be performed on) physically present in a manufacturing department, and sometimes of jobs about to arrive in the department. A sample dispatch list is shown in Figure 67.

DISPATCH LIST						
Department: **No. 12, Turret lathes**					Date: **447**	
Jobs in department						
Order #	Part #	Quantity	Operation #	Start date	Std. hours	Remarks
5987	B-3344	50	30	441	3.2	*Tooling in repair*
5968	B-4567	100	25	444	6.6	Eng. hold
5988	F-8978	30	42	446	4.8	
5696	12-133	300	20	447	14.5	
5866	A-4675	60	20	447	7.0	
5996	A-9845	200	30	448	6.2	
5876	F-4089	25	40	480	5.4	
Jobs scheduled to arrive this date						
6078	A-3855	160	30	446	6.5	In dept. 15
6001	D-8000	300	65	448	9.8	In dept. 08

FIGURE 67   Daily dispatch list.

The sequence of work established by the dispatch list is based on operation priorities which, in turn, are derived from order priorities. As order due dates are being revised via the MRP system, operation priorities must be reestablished accordingly. They may be expressed by means of operation start dates (as in the Figure 67 example) or operation finish dates, and if so, the affected orders must first be rescheduled by the operations scheduling system. Alternatively, the priorities can be expressed by means of one of a variety of priority ratios that are geared to order due dates.

A priority control system (i.e., dispatching or job sequencing) and its related instruments exist in every manufacturing plant, in some form. Without input from an MRP system, however, a priority control system cannot function very effectively because the information tends to be out of date, invalid, and untrue. Shop personnel do not, and cannot, rely on this information, and so the system must be supplemented by expediting of shortage lists. The shortage lists, incomplete as they usually are, then reflect the true priorities.

In the preceding discussion of priorities, the emphasis has been on manufactured items and on shop orders, because they involve operation priorities, which is not the case with purchase orders. Everything that has been said about priorities of shop orders, however, applies equally to purchase orders. Purchased component items have dependent priorities, the same as manufactured items, and they should, of course, be planned by the MRP system.

DETERMINING CAPACITY REQUIREMENTS

In Chapter 3, the point was made that an MRP system is capacity-insensitive, and properly so, as its function is to determine what materials and components will be needed and when, in order to execute a given master production schedule. There can be only one correct answer to that, and it cannot therefore vary depending on what capacity does or does not exist. The MRP system can be thought of as assuming that capacity considerations have entered into the makeup of the master production schedule, i.e., that the master production schedule being submitted to it for processing is realistic vis-à-vis available or planned capacity.

Capacity Requirements Planning

The term used in connection with long-range planning of capacity at the master production schedule level is *resource requirements planning,* and this function will be discussed in Chapter 11. *Capacity requirements planning* is the function of determining what capacities will be required, by work center by period, in the short-to-medium range, to meet current production goals. The output of the MRP system indicates what component items will have to be produced and when, and this output can therefore be converted into the capacities required to produce these items.

Such a conversion results in a machine load, or work load, projection that is then compared with available departmental and work-center capacities to help answer the day-to-day operating questions, such as:

- Should we work overtime?
- Should we transfer work from one department to another?
- Should we transfer people from one department to another?
- Should we subcontract some work?
- Should we start a new shift?
- Should we hire more people?

The tool that has traditionally been used to provide information on which answers to the above questions could be based is the so-called *load report*. This report is generated by the scheduling and loading system, which schedules individual operations of orders being released, converts the scheduling into hours of work load, and accumulates them by work center by period. The traditional load report reflects only the backlog of open orders, and the typical load pattern (for a work center, for a department, or for a plant) looks like that shown in Figure 68.

This pattern can still be found in the load reports of many manufacturing companies and plants. The manager evaluating the information understands that shop orders released in the current (first) period will add their load to the second period and those beyond, orders released in the next period will add their load to the third period and those beyond, etc. He can only estimate, or guess, what the total load in any of the future periods will turn

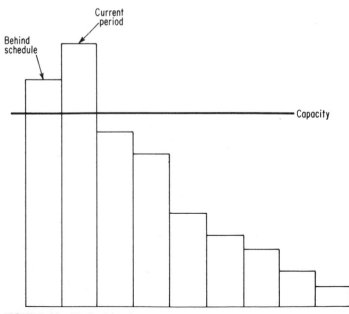

FIGURE 68   Typical load pattern.

out to be. But that would seem to be less important than the question of when the behind-schedule load will be worked off. It assuredly will not happen in the current period which is already overloaded. The manager knows, from experience, that next period's load report will likely indicate an overload in the *second* period, which will then be current. He also knows that a relatively heavy behind-schedule load appears to be a permanent condition, according to the load report.

The manager who tries to work with this type of load report may be baffled by the curious fact that, while the load report has always indicated a highly unsatisfactory capacity situation relative to current and behind-schedule work load, shipments of the product have been more or less on schedule. Accordingly, he views the load data with healthy skepticism and is loath to act on the information provided by the load report.

The load pattern illustrated in Figure 68 constitutes virtual proof that the load report exhibiting it is:

1. *Incomplete,* because it fails to include load that will be generated by planned orders

2. *Invalid,* because priorities are not being kept up to date

When planned orders do not enter into the load report, the indicated load is bound to decline following the current period and to trail off at a point that roughly corresponds to the span of the average item lead time. This type of load projection is incomplete in a way that offers very little "visibility" into the future beyond the current period. This is such a serious shortcoming that it all but defeats the purpose of projecting the work load. Because capacity-related corrective action, such as hiring or subcontracting, entails a lead time of its own, the very information that would be most desirable, i.e., a valid load picture several periods in the future, is missing.

The big "bulge" in behind-schedule and current-period load is a sure indication that priorities are not being kept valid. A good portion of the load classified as behind schedule is likely not *really* behind schedule, if requirements have been changing. The order due dates, and operation dates, have simply not been revised to reflect that. The same will be true for at least some of the work that constitutes the overload in the current period.

Usefulness of a Load Projection

A good, usable load projection has the following three attributes:

1. It is complete.
2. It is based on valid priorities.
3. It provides visibility into the future.

Under any inventory control system other than material requirements planning, the load report tends to fail on all three counts, if it is being generated at all. Its usefulness is limited in practice to comparing successive load reports for the purpose of trend detection. Capacity-adjustment action practically always lags behind the actual load development. Due to the load report not being trustworthy, the plant must usually get into actual trouble before management takes corrective action.

An MRP system has the potential for helping to solve the capacity requirements planning problem. An MRP system generates planned orders that can be converted into load and added to the load created by open orders. Whatever method is used to convert released orders into load can be used for planned orders also. This satisfies the requirements of completeness and visibility, as the entire planned-order schedule (spanning the full planning horizon) may be input to the scheduling and loading system.

The requirement of validity can be satisfied only if the MRP system is being used as a priority-planning system. When open-order due dates are being revised to stay valid, the entire load projection can be based on valid priorities, because the MRP system maintains the timing of planned orders continually up to date.

The MRP system does not, itself, plan capacity requirements, but it provides input to a capacity requirements planning system without which the latter cannot possibly function effectively. The load projection, or *capacity requirements report*, that is based on the outputs of an MRP system exhibits the kind of pattern illustrated in Figure 69. Depending on operations-scheduling practice, behind-schedule load may or may not disappear, but at any rate the former "bulges" are redistributed over a number of future periods, as some open orders have their due dates rescheduled to later dates.

The load projection is normally not perfectly level, as actual load tends to fluctuate from period to period, but it is roughly level (or trending) compared with the trail-off pattern of the traditional load report. Production rates, by department, can be set with reasonably high confidence that the

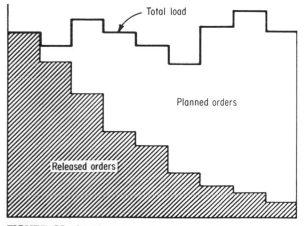

FIGURE 69 Load pattern based on both open and planned orders.

load in the foreseeable future will average what the capacity requirements report indicates. Short-term capacity adjustments must be made to compensate for load fluctuation from period to period, but there is ample notice provided by the information in the capacity requirements report.

To sum up the present discussion of the multiple functions, or uses, of an MRP system, it can be stated that such a system, in conjunction with the master scheduling function (discussed in Chapter 11) acts as a central planning system in the area of manufacturing logistics. Other systems, such as purchasing, scheduling, capacity requirements, dispatching, etc., are designed to execute the outputs of the MRP system. For their effectiveness, these systems are dependent on the completeness, validity, accuracy, and timeliness of their inputs. In this and the preceding chapters, the author trusts he has convincingly demonstrated that a time-phased material requirements planning system has the capability to generate such outputs.

In the area of manufacturing logistics, the inventory system is all-important. The material requirements planning approach guarantees that the inventory system will, in fact, be able to meet all the demands that management can reasonably place upon it. In companies that are developing or overhauling computer-based systems for production and inventory control applications, an MRP system should be the first goal.

CHAPTER EIGHT

SYSTEM EFFECTIVENESS: A FUNCTION OF DESIGN AND USE

The design, or "architecture," of MRP systems has by now been standardized, and it is embodied in the application software that computer manufacturers offer to their customers. The material requirements planning program packages are popular in the manufacturing industry, and in fact, most of the existing MRP systems utilize standard software; only a small minority of these systems have been designed and programmed by the user.

This is not to say that a large number of installed MRP systems are identical—there probably are not two exactly alike. This stems from the fact that the user of standard software has considerable freedom in how he constructs his particular system by configurating the *modules* (functions) making up the package, what decisions he makes about certain *parameters* of use, and whether he utilizes so-called *program exits* to supply his own programming of procedures not provided in the package. The effectiveness of the system that results depends, in part, on the decisions the user made at the time of system construction. But no matter how well the system may have been designed technically, its true effectiveness also depends on how well it is being used. Both of these considerations will be addressed in the present chapter.

CRITICAL SYSTEM DESIGN FEATURES

The three principal functions that an MRP system can provide—at the user's option—have been reviewed in the preceding chapter, and for purposes of design can be summarized in the following checklist of objectives:

1. INVENTORY
   - Order the right part.
   - Order in the right quantity.
   - Order at the right time.
2. PRIORITIES
   - Order with the right due date.
   - Keep the due date valid.
3. CAPACITY
   - A complete load.
   - An accurate (valid) load.
   - An adequate time span for visibility of future load.

A full and proper use of the MRP system, represented by the above checklist, will prove difficult or impossible unless the system's design anticipates such use. The intended use of the system should therefore dictate a number of critical design decisions, particularly:

1. The span of the planning horizon
2. The size of the time-bucket
3. The coverage of inventory by class
4. The frequency of replanning
5. The traceability of requirements
6. The capability to "freeze" planned orders

Planning-Horizon Span

For purposes of inventory ordering, the planning horizon should at least equal the (longest) cumulative product lead time, as defined in Chapter 3. If the horizon is shorter than that, the MRP system will be unable to time releases of planned orders for items at the lowest level correctly, with the result that orders for such items (purchased materials and component parts) will be *consistently* released too late. The system, in successively offsetting for lead time in the course of the level-by-level planning process, simply runs out of available time when it reaches the items on the lowest level.

This is illustrated in Figure 70, where the cumulative lead time is fifteen periods and the planning horizon is thirteen periods. The order for purchased material, developed by the system through the explosion of an end item inserted into the master schedule at the very edge of the planning horizon, should have been released two periods ago, according to the lead-time values supplied to the system. The best the system can do, under these

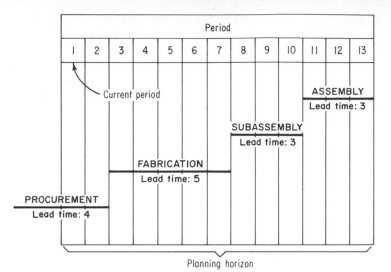

FIGURE 70   Planning horizon and cumulative lead time.

circumstances, is to plan the order release for the current period. The order is then two periods behind schedule before it is even released.

Because of the multilevel product structure and successive lead-time offsetting, there is a partial loss of horizon at lower levels. The *effective* planning horizon is successively diminished as the planning process progresses from one level to the next. The lower the level, the less visibility into the future. For example, in Figure 70 a planned-order release for the fabricated item can never be farther out than period 3. The effective planning horizon for this item is therefore only three periods. Although its time-phased inventory record would show thirteen time-buckets for planned-order releases, the last ten would always have zero contents.

One of the consequences of very short horizons at low component-item levels is the inability to apply a lot-sizing technique such as "least unit cost" or "least total cost" effectively, simply because of a lack of sufficient net requirements data. This has previously been discussed in Chapter 6.

Another, even more serious consequence of an inadequate planning horizon is a lack of visibility for purposes of capacity requirements planning. In the Figure 70 example, a complete load for fabrication operations cannot be projected beyond three periods (in period 4 and beyond, orders not at present planned by the system will eventually be released and will add to the load), which severely reduces the usefulness of the capacity requirements report or load report. It is, of course, precisely on the low (fabricated part) level that load visibility is most desirable.

A special case is the situation where the planning horizon is ample, both in the master production schedule and in the MRP system, but management insists on specifically authorizing each "manufacturing order" or "product lot" in the master production schedule, for release into production. This means that a quantity of an end item in the master production schedule cannot be processed by the MRP system unless and until management authorizes it. The lead time for this release that management recognizes tends to be arbitrary, and usually on the short side. Additional delay may also be caused by the "sign-off" procedure.

With time-phased material requirements planning, such a procedure for authorizing production is quite unnecessary and, in fact, undesirable. The MRP system plans the ordering of each component item on its individual merit, i.e., according to its lead time and those of its parents on higher levels. The system orders the right items at the right time, not sooner and not later, which means that the production commitment goes into effect gradually. The entire product lot is not actually committed at one time (as the authorization procedure implies), and cost is being incurred gradually, as dictated by individual item lead times. It is one of the advantages of working with an MRP system that management need not be concerned with authorizing individual product lots for production. All that is required is to maintain the best possible master production schedule at all times, and let the MRP system do the rest. The usefulness of this system should not be impaired by arbitrary interference and unnecessary delays in authorization.

Size of the Time-Bucket

Time-bucket size selected by the system user reflects a compromise, or tradeoff, between the desire to have planned events pinpointed in time and the cost of dividing time into very small increments that would then have to be represented by a large number of fields, and a large number of data elements that would have to be manipulated by the system. Experience has shown that buckets representing one-month periods are too coarse and the timing is too imprecise.

When the system indicates, for instance, that an order is to be released, or completed, in October, the question remains as to *when* in October. In this case, inventory planners and buyers will tend to "play it safe," order early and specify early deliveries, thus unnecessarily inflating the level of inventory.

From the foreman's point of view, specifying operation completions by month is less than helpful. The foreman needs to know what is needed this week and next week, or better yet, today and tomorrow. The foreman wants priorities, as he must follow some work sequence. When there are several hundreds, or thousands, of shop orders due in October, the foreman has been given little meaningful information and little help in getting his job done. When the time-buckets are too coarse (one month, two weeks, ten days), work priorities and sequences are invariably developed informally, via shortage lists and expediting.

A bucket size of one week has been found to be most practical. The division of time is sufficiently fine for purposes of order releases, completions, and priorities (as well as lot sizing and load reporting), and the MRP system that utilizes weekly time-buckets can be supplemented by a scheduling/ dispatching system that plans in terms of days or priority ratios.

System Coverage of Inventory Classes

Coverage of inventory by class is another important decision that the system user must make. The *ABC* classification of inventory has been discussed in the introduction to this book, where it has been noted that an MRP system is capable of according the same stringent treatment to any inventory item regardless of class. An MRP system user may feel, however, that *C*-items do not warrant such elaborate treatment, and he may exclude them from the system. There also exist MRP systems that cover *A*-items only, on the theory that if the most important and expensive inventory items are properly planned and controlled, the rest will take care of themselves, more or less. This is simply not so.

MRP systems that are limited in inventory-item coverage yield only a small fraction of the benefits that they are capable of. Such systems cannot displace the informal system that always has been, and under these circumstances will continue to be, the *modus operandi* in the factory. For purposes of assembling the product, the lowly *C*-item is as important as an *A*-item — both must be available in the right quantity at the right time. Furthermore, some *A*-items have components classified *B* and *C*, and shortage of one of the latter will prevent the completion of the *A*-item. As pointed out earlier in this book, no matter how much *C*-item safety stock there may be under an order point approach, there will be occasional shortages.

As to priority planning, unless all manufactured items are covered by the MRP system, relative shop priorities cannot be established. A manufactured *C*-item must be *manufactured* in the shop and must contend for productive capacity with *A*- and *B*-items. Unless a *C*-item order due date is maintained up to date through the MRP system, its validity is always questionable, but it will never do to assume that *A*-items have automatic priority over *C*-items. Unless the dates of actual need for both an *A*-item and a *C*-item are known, it is obviously impossible to tell which has priority over which. Here again, shortages and expediting will have to establish what the real priorities are.

Purchased *C*-items, when excluded from the MRP system, do not necessarily affect the priorities of other purchase orders, and they may be considered the exception to the rule that an MRP system should cover all classes of inventory for purposes of priority planning. The *C*-item purchase-order due dates will in this case tend to be invalid, however, causing some shortages and last-minute expediting.

Another reason why no inventory class should be excluded from system coverage lies in capacity requirements planning. All manufactured items, *A, B,* and *C,* must be covered by the MRP system if the capacity requirements report is to contain complete load data. If C-items are controlled by order point, only *open* C-item orders can be reflected in the load. Because some of these orders will carry invalid due dates, the scheduling of their operations will be incorrect, and this will affect the validity of the entire load projection. By excluding any manufactured items from the MRP system, the usefulness of capacity requirements planning information is impaired if not destroyed.

Replanning Frequency

The frequency of replanning is under complete user control, but it is of utmost importance to the effectiveness of system performance. As a general rule, the more dynamic or prone-to-change the environment, the more frequently the material requirements should be replanned. In most manufacturing companies, a longer than weekly replanning cycle will prove unsatisfactory, especially if the MRP system is used for purposes of priority planning.

Any MRP system that is used to replan cyclically (rather than continuously) can do no more than "take a snapshot" of inventory status at the time of replanning, and plan order priorities accordingly. Their validity gradually deteriorates following the replanning, as the inventory status changes. If the "snapshots" are not taken frequently enough to revalidate priorities, it becomes impractical to follow the priorities established by the formal system, and the informal system must take over. As pointed out earlier, without valid order priorities there can be no valid load projection. With insufficiently frequent replanning, the user cannot realize the potential of his MRP system. The subject of replanning frequency has previously been reviewed in some depth in Chapter 5.

Certain special capabilities can be incorporated into the basic MRP system that will enhance its usefulness. These system features are not absolutely essential to the system's operation, and they may therefore not be included in a given MRP-software package. They do, however, significantly increase the power of the MRP system as a planning tool and warrant inclusion in the system, even if the user has to supply his own programming. Of the various special system features, the most important ones are so-called *pegged requirements* and the *firm planned order*.

Pegged Requirements

The pegging of requirements provides the capability to trace item gross requirements to their sources. The process of material requirements planning, as described earlier, progresses from top to bottom of the product structure. The gross requirements for a component item, derived from its parent items and from external sources of demand, if any, are *summarized* by period. The contents of a given gross requirements bucket represent a total, the breakdown and the sources of which are obscured.

Pegging requirements means saving this information, which at one point in the requirements-planning process is known to the system, and recording it in a special file. Pegged requirements may be thought of as a *selective where-used file.* In comparison with a regular where-used file, which lists *all* parents of a component item, a pegged-requirements file lists only those parents that show planned orders (the source of component gross requirements) in their records. This permits the inventory planner to trace requirements upward in the product structure, to determine which parents a given gross requirement came from, where *their* requirements came from, etc. By following the "pegs" from one item record to another, the planner can trace the demand to its ultimate source, i.e., a specific bucket (or buckets) in the master production schedule.

Requirements pegging is effected by establishing a so-called *peg record* for each component item in which the breakdown, or detail, of gross requirements is recorded by period and tied to its source. An example is provided in Figure 71. Here the demand for item X comes from parent items A, C, D, and from an interplant or service-part order. The fields labeled "Parent Record" would, in the real situation, contain *addresses* of parent records in the computer file, rather than merely parent-item identification. This facilitates immediate retrieval of these records, which, of course, is the object of pegged requirements. Pegging provides a capability of specialized inquiry, for the benefit of the inventory planner.

The peg record may be incorporated into the item inventory record, or it may be stored in a separate pegged-requirements file. In the latter case, the address (pointer) of the corresponding peg record would be stored in the item inventory record in question, again to facilitate quick retrieval. In this case there are two retrieval steps involved: the item record points to the peg record, which points to the parent record(s). Pegged requirements

REQUIREMENTS RECORD – ITEM X

Period	I	2	3	4	5	6
Gross requirements	20		35	10		15

PEG RECORD – ITEM X

Period	Quantity	Parent record	External order
I	20	A	
3	15	A	
3	20	C	
4	10		No. 38447
6	15	D	

FIGURE 71 Pegged requirements.

constitute an important MRP system capability and an important tool of the inventory planner, the use of which will be discussed in the next section of this chapter.

The preceding discussion of pegged requirements covers the so-called *single-level peg*, i.e., the capability to trace the source of item demand to the immediately higher level only. With the single-level peg, a succession of peg inquiries is required to trace item demand to an end-item lot (or lots) called for by the master production schedule. In order to link item demand to that schedule by means of a single inquiry, the so-called *full-peg* capability would be required. Under the full-peg approach, each individual requirement for a component item is identified with a specific product (or end-item) lot, or customer order, listed in the master production schedule.

This principle can be extended to orders and even on-hand quantities of the component item, so that it may always be known which group of parts "belongs" to which product lot. It is rarely practical to program a full-peg capability, however, because in most manufacturing environments it is intended that individual requirements for a component item stemming from multiple parents be combined, that an order cover multiple net requirements, and that parts on hand or in process be commingled. Lot sizing, safety stock, scrap allowances, and the level-by-level planning process itself tend to obscure (or even erase) a clean path connecting noncontiguous levels.

Full pegging is feasible, and desirable, in a limited number of situations, such as when the product is custom-engineered and made to order, when the different standard products have few or no common components, or when the master production schedule consists of special contracts. Common component usage and repetive production tend to make full pegging impractical. With material requirements planning, "eggs" are deliberately "scrambled," as it were. Full pegging attempts to keep the eggs from getting scrambled in the pan—an awkward and often impossible task.

The Firm Planned Order

This term denotes a capability by the system to accept a command to "freeze" the quantity and/or timing of a planned-order release. This is another important tool of the inventory planner, by means of which he is able to solve certain types of problems, reviewed below.

The ability to freeze a planned order requires special programming in the MRP system, because it is contrary to its regular logic. Planned orders are otherwise under the exclusive control of the system, which plans and replans the planned-order release schedule in each time-phased item record according to the lead time and lot-sizing rule specified. The schedule is revised (status is rebalanced) as net requirements change, automatically. The result is that the system, over a period of time, tends to move a given planned order around and to change its quantity, perhaps several times before the order matures for release.

The firm-planned-order command immobilizes the order in the schedule, forcing the MRP system to "work around" it in adjusting coverage of net requirements. The firm planned order forbids the system to put another planned order into the "frozen" bucket, which in some cases may result in a given net requirement not being fully covered. This special capability should therefore be used judiciously and for a specific planned order only, rather than for the whole planned-order release schedule.

THE SYSTEM AND THE INVENTORY PLANNER

The inventory planner (also called inventory analyst, inventory controller, etc.) is responsible for the planning and control of a group of specific inventory items, and in a material requirements planning environment, he interacts continuously with the MRP system. He is the recipient of the system's principal outputs, and his first duty is to take inventory order action based on information supplied by the system. He inquires into the system's files for data needed for purposes of analysis, and he handles a miscellany of problems that arise in the course of his work. The inventory planner's specific job description varies from company to company, but in the typical case his function consists essentially of the following responsibilities:

- Release orders for production
- Place purchase requisitions
- Change the quantity of orders and requisitions, including cancellation
- Change the timing of (i.e., reschedule) open shop orders
- Request change in the timing of open purchase orders
- Activate special procedures for the handling of engineering changes affecting items under the planner's control
- Approve requests for unplanned stock disbursements
- Monitor inventory for inactivity or obsolescence and recommend disposition
- Investigate and correct errors in inventory records
- Initiate physical inventory counts
- Analyze discrepancies or misalignments between item requirements and coverage, and take appropriate corrective action
- Request changes in the master production schedule

Most of the above are routine and require no further elaboration, but a few of the inventory planner's duties warrant a more detailed review. Transactions continually modify inventory status which, in turn, provides the clues to inventory action. The principal types of this action are related to orders, i.e., the releasing of planned orders and the changing of the quantity and/or timing of open orders. The inventory planner is constrained by the fact that it may be difficult or costly to change the quantity of an open purchase order, and usually impossible (other than by splitting the lot) to change the quantity of an open shop order. His field of order-related action is, in practice, generally limited to:

- Releasing the order in the right quantity at the right time
- Rescheduling the due date of an open order if and as required to make it coincide with the date of actual need.

In both of these functions, the inventory planner is fully supported by the MRP system, which determines both the quantity and the timing of planned-order releases and which also constantly monitors the validity of all open-order due dates. The following examples illustrate how the MRP system determines when to generate the two basic outputs or messages, "release the order" and "reschedule the order."

Releasing a Planned Order

A planned order is *mature* (for release) when the planned release quantity appears in the current-period bucket. This happens either as a result of offsetting for lead time in the course of the requirements explosion or by passage of time, which gradually brings a planned-order release toward the first or current period. The current-period bucket in the planned-order release schedule is known as the *action bucket*. The (material requirements planning) computer program tests the contents of this bucket, and when it exceeds zero, the system generates a message (report) to the inventory planner that the order is due for release. Figure 72 shows such a condition.

The planner, who reviews the request and takes the actual action, normally has the privilege of overriding the system in terms of changing the quantity of the order at this point. For example, a shortage of raw material may not allow the order to be released in the full quantity planned by the MRP system, and the planner may decide to reduce the order quantity rather than to delay the order release.

Conversely, the planner may wish to increase the order quantity for some reason. He should not do this without assuring himself that the action will

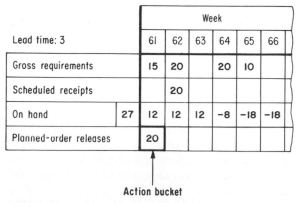

		Week					
Lead time: 3		61	62	63	64	65	66
Gross requirements		15	20		20	10	
Scheduled receipts			20				
On hand	27	12	12	12	−8	−18	−18
Planned-order releases		20					

Action bucket

FIGURE 72   A planned order mature for release.

+20

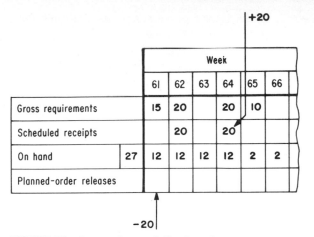

	Week					
	61	62	63	64	65	66
Gross requirements		15	20		20	10
Scheduled receipts			20		20	
On hand	27	12	12	12	12	2	2
Planned-order releases						

−20

FIGURE 73   Status change following planned-order release.

not cause a problem at the level of component material that has been planned by the MRP system to cover requirements of perhaps several parent planned orders, in quantities that the *system* planned for these orders. If the planner exceeds one of these quantities, he may short another one.

In net change MRP systems (Chapter 5), changing planned-order quantities at the time of shop-order release means upsetting the interlevel equilibrium that the system continuously strives to maintain. Such changes, in effect, introduce errors into the system's records which the planner should immediately correct (through special transactions) if he must override the system's recommendation. Note that the preceding comments pertain to shop orders; planned purchase orders are not so critical as they do not involve component materials within the system. When the planned order shown in Figure 72 as mature is released, the transaction reporting this will change the status of the item to that shown in Figure 73. At this point, both open orders are correctly scheduled, i.e., aligned against the dates of need. If the gross requirements subsequently change, however, the dates of need may no longer coincide with the order completion times (due dates). Such a condition is illustrated in Figure 74. Note that in this example only

	Week					
	61	62	63	64	65	66
Gross requirements		30	5		10	10	10
Scheduled receipts		←20			20→	
On hand	27	−3	12	12	22	12	2
Planned-order releases						

FIGURE 74   Open orders do not coincide with dates of need.

the timing, not the quantity, of the total requirements has changed. The coverage is therefore still adequate—no additional orders are required—but the timing of the open orders is now wrong.

Rescheduling an Open Order

A net change MRP system detects this condition immediately upon processing the transaction that caused the gross requirements to change. A regenerative MRP system detects this during the requirements planning run. A changed gross requirements schedule necessitates a recomputation of the projected on-hand schedule, and the new schedule contains the clues to the action required. In Figure 74, there is a net requirement (for 3) in the first period, followed by open orders in subsequent periods. The system is programmed not to generate a new planned order to cover the net requirement (regular logic) but to request the rescheduling of the closest open order.

In the third period (week 63 in the example), there are 12 on hand and the gross requirement in the subsequent period is only 10. This requirement can be covered in full by the quantity on hand, and there is clearly no need for the open order to arrive in week 64, as originally scheduled. This order should be rescheduled (its due date changed) to week 65, when it is actually needed. The two tests for open-order misalignment are as follows:

1. Are there any open orders scheduled for periods following the period in which a net requirement appears?
2. Is there an open order scheduled for a period in which the gross requirement equals or is less than the on-hand quantity at the end of the preceding period?

The MRP program carries out these two simple tests whenever the projected-on-hand/net-requirements schedule is being recomputed. If a test is positive, the system generates the appropriate rescheduling message. Note that the extension of the second test to subsequent periods will indicate that an open order should be canceled when the on-hand quantity in the period preceding the scheduled receipt of the order is sufficient to cover *all* remaining gross requirements. This is equivalent to rescheduling the order beyond the far edge of the planning horizon. Note also that the system recomputes the planned-order schedule so as to align it properly with net requirements, which means that *planned orders* are being rescheduled automatically, without action on the part of the inventory planner.

If the relative priorities in the shop (and those of open purchase orders) are to be kept valid, the planner must reschedule due dates not only for orders needed earlier than originally planned, but also for those needed later. The tendency is to concentrate on orders that need to be completed early to prevent shortages, and to delay action or ignore the others.

It is understood that following the rescheduling action by the inventory planner, which is reflected in the MRP system, the revised shop-order due dates will be input to the operations scheduling system and to the dispatching (operations sequencing) system. The former reschedules all remaining operations of the affected shop orders in accordance with the new order due dates; the new operation start (or finish) dates may then serve as a basis of dispatching and are also used to recompute work load. When priority ratios (rather than operation start dates) are used for purposes of dispatching, the new order due dates enter into the preparation of the daily dispatch list. As far as revising purchase-order due dates is concerned, the inventory planner recommends action, by submitting the revised dates of need, to the purchasing department. Only when the latter actually acts does the MRP system reflect the rescheduling.

The planner may decide not to advance the order due date (contrary to an indication by the MRP system) when there is safety stock or when the new date would be impossible to meet. In the latter case, the proper course of action is to peg upward in an effort to solve the problem, possibly all the way to the master production schedule, which may have to be changed.

Problems of Net Requirements Coverage

Probably the most serious problems that the inventory planner must cope with are discrepancies or misalignments between net requirements and coverage, resulting from unplanned events or increases in gross requirements. The planner has limited means at his disposal when trying to rebalance the status of a given inventory item. He cannot change the quantity on hand, nor can he change gross requirements by direct intervention. He can only change orders, i.e., the timing of an open order and both the quantity and timing of a planned order, as discussed previously. Thus to change the gross requirements for a given item, he must change the planned-order schedule of its parent item(s).

To be able to do so, the inventory planner depends on the two special capabilities of the MRP system that were mentioned previously, i.e., *pegged requirements* and *firm planned order*. How he would use these is illustrated in Figures 75, 76, and 77. Following the original status of item Y, a pur-

Lead time: 5		Week									
		28	29	30	31	32	33	34	35		
Gross requirements					20			25			Item Y
Scheduled receipts			15								
On hand	5	5	5	20	0	0	0	-25			
Planned-order releases			25								

FIGURE 75   Original status of item Y.

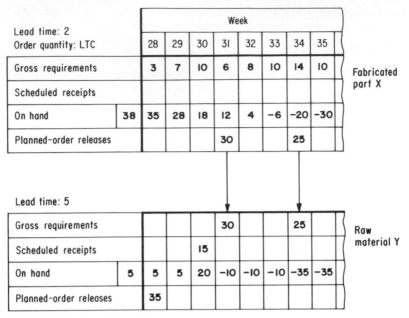

Lead time: 2
Order quantity: LTC

	Week								
		28	29	30	31	32	33	34	35
Gross requirements		3	7	10	6	8	10	14	10
Scheduled receipts									
On hand	38	35	28	18	12	4	-6	-20	-30
Planned-order releases					30			25	

Fabricated part X

Lead time: 5

		28	29	30	31	32	33	34	35
Gross requirements					30			25	
Scheduled receipts				15					
On hand	5	5	5	20	-10	-10	-10	-35	-35
Planned-order releases		35							

Raw material Y

FIGURE 76   A problem of coverage.

chased material with five weeks' lead time (Figure 75), gross requirements in week 31 increase from 20 to 30. As a result, the MRP system requests an immediate order release for 35 units (Figure 76). The inventory planner reviews this request against the current status of the item, and he detects a problem: the item, which has a procurement lead time of five weeks is needed in three weeks.

Before placing a purchase requisition on a rush basis, the planner decides to peg to parent items, to see if the problem might be solved some other way. The record of fabricated part X (Figure 76), from which the gross requirement stems, indicates that the planned order scheduled for release in week 31 covers net requirements of weeks 33, 34, and 35, and is computed by (let us say) a "least total cost" lot-sizing algorithm. The solution is evident: the parent planned order can be reduced without causing a problem in the status of item X.

The planner reduces the planned order in question to 20 via a transaction and designates it as a *firm planned order* by means of a special command input to the system. This is necessary so as to prevent the system from increasing the planned order back up to 30 during the next replanning cycle. This planned order is now "frozen," and after replanning, the two records appear as in Figure 77. The problem is solved, and an order for 25 units of item Y will be released under normal lead time. Note that because the planned order for item X has been reduced, the MRP system has compensated by moving the next planned order in the parent record forward. In the real situation, the quantity of the second planned order (recomputed under LTC) might also be affected.

The preceding example illustrates a problem of coverage caused by an increase in component-item gross requirements, but the same type of problem would have arisen if the vendor of the open order for 15 had indicated that he was unable to ship on time. If item Y were a fabricated part, the scrapping of 10 out of the 15 in process would have the same effect. In our example, the inventory planner was able to reduce the parent planned order because lot sizing covered multiple periods' net requirements. Had the planned order covered a single period, it could still have been reduced by an amount within its scrap allowance or other excess over the quantity of the net requirement. Safety stock at the parent level would also allow a reduction in the planned order.

The type of problem illustrated in the preceding examples can sometimes be solved without having to reduce the *quantity* of the parent planned order; instead, only its *timing* is changed. If the parent item's planned lead time can be compressed (as it often can be — see discussion of lead time flexibility in Chapters 4 and 12), the respective planned-order release can be rescheduled for a later period and held in place as a firm planned order. Rescheduling a parent planned-order release will consequently (after the next explosion) reschedule the corresponding component gross requirement and thus solve the problem of net requirements coverage. In Figure 76, for example, if the lead time of parent item X were reduced by one week

		Week							
		28	29	30	31	32	33	34	35
Gross requirements		3	7	10	6	8	10	14	10
Scheduled receipts									
On hand	38	35	28	18	12	4	-6	-20	-30
Planned-order releases				(20)		25			

Fabricated part X

FIRM PLANNED ORDER

		Week							
Gross requirements					20		25		
Scheduled receipts				15					
On hand	5	5	5	20	0	0	-25	-25	-25
Planned-order releases		25							

Raw material Y

FIGURE 77   Solution of problem of coverage.

(for purposes of the first planned-order release only), it would result in the net requirement for component item Y occurring one week later. This would alleviate the problem of net requirements coverage by allowing an extra week for the procurement of the material.

If the inventory planner is unable to solve a problem of coverage by pegging to the next-higher level and manipulating planned-order or open-order data, he may peg from the parent record to *its* parent records in an attempt to find a solution. Successive pegs may lead to the master production schedule, which may have to be changed in order to solve a particular component-item problem.

Considerations of system design and system use, the topic of discussion in the present chapter, extend also to the chapter that follows next. While thus far we have been examining aspects of system design from the user's point of view, in Chapter 9 we shall review considerations of a more technical nature: the design of an inventory record, the means for updating this record, and the linkage of files used by the MRP system.

PART FIVE

DATA

After all, the engineers create the bill so that, by definition, somebody other than the designer can make the product. The bill of material is, therefore, really made for others in the first place. And it would seem to follow that it should be structured for the user's, not the designer's, convenience.

GEORGE W. PLOSSL in "MRP and Bill of Material Structure," film produced by International Business Machines Corp., 1972.

CHAPTER NINE

SYSTEM RECORDS
AND FILES

An MRP system can be thought of as a set of logically linked item inventory records, coupled with a program (or programs) that maintains these records up to date.[1] The design of the inventory record, as well as the way the data it contains are being manipulated to produce valid system outputs, is crucial to both the effectiveness of the system and the understanding of the subject of material requirements planning.

THE TIME-PHASED INVENTORY RECORD

Under the material requirements planning approach, a separate time-phased inventory record is established and maintained for every inventory item. Each record consists of three portions, or *segments,* as follows:

1. Item master data (record header)
2. Inventory status data (the body of the record)
3. Subsidiary data

The inventory status segment is either reconstructed periodically or kept up to date continuously, depending on which of the two basic alternatives of implementing an MRP system—schedule regeneration or net change (discussed in Chapter 5)—had been chosen. At this point in the discussion, however, we need not be concerned with the distinction. Thus far we have been dealing only with the status data (the most important segment of the record), and there are a few more aspects of this segment to be reviewed before describing the header and subsidiary segments.

---

[1] For an alternative definition, see Chapter 1.

Time-phased Record Format

The most compact format of recording and displaying time-phased inventory status data is the one introduced in Chapter 4 and used in several previous examples. It consists of four rows of time-buckets representing the following:

1. Gross requirements
2. Scheduled receipts (open orders)
3. On hand (current and projected by period)
4. Planned-order releases

This format accommodates all the information that is essential for the proper manipulation of the status data and for the operation of the MRP system. The four rows of buckets define inventory status in summary form, and the format contains implicit information that can be inferred from the data that are displayed directly. This is the standard format favored by many MRP system users, and it is the format normally used for purposes of communication and instruction.

At the option of a given user, however, the format can be expanded in such a way as to provide more detail and/or to state more of the information explicitly. Figure 78 shows both the compact and the expanded format, based on the same status data. The example illustrates the possibilities of expansion rather than the format of an actual record. In practice, the expansion is usually limited to adding separate net requirements and/or planned-order receipt buckets.

Optional Fields

In addition to what is shown in Figure 78, the status segment of the inventory item record may include a field labeled "allocated on hand." Allocation has previously been discussed in Chapter 5. The quantity allocated indicates the quantity of the item earmarked for a parent order (or orders) that has been released but for which the material requisition has not yet been filled. The allocated parts "belong" to the respective parent orders, and they are still physically on hand in the stockroom only because of the time gap between order release (by the inventory planner) and the filling (by the stockroom) of the supporting requisition for component materials.

Where a single allocation field in each inventory record is being maintained, it is understood that parent orders will normally be released during the period for which the release is planned, and not before. Also, it is assumed that *all* the component items are required at the time the parent order is released. Both of these conditions will prove to be true in the typical manufacturing environment, and the single allocation field is standard. In the exceptional cases where either orders must often be released prematurely for some reason or the requirement for the different compo-

A COMPACT FORMAT

Lead time: 3		Period			
		1	2	3	4
Gross requirements		10	15	75	17
Scheduled receipts		8		25	
On hand	72	70	55	5	−12
Planned-order releases		20			

B EXPANDED FORMAT

		Period			
Lead time: 3		1	2	3	4
GROSS REQUIREMENTS	From parent items	10	10	15	12
	Service part orders		5		5
	Interplant			60	
	Total	10	15	75	17
SCHEDULED RECEIPTS	Supply source A			25	
	Supply source B	8			
	Total	8		25	
PLANNED-ORDER RECEIPTS					20
NET REQUIREMENTS					12
ON HAND	Stockroom #1	50	40	30		8
	Stockroom #2	22	30	25	5	
	Total	72	70	55	5	8
PLANNED-ORDER RELEASES		20			

FIGURE 78 Time-phased record: compact and expanded formats.

nents of an assembly is staggered over a long assembly lead time, the allocated quantities would be time-phased; i.e., a separate row of time-buckets would be maintained. An example of this appears in Figure 79. Note, in this example, that the use of a single allocation field would distort the component item's projected on-hand schedule (Figure 79B), which would then show 15 in period 1, and 3 in period 2.

Another field that can optionally be maintained in the time-phased inven-

A

ORIGINAL STATUS
OF COMPONENT
ITEM

		Period		
PARENT	1	2	3	4
Planned-order releases	10		15	

COMPONENT

Gross requirements	30	12	25	20
Scheduled receipts				
On hand	60	30	18	−7	−27
Planned-order releases	27			

B

STATUS FOLLOWING
PARENT ORDER
RELEASES

PARENT

Planned-order releases	0		0	

+10   −10 +15   −15

COMPONENT

Gross requirements	20	12	10	20
Allocated	10		15	
Scheduled receipts				
On hand	60	30	18	−7	−27
Planned-order releases	27			

FIGURE 79 Time phasing of allocated quantities.

tory record is the "quantity past due." One time-bucket immediately preceding the first period is provided for this purpose in each of the schedules (rows). In the "on-hand" schedule, this field shows the current quantity on hand, as the notion of "past due" does not apply to these data. Past-due quantities, if any, are recorded in the respective fields, as shown in Figure 80. In the computation of net requirements, the past-due quantities must be added to those in the first period (the assumption here is that where performance fell behind schedule, it will catch up in the first, or current, period) so as not to distort the projected-on-hand/net requirements schedule. This is shown in Figure 80A. An alternative treatment is to include the past-due quantities in the first-period buckets, as shown in Figure 80B. In either case, the net requirements computation must produce identical results.

The respective quantities are recorded as past due either as a result of the lead time exceeding the available time, in the case of planned-order releases, or because of lack of planned performance in any of the schedules. If the master production schedule that is being input to the MRP system for processing contains past-due buckets, it will also cause quantities on component levels to be timed as past due.

The past-due timing in the time-phased inventory record should be avoided except where it may aid in following up and expediting behind-schedule performance on open-order completions and planned-order releases. Recording a planned order as past due when there is insufficient time left for the full lead-time offset, as shown in Figure 81, makes little sense, as there is no delinquent performance involved that should be expedited, and the order-release action cannot take place in the past but only in the present, i.e., in the current period.

A

	Past due	Period 1	2	3	4
PARENT					
Planned-order releases	12	5		18	20

COMPONENT

	Past due	1	2	3	4
Gross requirements	12	5		18	20
Scheduled receipts	10	15			
On hand	36	44	44	26	6
Planned-order releases					

B

PARENT

	Past due	1	2	3	4
Planned-order releases	12	17		18	20

COMPONENT

	Past due	1	2	3	4
Gross requirements	12	17		18	20
Scheduled receipts	10	25			
On hand	36	44	44	26	6
Planned-order releases					

FIGURE 80   Treatment of quantities past due.

Lead time: 5	Past due	Period			
		I	2	3	4
Net requirements					25
Planned-order releases	25				

FIGURE 81   Past-due order release caused by insufficient lead time.

It is possible to time-phase past-due quantities and to display them in the inventory record, as shown in Figure 82, but there is little benefit to such practice. A past-due order (assuming its due date is valid) is past due and needs to be expedited for earliest possible delivery—irrespective of *how much* past due it is. Its original due date can be carried in the subsidiary segment of the inventory record. The status segment of this record is being unnecessarily complicated by the inclusion of several "past-due" fields.

	Weeks past due				Week			
	4+	3	2	I	34	35	36	37
Scheduled receipts	6			50			60	

FIGURE 82   Time-phased quantities past due.

In MRP systems of the net change variety the function of the "past-due" field is taken over by the control-balance bucket, in which both delinquent and premature performance is being recorded in terms of, respectively, positive and negative values. The function of the control-balance field has previously been discussed in Chapter 5.

The last special field in the status segment of the inventory record that merits brief mention is the "total" bucket which appears at the end of each time-bucket row. Inclusion of this field is optional. It would be used for purposes of reconciliation or a validity check of the status data that the computer would be programmed to carry out whenever the net requirements are recomputed.

For example:

Current on hand:		115
Total scheduled receipts:		100
		215
Allocated on hand:	35	
Total gross requirements:	380	−415
Total net requirements:		−200
Total planned orders:		225
Planned coverage excess:		25

This type of reconciliation will detect irregularities in the status data, or conditions calling for scrutiny and possible action. For example, if the projected on-hand quantity (equivalent to net requirements) at the end of the planning horizon is a positive value ("negative" net requirements), it is indicative of excessive coverage, probably caused by a reduction in gross requirements. If there are any open orders outstanding, they should be reduced or canceled, if possible.

The Complete Logical Record

In addition to the status data segment, the item master data (header) and subsidiary data segments make up the item inventory record. All these data together are termed the *logical record* (data that are logically related) as against the *physical record* or records stored in possibly different format and different locations of computer storage. The data that constitute a logical record are not necessarily stored together physically. Some of them may not be stored at all but are re-created in the computer's main memory for purposes of computation and/or display. This is a matter of programming and the design of data-base software which the system user, generally speaking, need not be concerned about. The full item inventory record (for an example, see Figure 83) consists of the following:

1. ITEM MASTER DATA SEGMENT
   - Item identity
   - Item characteristics
   - Planning factors
   - Safety stock
   - Pointers to other files
2. INVENTORY STATUS SEGMENT
   Gross requirements
   - Control balance or past-due field
   - Time-phased data fields
   - Total
   Scheduled receipts
   - Control balance or past-due field
   - Time-phased data fields
   - Total
   On hand
   - Current on hand
   - Allocated on hand
   - Projected on-hand fields
   - Total (ending inventory or net requirements)
   Planned-order releases
   - Control balance or past-due field
   - Time-phased data fields
   - Total

	Part No.	Description		Lead time		Std. cost		Safety stock
ITEM MASTER DATA SEGMENT	Order quantity		Setup		Cycle	Last year's usage		Class
	Scrap allowance		Cutting data		Pointers		Etc.	

	Allocated		Control balance	Period								Totals
				I	2	3	4	5	6	7	8	
INVENTORY STATUS SEGMENT	Gross requirements											
	Scheduled receipts											
	On hand											
	Planned-order releases											

Order details	
SUBSIDIARY DATA SEGMENT · Pending action	
Counters	
Keeping track	

FIGURE 83   Logical record of an inventory item.

3. SUBSIDIARY DATA SEGMENT
Order details
- External requirements
- Open (shop and purchase) orders
- Released portion of blanket orders
- Blanket order detail and history
- Other (user's choice)

Records of pending action
- Purchase requisitions outstanding
- Purchase-order changes requested (quantity, due date)
- Material requisitions outstanding
- Shop order changes requested (rescheduled due dates)
- Planned (shop) orders held up, material shortage
- Shipment of item requested (requisition, etc.)
- Other (user's choice)

Counters, accumulators
- Usage to date
- Scrap (or vendor rejects) to date
- Detail of demand history
- Forecast error, by period
- Other (user's choice)

Keeping-track records
- Firm planned orders

- Unused scrap allowance, by open shop order
- Engineering change action taken
- Orders held up, pending engineering change
- Orders held up, raw material substitution
- Other interventions by inventory planner

UPDATING INVENTORY RECORDS

The inventory status data are maintained up to date by means of processing (posting) *inventory transactions* against the item inventory record. An inventory transaction is defined as a notice of an event that changes the inventory status. *External* inventory transactions are reported to the system, whereas *internal* transactions are generated by the system itself, in the course of requirements planning. Reports of certain events that do not affect inventory status but are posted to the subsidiary data segment of the record are called *pseudotransactions*.

Transactions and Other Entries

The status data on which an MRP system depends are maintained up to date by means of processing transactions against item inventory records. Inventory transactions are not, however, the only entries processed by the system that affect these records. The several types of entries that the system processes in order to update inventory records may be categorized as follows:

1. Inventory transactions
2. User-controlled exceptions to regular processing logic
3. Pseudotransactions
4. Final assembly schedule entries
5. Error-correction entries
6. File maintenance entries

Inventory transactions act to modify the status of inventory items; i.e., status is changed following the processing of any inventory transaction. A given transaction may cause subsidiary records to be processed, in addition to processing the status data segment of the inventory record. A transaction may change the status in such a way as to require also the updating of component-item status (in net change implementations of MRP systems), thus affecting multiple inventory records. A transaction may report a normal or planned event, such as a stock receipt, or an unexpected event, such as a stock return. While both may have the same physical effect, the regular processing logic must be modified (as will be shown later) to register unexpected events.

User-controlled exceptions to regular processing logic represent another category of entries processed against inventory records. Such entries serve as a means of intercession by the inventory planner. In certain situations, human judgment is required to evaluate and solve a problem, and the planner must be able to override the system's regular logic. In this category belong several types of commands that the MRP system can be programmed to obey. One example is a *hold* command to prevent a (mature) planned order from being issued, perhaps because of a contemplated substitution in raw material. Another example is a *scrap tag* command that tells the system not to call for release of a new order if its quantity is smaller than the scrap allowance of an existing open order. A *firm planned order* command, which freezes a planned order in place, is another example. The use of this command has been discussed in the preceding chapter.

Pseudotransactions are entries to the subsidiary data segment of the item inventory record. Pseudotransactions do not affect inventory status. Examples are a purchase requisition issue (status will be affected only upon the release of the purchase order) and a change in an open order detail. Another example is the recording of a subcontractor's work authorization.

Final assembly schedule entries apply to highest-level items only, in those cases where the end products themselves (because of their complexity) do not appear in the master production schedule. When the final assembly schedule, which is stated in terms of product models, is put together, the high-level components on which it will draw may be allocated in the respective inventory records. In another type of manufacturing business, a customer order may be processed this way upon receipt. In an assembly-line environment, a day's or week's final production may be broken down into high-level components consumed, summarized by component, and processed against the respective component inventory records in lieu of stock disbursement transactions, which are not otherwise reported for highest-level items.

Error-correction entries are not genuine transactions, as they do not affect real status. In some MRP systems, special transaction codes are being used to distinguish error-correction entries from genuine transactions that have the same effect. For example, the inventory planner releases an order for item A but erroneously reports it as item B. In the record of B, there now appears an open order. The error is corrected by processing an entry that reverses the previous transaction, rather than by an order-cancellation transaction. The effect would be the same, but the distinction is made for purposes of record.

File maintenance entries affect the item master data segment (header) of the item inventory record. Such entries update the record for changes in the attributes of the item, e.g., standard cost, classification, item description, etc., or for changes in planning factors such as lead time or scrap allowance. File maintenance entries do not affect inventory status, or rather, their processing does not trigger the replanning process in standard implementations of material requirements planning.

Transaction Effects

The designer of an inventory control system must decide how many different types of transaction are to be recognized, how they are to be coded, and how they are to be processed by the system. The choices are virtually unlimited, and dozens of transaction types may be recognized in a given system. The range and treatment of both transactions and pseudotransactions will be reviewed later in this section. While there is no limit to the number of different transaction types that may be used, there is a limited number of *effects* that these transactions can have on inventory status. Thus a number of different transaction types will affect inventory status the same way. For example, a stock receipt of an overrun, a customer return, and an inventory adjustment "up" (the result of a physical count) will increase the quantity on hand and reduce net requirements. The different effects that various transactions can have on a time-phased inventory record are as follows:

EXTERNAL TRANSACTIONS AFFECTING ONE RECORD

1. *Change quantity of gross requirements*
   Secondary effect: recompute projected on hand
                           recompute planned-order releases
2. *Change quantity of scheduled receipt*
   Secondary effect: recompute projected on hand
                           recompute planned-order releases
3. *Reduce scheduled receipt and increase quantity on hand*
4. *Change quantity on hand*
   Secondary effect: recompute projected on hand
                           recompute planned-order releases
5. *Reduce quantity on hand and reduce gross requirements*
6. *Reduce quantity on hand and reduce quantity allocated*

EXTERNAL TRANSACTIONS AFFECTING MULTIPLE RECORDS

7. *Change quantity of planned-order release (parent record) and change quantity of gross requirements (component records)*
   Secondary effect: recompute projected on hand and planned-order release in component records
8. *Reduce quantity of planned-order release and increase scheduled receipts (parent records); reduce gross requirements and increase quantity allocated (component records)*
   Secondary effect: recompute projected on hand in parent record
9. *Increase quantity of planned-order release and reduce scheduled receipts (parent record); increase gross requirements and reduce quantity allocated (component records)*

INTERNAL TRANSACTIONS AFFECTING MULTIPLE RECORDS

10. *Change quantity of planned-order release (parent record) and change quantity of gross requirements (component records)*
Secondary effect: recompute projected on hand and planned-order releases in component records

Any given inventory transaction has one (and only one) of the ten possible effects listed. The comments that follow refer to these effects by their number.

Effect No. 1 (Change quantity of gross requirements) is a result of either increasing or reducing the contents of a gross requirements bucket or multiple buckets. Note that a change in the *timing* of a gross requirement is effected by reducing the quantity in the original bucket and increasing the quantity in the new bucket. An addition of a new requirement in a new bucket is tantamount to increasing that bucket's contents from the original zero to the new quantity. Effect No. 1 results from transactions reporting demand for the item (including an increase, reduction, or cancellation of this demand) originating from external sources. Orders or forecasts for service parts, interplant items, etc., are an example.

Effect No. 2 (Change quantity of scheduled receipt) results from increasing, reducing, canceling, or rescheduling an open order. Rescheduling, as in the case of gross requirements, means reducing the contents of one bucket and increasing that of another one. Transactions that will have this effect are, for example, a purchase-order increase, a scrap report, and a change in the order due date.

Effect No. 3 (Reduce scheduled receipt and increase quantity on hand) is caused by a stock receipt, partial or full, of an order. Note that this does not apply to an unplanned receipt for which no order had been previously placed, nor to the quantity of an overrun or overdelivery. Unless delivery is premature, neither the projected on hand nor the planned-order release schedules need be recomputed.

Effect No. 4 (Change quantity on hand) is the result of transactions that increase or reduce the quantity on hand without affecting any open orders. Stock returns, overdeliveries, inventory adjustments "up" or "down," and unplanned disbursements belong in this category. The unanticipated change in the quantity on hand causes a recomputation of the projected on-hand schedule and consequently, the planned-order release schedule.

Effect No. 5 (Reduce quantity on hand and reduce gross requirements) results from a disbursement or shipment of an external (service part, interplant, etc.) order. There are no secondary effects on the other status data in the record.

Effect No. 6 (Reduce quantity on hand and reduce quantity allocated) results from a planned (anticipated) disbursement of a component item against a parent order. As the material requisition or picking list, previously released to the stockroom, is filled, the transaction reporting it reduces the quantities on hand and allocated.

Effect No. 7 (Change quantity of planned-order release in the parent record and change quantity of gross requirements in the component record) is a result of an intervention by the inventory planner who, as discussed in the preceding chapter, solves certain problems by changing the quantity or timing of a planned order and "freezing" this change so that the MRP system will not try to recompute or reposition this particular planned order the next time that the net requirements change. The transaction reporting this intervention to the system is the previously discussed firm planned order. The change in the planned-order schedule affects the gross requirements of component items and causes their status to be recomputed. The firm planned order is one of several types of inventory transaction that affect more than one record, in cases of *manufactured* items. Purchased items have no components (in the system) and transactions reported against them never affect other inventory records.

Effect No. 8 (Reduce quantity of planned-order release and increase scheduled receipts in parent records; reduce gross requirements and increase quantity allocated in component records) is caused by a release of a planned order, which the respective transaction converts to an open order (scheduled receipt) in the inventory record. This transaction also affects component records, whose gross requirements are reduced and the allocated quantity increased.

Effect No. 9 (Increase quantity of planned-order release and reduce scheduled receipts in the parent record; increase gross requirements and reduce quantity allocated in component records) nullifies a previous order-release transaction. This happens when the inventory planner, for some reason, decides to rescind the release of an order. Once a shop order has started into the manufacturing process, this, of course, is no longer possible.

Effect No. 10 (Change quantity of planned-order release in the parent record and change quantity of gross requirements in the component records) is caused by the only internal transaction that exists, i.e., a change in a parent planned-order schedule being reflected in the gross requirements of component items. This effect is identical to No. 7, except that here the "transaction" is generated by the system internally, in the course of requirements planning (explosion).

The Basic Transaction Set

As pointed out earlier, different transaction codes may be used for several entries that are identical logically, i.e., that have the same effect on inventory status. The reason for creating a transaction set larger than the minimum that is essential lies in the desirability of being able to log transaction history (audit trail) by recording and measuring their sources, reasons, etc., and also of being able to trigger different treatments of these various transactions in the subsidiary data segment of the inventory record.

It is not practical to attempt a comprehensive review of inventory transactions by type and variety, because each user of an MRP system is free to create, without limit to number and type, a transaction set best suited to his needs. It is possible, however, to list the basic transactions that would permit the essential job to be done. The following list comprises the basic transactions that are *reported* to the system, as against transactions that the system generates internally.

Transaction Type	Sample Code
REQUIREMENTS FROM EXTERNAL SOURCES	
■ Enter	A1
■ Cancel	A2
■ Increase	A3
■ Reduce	A4
■ Change timing	A5
ORDER RELEASE	
■ Place order	B1
CHANGE IN SCHEDULED RECEIPTS	
■ Cancel order	C1
■ Increase quantity	C2
■ Reduce quantity	C3
■ Reschedule	C4
■ Scrap in process	C5
RECEIPTS	
■ Scheduled receipt	D1
■ Unplanned receipt	D2
■ Inventory adjustment upward	D3
■ Stock return	D4
REJECTED SHIPMENTS	
■ Reject	E1
■ Cancel rejection	E2
DISBURSEMENTS	
■ Scheduled disbursement	F1
■ Unplanned disbursement	F2
■ Inventory adjustment downward	F3
■ Scrap in storage	F4

Reporting Receipts and Disbursements

As mentioned in Chapter 2, an MRP system is based on the assumption that each item under its control passes into and out of stock and that reports of receipts and disbursements, i.e., transactions, will be generated. In many manufacturing operations, however, it is not practical to route each inventory item through a stockroom. In these cases, the reporting, which is mandatory under the MRP system, may be based on events other than physical arrival in stock and departure therefrom. Under the following options in the treatment of receipts and disbursements, the posting of transactions is:

1. Initiated on report from stockroom
2. Initiated on report from receiving dock
3. Triggered by shop floor events
4. Anticipated from other transactions

Reporting from the stockroom is the normal practice. Receipts of purchased items may alternatively be reported from the receiving dock, but if the stockroom is to be bypassed entirely, such transactions signal both a receipt and a disbursement. The posting of receipts and disbursements to inventory records can be triggered by certain designated events on the shop floor. The completion of the last (or other designated) operation on a shop order may be considered as a receipt, or a simultaneous receipt and disbursement. The completion (receipt) of a parent order may be treated as a disbursement of component items. A production report (mentioned earlier in this section, in connection with assembly lines) may be broken down and translated into component-item disbursements. A disbursement can also be anticipated from the posting of a related transaction. For example, the release of a parent planned order may be treated as tantamount to component-item disbursement.

THE DATA BASE

In a computer-based system such as material requirements planning, files constitute the foundation on which the superstructure of the application is built. As with any foundation supporting a structure, it codetermines the soundness and utility of such a structure. The effective operation and efficiency of an MRP system is, to a considerable degree, a function of *system file quality*. This quality, in turn, is reflected in the relative accuracy, up-to-dateness, and accessibility of file-record information.

The importance of file organization and file management to the success of a computer-based system is great, particularly so because of a universal tendency on the part of management to *underestimate* both the importance and the requirements of this part of the system. Lack of file integrity is one important reason why some MRP systems installed in industry have failed to live up to expectations. Emphasis must therefore be put on system files, their organization, maintenance, and accessibility. Computer manufacturers have invested heavily in the development of file management programs (data-base software), a tool that helps greatly in coping with the problem of maintaining file integrity.

Problems of File Maintenance

A computer-based system such as material requirements planning will not work satisfactorily with poor files, but in the average manufacturing company the files in question, at the time the system is being implemented, normally *are* in a rather poor condition. This seems invariably true particularly with manually maintained files of records related to product structure (bills of material), to inventory status, and to the manufacturing process proper (routings, operation sheets). It is due to the fact that the rate of change affecting these records is typically not matched by a corresponding capacity of the responsible departments to incorporate the changes into the files fully and properly.

When the functions of inventory management and production control that utilize the information contained in these files are to be automated, the respective files must normally be overhauled, restructured, recoded, and updated. This is usually recognized, and file cleanup is carried out as a subproject of the system implementation effort. But *fixing* something is one thing, and *keeping it fixed* is another. Files tend to deteriorate following the conclusion of the fixup effort. The reason for this is the extreme difficulty of manually maintaining any file that contains other than static information.

The task of file maintenance is not only difficult but requires such a large effort that it becomes, in practice, virtually impossible to keep a voluminous file complete and updated under manual methods, with the meager resources normally allocated for this function. A classic example is the typical bill of material, or a manufacturing routing file, which consist of several tens of thousands of records encompassing active, inactive, semiobsolete, and obsolete parts. These files are constantly affected by so many changes that true file maintenance can become a nightmare. This is so because many types of change literally explode throughout the file. A single such change may affect hundreds, and sometimes thousands, of individual records.

The key to this problem is the staffing and budget provided for file maintenance which, in most cases, is simply insufficient. The planners of a new MRP system usually recognize that pertinent files may have to be reorganized and updated, that in some cases they must be enlarged and the complexity of their structure must be increased (see next chapter), and that these files will have to be rigorously maintained in the future if the new system is to function properly. Such demands often run into strong opposition by the heads of departments responsible for maintaining these files, because they foresee the increase in the file maintenance cost, which *has not been budgeted.*

Furthermore, these department heads are sensitive to the cost-performance of their functions, and that is why they may be reluctant to request additional funds for the maintenance of files to new, higher standards, particularly when they themselves are not the primary beneficiaries of increased file data integrity. Even when forced to augment their capacity for file maintenance, they may tend to bleed it at times of various departmental crises and, particularly, during cost-cutting drives. File maintenance may be economized on without the consequences becoming immediately apparent — but it may eventually prove very costly in terms of impaired system effectiveness.

Management has traditionally been reluctant to face up to the problem of file maintenance, yet even the old manual systems were built around the implicit assumption of file data integrity, and violations of this assumption impaired the effectiveness of such systems. Because these systems were entirely people-based, however, they got by without rigorous file maintenance thanks to the ability of human beings to improvise and to make up for deficiencies of procedure and file information. Because a machine lacks this ability, however, rigorous file maintenance is *imperative* in computer-based systems.

Files and the Data Base

There are two classes of data that computer programs operate on, i.e., *input data* (transactions) and *file data.* In data-processing terminology, terms such as *data control, data management, data base,* etc., pertain to file data alone. The data base consists of one or more data files, and various functions pertaining thereto are collectively known under such labels as *file management, data management,* and *data base management.* The term *data base* (sometimes also *data bank*) has some special connotations as to the characteristics of the files that constitute it. The most significant attribute of a data base is its *commonness,* i.e., system files serving as a common base for several applications and subsystems.

Under older methods, the various departments and functional groups in a manufacturing company maintained their own files, with file-record information being organized so as to suit the particular needs of each individual department. This included a considerable amount of redundancy and data duplication. For example, a typical inventory record contained data such as:

- Part number
- Part description
- Standard cost
- Raw material used (for manufactured parts)

- Purchase-order quantity or quantity discounts (for purchased parts)
- Where-used information
- Etc.

All the above was duplicated in at least one, and sometimes all, of the following, different record files:

- Cost sheets
- Purchased parts records
- Routings
- Engineering drawings
- Service part price (billing) records
- Stores location records

When files are transferred to, and centralized in, a computer system, such duplication would be unnecessarily costly in terms of both cost of storage and cost of maintenance. In setting up a data base for a computer-based system, the goal of file efficiency is reflected in the twin objectives of:

1. Eliminating or minimizing data duplication, redundancy, different file "versions," and different update levels

2. Optimizing file access and its economy

These are *conflicting objectives*. If the files were stored in their original state, with the duplicated data that made them self-sufficient, access would be fast and economical but cost of storage and maintenance would be excessive. If the duplication is eliminated, it means either that several files must be accessed to retrieve a set of data required for a given application or that files have been consolidated and now contain large records. In the latter case, sequential processing will have become relatively inefficient, and in random-access processing, multiple accesses for selective data retrieval may be necessary.

It can be seen from this dilemma that the problem is one of determining the best file organization that would balance the advantages and disadvantages. The problem is further compounded, however, by another objective of the data-base concept, called *application independence*. If the number, nature, and frequency of applications were fixed, it would be possible to tailor file organization to these applications in a way that would optimize overall efficiency. But the goal is the opposite—a data base should be organized independently of applications and should serve as a common foundation for all applications and subsystems, both *planned* and *unplanned*. The term *application independence* also implies that changes in the application program (such as material requirements planning) should not affect the organization of the data base.

This is a sound objective, because applications are subject to change and unknown future applications must not require a reorganization of the data base, which is a major and costly undertaking. How best to meet the requirements of storage efficiency, file maintenance, and data retrieval is a technical system problem that is, in practice, solved by some form of compromise between the conflicting objectives. Different data-base software packages embody different approaches to this solution.

When we consider what happens (and must happen) to files when they become a part of a system data base, another significant characteristic of the data-base concept emerges. It is the requirement that files can no longer "belong" to the departments in which they originated. In a modern computer-based system, information is not "owned" by any one business function, in the sense that departments which traditionally had autonomous jurisdiction over the contents and format of the respective file records can no longer exercise such authority. This is due to the fact that records have been stripped of redundant and duplicate data and that files have been reorganized and perhaps consolidated and now serve as a *common* base for multiple applications. The file management functions mentioned earlier consist of the following:

- File creation
- File organization
- Providing for file access
- File updating (i.e., transaction processing)
- File maintenance
- Establishing inquiry capability
- Report generation

Some of the above represent largely technical data-processing considerations that will not be elaborated on here. Three of these functions, and the problems associated with them, however, merit a review. They are file maintenance, already discussed, and the closely related functions of file organization and file access or data retrieval.

File Organization and File Access

A file is made up of a set of like records. Each record, in turn, consists of a number of *fields* containing the various pertinent data or *data elements*. Each record has a *key,* i.e., a field or data element that serves as the main identification of that record. The key is the identifier by which the record is found in the file. An example is the part number in an inventory-record file. Each file is organized in the sequence of its key. The file organization and file access problems arise when some data other than the key are to be retrieved. Such data, while they occupy the same field in each of the records, are not (and cannot be) sequenced in their own right, and therefore it is not possible to find (access and retrieve) them directly, without more or less excessive scanning of the file. In a data-base arrangement, this problem is crucial and must be solved through one or more techniques of information retrieval.

If the record (or records) containing the desired data cannot be accessed directly, it must be accessed indirectly, through one of the following:

- A *file scan* (always possible but most inefficient)
- A separately maintained *index*
- A linked record or *chain*

The problem, and some of the available solution techniques, can best be illustrated using a commonly known file, such as a telephone directory. A phone book is, in effect, a set of records pertaining to telephone users. Each of these records is made up of three or four fields, i.e.:

1. Name
2. Business or occupation (optional)
3. Street address
4. Telephone number

The name is the key, and the file is, of course, organized in alphabetic sequence. It is not difficult to envision this file as residing in computer random-access storage and to pretend that in retrieving information from the phone book we act as a computer program. To learn the telephone number of someone named Morris, for instance, we break the book open somewhere beyond its middle, as we are familiar with the key and its sequence and know approximately where to look for the letter M. From the page we have opened, we then conduct a partial file scan, either forward or backward, until the desired record is located.

The logic of this technique can be programmed for a computer to follow, by setting up a subsidiary record or *index* (which we carry in our head), which might indicate, for instance, the range of storage addresses (phone-book pages) for each letter of the alphabet. This index would be consulted first, and the subsequent scan would be accordingly limited. But here we are dealing with the name, i.e., the key itself, which in computer systems is not a problem at all, as a number of techniques for minimizing scans, or even accessing the record directly, are available.

The real problem would arise were we to seek information such as:

1. Whose number is 322-7593?
2. Which names represent lumberyards?
3. What are all the names with a 48th Street address?

The telephone directory contains all this information, but how do we locate it short of a total scan? The phone book solves problem No. 2 by means of yellow pages, which represent a duplicate file of the same records organized by a different key, i.e., occupation or business. In a computer system, such record duplication would be unnecessary, as the yellow-pages file would need to contain only the storage addresses of the lumberyard records but no names, street addresses, or telephone numbers, which can be extracted by going back to the name records. Such record linkage represents *chaining*, as the contents of one record point to the location of another record. The technique of chaining will be described in more detail below.

If query No. 1 above were frequent, an index to telephone numbers could be constructed; e.g., all pages on which the prefix 322 appears could be listed in a separate record, along with similar records for all the other prefixes. This would create another small subsidiary file, to be consulted for purposes of limiting file search. Obviously, a more extensive index would limit the search still further, but at the expense of storing a larger subsidiary file. Problem No. 3 could be solved similarly.

It can be seen that if a file is to serve multiple applications, including unspecified future ones, a host of file organization and data-retrieval problems arise. The objective of eliminating duplication must be compromised to some extent, and various indexes, new chain fields in existing records, and subsidiary record files must be created. Note that all the data being stored to facilitate retrieval must be *maintained*. As changes are made in the primary records, they must be reflected in the chain structures, indexes, etc. The cost of storing and maintaining the subsidiary records represents the tradeoff between the economy of file storage on one hand and the efficiency of data retrieval on the other.

The Chaining of Records and Files

A special case of the file organization and record-retrieval problem involves two or more files that are logically related but differently organized, which cannot, due to their nature, be made similar in organization or consolidated. The classic example of this phenomenon is the relationship between a product-structure (bill of material) file containing part numbers repetitively listed by product subassembly, and a file containing a single record for each part number, such as an inventory-record file.

For the material requirements planning application, in the course of requirements explosion the pair of related files must be processed in conjunction. The problem is one of record linkage, and it is aggravated by the fact that there is no one-for-one relationship between part-number records of the two files. The problem is solved through *chaining*, i.e., the storing in one record of the (storage) address of a related record which, in turn, may contain the address of another related record. An address stored for purposes of chaining is referred to as a *pointer*.

Computer manufacturers have developed, and made available to their customers, generalized application software packages to handle this prob-

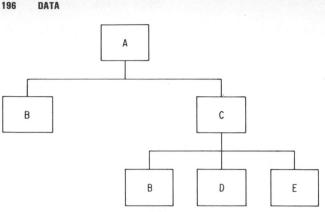

FIGURE 84   Product structure, item A.

lem. These programs are called *bill of material processors* or chained-file management systems. Such programs normally combine the capabilities of file organization, retrieval, and maintenance. They depend on the technique of chaining for their effectiveness.

Chaining and its use will be demonstrated in examples that follow. Note that these are *examples*; other ways of chaining the records in question are possible. A bill of material containing five part numbers is depicted in Figure 84. The chaining of this bill to the respective inventory records, as represented graphically in Figure 85, is of two kinds, tracing either down (explosion) or up (implosion, where used) the product structure. Thus when planning material requirements, the chain from assembly-record A in the inventory file leads to the bill of material record of A, which lists as its components B and C. These component records, in turn, chain back to their respective inventory records in the first file, so that these can be updated.

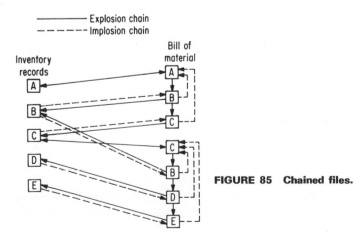

FIGURE 85   Chained files.

As component item C is an assembly, it has its own bill of material record in the product-structure file, to which it is also chained. For purposes of tracing up the product structure, chains lead from each record in the inventory file to *all* corresponding records in the other file (see part B). Each component record in the bill of material file is linked to its parent-assembly record in that file.

In a standard-cost-buildup application, if the cost of part B increased by $1, the where-used chaining will assure that the cost increase is carried from inventory record B to product-structure records B and C, from there back to inventory record C and again to product-structure records C and A, and finally back to inventory record A, increasing its cost by $2.

The examples used thus far illustrate the chaining of records within one file and the chaining of two files, but the technique may be extended to any number of files that are logically related. The software called chained-file management systems, referred to earlier, is capable of linking several files used for material requirements planning and for applications related to material requirements planning. An example of chained files that would be used if the MRP system were complemented by operations scheduling and capacity requirements planning systems is shown in Figure 86.

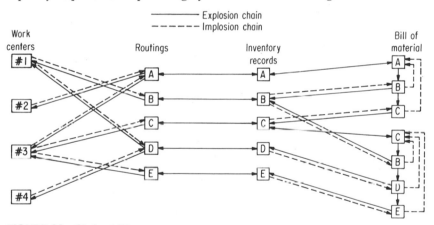

FIGURE 86   Chained-file management system.

As mentioned earlier, data that constitute the *logical* inventory-item record may be stored *physically* together, or they may be stored as separate record files linked to the item-master segment of the record. This is a programmer's choice, which is largely dictated by the particular data-base software being used. When logically related records must be stored physically apart, they are linked by chaining. A good example would be requirements-data fields and peg records in an MRP system, which are often stored in separate files, as illustrated in Figure 87. This example, as well as the preceding two, is based on the bill of material in Figure 84.

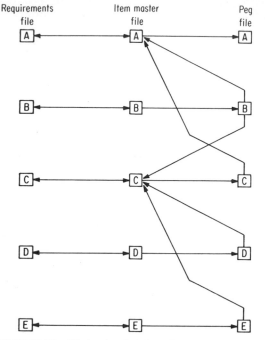

FIGURE 87   Chained subsidiary files.

Bill of Material Format

Note that in Figure 84, the product-structure data of item A are depicted in a single, composite bill of material but are shown in Figure 85 as being stored in the form of two separate bills for items A and C. This is related to the question of *bill of material format*. Under manual methods, product-structure data can be maintained in a variety of formats, and it is not unusual for different departments in a plant to maintain their own versions of the bill of material, in a format to suit their respective needs. Thus an engineering bill, a purchasing bill, a costing bill, an assembly bill, and an inventory-planning bill may exist simultaneously. Needless to say, this is a costly and inefficient way to maintain product-structure data files.

When product-structure data are stored in a computer system, duplication of effort (and cost) in maintaining the bill of material can be eliminated. Only one set of data, in a format best suitable for storage, is maintained, but the data can be retrieved and "assembled" by the computer in a variety of formats, to be printed out (or otherwise displayed) for the benefit of the various users.

The format used for purposes of storage is the so-called *single-level bill,* which minimizes both storage space and maintenance requirements. Under this approach, a single product-structure record for each assembly and

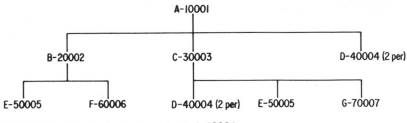

FIGURE 88   Product structure, item A-10001.

subassembly is established, and it simply lists the parent item's components (identity, quantity per, pointer, and sometimes a code identifying those component items that are subassemblies) on the immediately lower level only. Multilevel bills are then reconstructed via chaining, as and if required. The single-level bill format, as well as several other formats in which product-structure data can be displayed, will be illustrated in the next example.

Product-structure data of item A-10001, shown in Figure 88, would be stored in single-level bill format, as follows:

Parent:	A-10001	B-20002	C-30003
Components:	B-20002*	E-50005	D-40004 (2 per)
	C-30003*	F-60006	E-50005
	D-40004 (2 per)		G-70007

In the above example of three single-level bills, asterisks represent subassembly codes. Pointers and quantities of 1 per are omitted. The data can be formatted and displayed in various ways; the six most popular formats are termed as follows:

1. Single-level explosion
2. Indented explosion
3. Summarized explosion
4. Single-level implosion
5. Indented implosion
6. Summarized implosion

The single-level explosion format is that of a single-level bill. For item A-10001, the following data would be displayed:

A-10001
B-20002*
C-30003*
D-40004 (2 per)

The indented explosion format lists components on all lower levels, and the number of levels involved is indicated in the display by an indentation of component-item numbers under the respective parent-item number. For item A-10001, the printed output, also known as an indented parts list, would appear as follows:

```
A-10001
  B-20002
    E-50005
    F-60006
  C-30003
    D-40004 (2 per)
    E-50005
    G-70007
  D-40004 (2 per)
```

The summarized explosion format lists all the components of a given assembly or subassembly irrespective of level, with quantities per reflecting use per unit of the assembly in question rather than per unit of the component's parent. For item A-10001, the printed output, also known as a parts list, would appear as follows:

```
A-10001
B-20002
C-30003
D-40004 (4 per)
E-50005 (2 per)
F-60006
G-70007
```

The single-level implosion format is that of a where-used list. The output lists all the parents (on the immediately higher level only) of a given item, such as, in the case of item E-50005:

```
E-50005
B-20002
C-30003
```

The indented implosion format traces the usage of a given item in its parent, and, in turn, the parent's parent, etc., until the end item is reached. Indentations signify levels. For example, the output for item F-60006 would appear as follows:

```
  A-10001      or      F-60006
  B-20002              B-20002
F-60006                  A-10001
```

The summarized implosion format is an expanded where-used list in which all the items on higher levels that contain the item in question are listed. The quantities per are total quantities of the item used in each of the higher-level assemblies. For item E-50005, the output would appear as follows:

```
E-50005
A-10001 (2 per)
B-20002 (1 per)
C-30003 (1 per)
```

The six display formats just described correspond to the six retrieval programs usually supplied by computer manufacturers as part of the bill of material processor software. These programs may be used in the process of exploding requirements in an MRP system, preparing material requisitions or picking lists, product costing, engineering changes, etc. To meet specialized needs, additional display formats can be created via special user-written retrieval programs.

A layman might be under the impression that the tremendous speed of a computer enables it to find anything in a file almost instantaneously and that considerations of file organization, maintenance, and data retrieval are not very important. Why are they important? Because even microseconds add up. If the Manhattan telephone directory, which contains just under 1 million names, were to be scanned from a random-access storage device, and assuming that each record were accessed individually (rather than in blocks of records) at 20 milliseconds per access cycle, the total search time would amount to 5 hours.

INPUT DATA INTEGRITY

Because an MRP system entails processing of data on a massive scale, it is virtually impossible to implement such a system without a computer. A computer, however, functions with full success (unlike a human being) only in a "perfect" environment, which would include error-free, complete, and timely data. When data lack integrity, any computer system tends to fail. In a system such as material requirements planning, the computer is programmed to make many decisions (order size, order release, etc.), and thus because day-to-day tasks and functions of the business are being performed automatically, system failure may have far-reaching consequences. Low-quality input data heavily contribute to such failure and particularly plague newly developed systems once these go into operation. The quality of input data varies with their source, and the incidence of errors is always the highest in the data being generated in factory operations. For purposes of material requirements planning, data are being contributed by planners, stockroom employees, expediters, dispatchers, inspectors, truckers, and foremen, all in a position to introduce errors into the system.

Input-data errors cannot be entirely prevented, but it is important that their impact on the functioning of the system be minimized. It is feasible to incorporate a variety of external and internal system checks as part of the overall MRP system design, and a qualified programmer can incorporate many auditing, self-checking, and self-correcting features into a program. The "war" against input errors should be conducted on three separate fronts, i.e.:

1. Erection of a *barrier* to keep errors from entering the system

2. Programmed capability to *detect internally* most of the errors that got through the barrier

3. A procedure for *washing out* of the system the residue of undetected errors

The barrier, or filter, against input errors may consist of a number of procedures and techniques. Some form of input audit, testing the formal correctness (does such a part number exist, is this a legitimate transaction code, are any of the data missing, etc.) is always desirable. The barrier against the entry of erroneous input is a programmed capability of the computer system to detect and *reject* incorrect transactions at the point of entry, i.e., immediately following the input step and before processing begins.

Beyond a formal check at the point of entry, so-called *diagnostic routines* can be programmed that will conduct other tests prior to the actual processing of input data. For example, the part number, transaction code, etc., may be correct but a diagnostic test against open-order records indicates that no order has been issued for this item. Diagnostic tests conducted against files other than those to be updated, or against special tables set up for this purpose, cost something in terms of extra processing time, but for computer applications in areas of high input-data error rates they should by all means be programmed. A great variety of this type of check is possible, and when carried out in a computer, it is the swiftest and most efficient way of "catching" errors.

Internal detection, during the actual processing, of errors that got past the barrier discussed above, is also an important system capability that can usually be programmed. It is distinguished from diagnostic tests mainly by the fact that the checks are made against the file being updated. An example might be a stock-disbursement transaction that passes both input audit and diagnostic tests but is *substantively* incorrect, i.e., reports a withdrawal quantity which exceeds the quantity previously on hand.

An entirely different kind of test, called *test of reasonableness*, can sometimes also be employed. For example, if the usage of a given inventory item averages 100 per period, a gross requirement of 1,000 or 5,000 for period X is almost certainly invalid. A man spots and questions such absurdities immediately. A computer can be programmed to do the same. As far as a test of reasonableness is concerned, the computer program, by applying this test, can always flag the results that are suspect. The computer can tell the recipient of its output not to use the information without verifying it first.

Washing out residues of errors that escaped detection by other means is a must if the MRP system is to be kept from gradually (perhaps very gradually) deteriorating. It should always be assumed that at least some small proportion of errors in input data will penetrate the system despite all barriers and checks. These errors may be forever undetectable as such, but procedures should be devised to detect their *effect* on system files, and it is this effect that must be removed.

This is accomplished by means of various *reconciliation*, *purging*, and *close-out* procedures, which are analogous to writing off, periodically, miscellaneous small unpaid balances in an accounts-receivable file. Examples of this type of procedure are the reconciliation of planned versus actual requirements for an item at the master production schedule level, and the closing-out of ancient shop or purchase orders that still show some small quantity due.

It is a safe assumption that most MRP systems installed in industry contain some (small, we hope) percentage of error at all times. This can be tolerated as long as such system-resident errors do not accumulate. Even an accumulation at a minute rate must eventually smother an MRP system. As far as the washing-out of error residues is concerned, it is less important how soon after the fact the effect of an error is removed, but all-important that it be removed at some scheduled interval. If a certain level of residual error is inherent to the system, it should be kept constant.

Equally as important as the technical aspects of preserving data integrity—or perhaps more so—is the training, discipline, and attitude of people. Those who contribute input data to the system, and those who use the system in the performance of their job, must be educated to the fact that a computer's outputs cannot be better than its inputs. If an MRP system is to be successful, management has to accept responsibility for convincing everyone who interacts with the system that he has an important new role in "feeding" the computer and thus helping to keep the system effective.

REFERENCES

Data Base Organization and Maintenance Processor, general information manual form no. GH20-0771, International Business Machines Corp., 1971.

Introduction to Data Management, student text form no. SC20-8096, International Business Machines Corp., 1970.

Orlicky, Joseph: *The Successful Computer System*, McGraw-Hill, 1969, pp. 151-168.

System Data Base, Communications Oriented Production Information and Control System (COPICS), vol. 8, form no. G320-1981, International Business Machines Corp., 1972.

CHAPTER TEN

PRODUCT DEFINITION

Throughout the discussions in previous chapters, it has been assumed that a master production schedule exists to which an MRP system can be geared—and that such a schedule states the overall plan of production completely and unambiguously. Implied in this assumption is a bill of material that defines the product line not only from the customer's (and final assembly) point of view but also in a way that is suitable for purposes of procurement, fabrication, and subassembly. In other words, if an MRP system is to function properly, the product must be defined in such a way as to make it possible to express a valid master production schedule *in terms of bill of material numbers*, i.e., assembled-item numbers.

Unlike the order point approach, material requirements planning works with products and the relationships of their component items, using the bill of material as the basis for planning. Material requirements planning thus puts the bill of material to a wholly new use, and the bill of material acquires a new function—in addition to serving as part of product specifications, it becomes a framework on which the entire planning process depends. In some cases, however, the bill of material maintained by the engineering department is not usable for purposes of material requirements planning without a certain amount of modification.

As an important input to the MRP system, the bill of material must be accurate and up to date if the system's outputs are to be valid. But in addition, it must be unambiguous and so structured as to lend itself to material requirements planning. The mere existence of a bill of material is no guarantee that an MRP system can function properly. The bill of material is essentially an engineering document, and its traditional function has been to define the product from the design point of view. With the advent of material requirements planning, the product may have to be redefined so as to fit the needs of planning and manufacturing. Such redefinition is termed *structuring*, or restructuring, the bill of material.

The term *bill of material structure* pertains to the *arrangement* of component-item data within the bill of material file rather than to the organization of this file on a storage medium or in a storage device of a computer. Bill of material processors, software packages mentioned previously, edit, organize, load, maintain, and retrieve bill of material records but do not structure them. These programs assume that the bill of material file is already properly structured to serve the needs of material requirements planning. The intent of the present chapter is to clarify the subject of bill of material structuring and to describe the basic techniques used to achieve good bill of material structure.

When an MRP system is about to be introduced into a manufacturing company or plant, the existing bill of material should be reviewed to ascertain its suitability for purposes of material requirements planning. The following checklist will aid in spotting its structural deficiencies:

■ *The bill should lend itself to the forecasting of optional product features.* This capability is essential for purposes of material requirements planning.

■ *The bill should permit the master production schedule to be stated in the fewest possible number of end items.* These items will be products or major assemblies, as the case may be, but in either case they must be stated in terms of bill of material numbers.

■ *The bill should lend itself to the planning of subassembly priorities.* Orders for subassemblies have to be released at the right time, with valid due dates, and the due dates should be kept up to date.

■ *The bill should permit easy order entry.* It should be possible to take a customer order that describes the product either in terms of a model number or as a configuration of optional features and translate it into the language that the MRP system understands: bill of material numbers.

■ *The bill should be usable for purposes of final assembly scheduling.* Apart from material requirements planning, the final assembly scheduling system needs to know, specifically, which assemblies (assembly numbers) are required to build individual units of the end product.

■ *The bill should provide the basis for product costing.*

■ *The bill should lend itself to efficient computer file storage and file maintenance.*

In a given case, when these criteria are applied to the existing bill of material, it will often be found that some, but not all, of the above requirements can be satisfied. The bill of material may have to be restructured, and this can be done without affecting the integrity of product specifications. The severity of the problem of bill of material structure varies from company to company, depending on the complexity of the product in question and the nature of business. The term *bill of material structuring* covers a variety of types of change made in the bill of material, and several different techniques for effecting such changes. The subject of bill of material structure, as reviewed in this chapter, comprises the following:

1. ASSIGNMENT OF ITEM IDENTITIES
   - Elimination of ambiguity
   - Levels of manufacture
   - Treatment of transient subassemblies
2. PRODUCT MODEL DESIGNATIONS
3. MODULAR BILL OF MATERIAL
   - Disentangling product option combinations
   - Segregating common from unique parts
4. PSEUDOBILLS OF MATERIAL
5. INTERFACE TO ORDER ENTRY

ASSIGNMENT OF IDENTITIES TO INVENTORY ITEMS

If a bill of material is to be used for purposes of material requirements planning, each inventory item that it covers must be *uniquely identified*. One part number must not identify two or more items that differ from each other, if ever so slightly. This includes raw materials and subassemblies. The assignment of subassembly identities tends to be somewhat arbitrary, as actually a new entity is created every time another component is attached in the course of the assembly process. The product designer, the industrial engineer, the cost accountant, and the inventory planner might each prefer to assign them differently.

Elimination of Ambiguity

The question is when do unique subassembly numbers have to be assigned for purposes of material requirements planning, and when do they not. In reality, it is not the design of the product but the way it is being assembled that dictates the assignment of subassembly identities. The unit of work, or task, is the key here. If a number of components are assembled at a bench and are then forwarded, as a completed task, to storage or to another bench for further assembly, a subassembly number is required. Without it, the

MRP system could not generate orders for these subassemblies and plan their priorities.

Some engineering departments are overly conservative in assigning new part numbers, and the classic example of this, encountered quite often, is a raw casting that has the same part number as the finish-machined casting. This may suit the engineer, but it is difficult to see how an automated inventory system such as material requirements planning is supposed to distinguish between two types of items that must be planned and controlled separately. They have different lead times, different costs, and different dates of need.

Another requirement is that an identifying number *define the contents* of the item unambiguously. Thus the same subassembly number must not be used to define two or more different sets of component items. This sometimes happens when the original design of a product subsequently becomes subject to variation. Instead of creating a new bill of material for the assembly affected, with its own unique identity, the original bill is specified with instructions to substitute, remove, and add certain components. This shortcut method, called *add and delete*, represents vulnerable procedure, undesirable for purposes of material requirements planning, as will be discussed later.

Levels of Manufacture

The bill of material should reflect, through its level structure, the way material flows in and out of stock. The term *stock* in this connection does not necessarily mean a stockroom but rather a *state of completion*. Thus when a fabricated part is finished or a subassembly is completed, it is considered to be on hand, i.e., in stock, until withdrawn and associated with an order for a higher-level (parent) item as its component. An MRP system is constructed in a way which assumes (as discussed in Chapter 2) that each inventory item under its control goes into and out of stock at its respective level in the product structure. Material requirements planning also assumes that the bill of material accurately reflects this flow. Thus the bill of material is expected to specify not only the *composition* of a product but also the *process stages* in that product's manufacture. It must define product structure in terms of levels of manufacture, each of which represents the completion of a step in the buildup of the product. This is vital for material requirements planning because it establishes, in conjunction with item lead times, the precise timing of requirements, order releases, and order priorities.

Sometimes there is reluctance toward assigning separate identities to semifinished and finished items, where the conversion to the finished stage is of minor nature. An example might be a die casting that is first machined and then receives one of three finishes, chrome, bronze, or paint, as shown

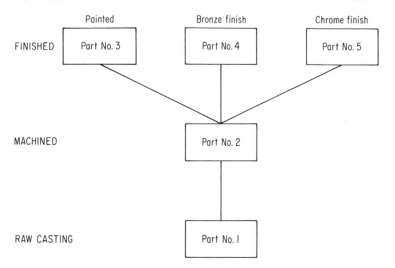

FIGURE 89   Unique identity of semifinished and finished items.

in Figure 89. The three finished items will have to be assigned separate identities if they are to be ordered, and their order priorities planned, by the MRP system. This is an example of a situation where unique item identity (of the finished casting) would normally not exist, but should be established prerequisite to material requirements planning, as otherwise such items would fall outside the scope of the system and result in loss of control.

Treatment of Transient Subassemblies

Another example of an item identity problem that is almost the opposite of the preceding one is the *transient subassembly,* sometimes called a "phantom." Assemblies of this type never see a stockroom, because they are immediately consumed in the assembly of their parent items. An example of this is a subassembly built on a feeder line that flows directly into the main assembly line. Here the subassembly normally carries a separate identity. Because it is recognized in the bill of material, the MRP system would treat it in the same way as any other subassembly. This may be undesirable, because if this kind of item is planned under an MRP system, its logic assumes that each component item goes into and out of stock and that all receipts and disbursements are being reported. That is the way the time-phased inventory record is designed and updated, and the question arises as to how to handle such subassemblies within an MRP system.

A transient subassembly would not have to be identified in the bill of material at all if there were never an overrun, a customer return, or service-part demand. Otherwise it must be separately identified in the bill of material and its inventory status must be maintained. In MRP systems of the net change variety, this would pose a particular problem because all transactions for transient subassemblies would continuously have to be reported to the system, in order to maintain the respective inventory records up to date. This is really quite unnecessary and a waste of effort in the case of order releases, order completions (receipts), and disbursements, in view of the ephemeral existence of transient subassemblies. Fortunately, there is no need to do this, thanks to a technique called the *phantom bill.* While transactions of the type mentioned do not have to be reported and posted under this approach (this applies to assembly activities but not to stock-room receipts and disbursements), the system will pick up and use any transient subassemblies that happen to be on hand. Service-part requirements can also be entered into the record and will be correctly handled by the system. But otherwise it will, in effect, bypass the phantom item's record and go from its parent item to its components directly.

To describe the application of this technique, let us assume that assembly A has a transient subassembly B as one of its components and that part C is a component of B. Thus, for purposes of illustration, item B, the phantom, is envisioned as being sandwiched between A, its parent, and C, its component. To implement this technique, the transient subassembly is treated as follows:

1. Lead time is specified as zero.
2. Lot sizing is lot for lot.
3. The bill of material (or the item record) carries a special code so that the system can recognize that it is a phantom and apply special treatment.

The special treatment referred to means departing from regular procedure, or record update logic, when processing the phantom record. The difference between the procedures can best be described through examples.

In Figure 90, inventory status data for items A (top), B (middle), and C (bottom) are shown. Note that the zero-lead-time offset on the item in the middle places the planned-order release for eighteen pieces in the same period as the net requirement. This, in turn, corresponds to the requirement for eighteen C's in the same period.

Following the release of the planned order for A, the update procedure for item record B will vary, depending on whether or not it is coded as a phantom. In the absence of such a code, regular logic applies. The regularly updated records of items A and B are shown in Figure 91. Record C continues unchanged. Following the release of the planned order for B, item record C is updated as shown in Figure 92.

Had item B been coded as a phantom, all three records would have been updated in one step, illustrated in Figure 93, as a result of the planned-order release of item A. Note that the release of planned order A, which normally would reduce only the corresponding gross requirement B (as in Figure 91), in this case also reduces the gross requirement for C, as though C were a direct component of A. Note also that the two units of B in stock

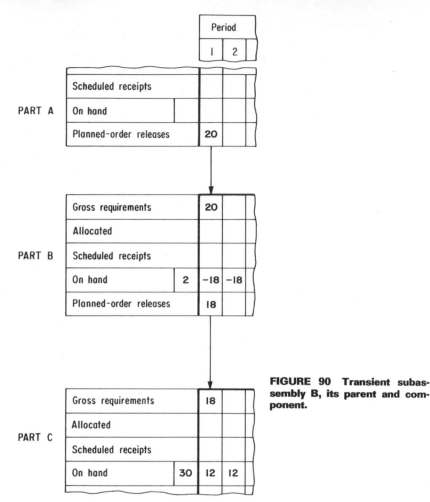

FIGURE 90 Transient subassembly B, its parent and component.

(perhaps a return from a previous overrun) are applied to the gross requirements for A and that the allocation has been *distributed* between B and C.

Upon closer examination of these examples it can be seen that the phantom logic is nothing more than a different treatment of allocation. (Zero lead time and lot-for-lot ordering are assumed, but these can be specified for some regular subassemblies also.) Once this step is carried out, regular processing logic applies, causing the records to be updated and their status data aligned correctly.

The phantom bill technique, as pointed out earlier, applies primarily to net change MRP systems. In regenerative systems the question of posting or not posting transactions to phantom records to cover assembly activities is not crucial, because a planned-order release does not update component gross requirements data. Hence, the problem of rebalancing (realigning)

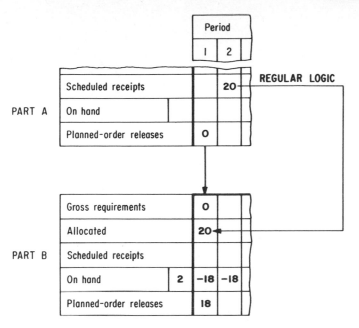

	Period		
	1	2	

REGULAR LOGIC

PART A

Scheduled receipts		20
On hand		
Planned-order releases	0	

PART B

Gross requirements		0	
Allocated		20	
Scheduled receipts			
On hand	2	−18	−18
Planned-order releases		18	

PART C

Gross requirements		18	
Allocated			
Scheduled receipts			
On hand	30	12	12

FIGURE 91   Regular update logic following release of order for item A.

the planned-order and gross requirements data of the three records does not arise. Following the planned-order release of the transient subassembly's parent, the next requirements planning run will wash out both the gross requirement and the planned-order release for the transient subassembly.

The objective of not having to report phantom transactions still remains, however, and it can be achieved by, again, specifying lead time as zero, lot-for-lot ordering, and coding the inventory record of the transient subassembly so that notices for planned-order releases are either suppressed or flagged to be disregarded. The MRP system will function correctly.

The problem then becomes one of component requisitioning (for the transient subassembly's parent orders), and it must be solved by modifying

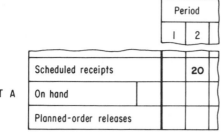

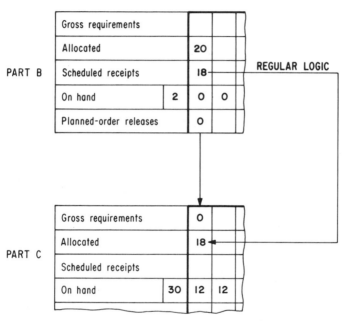

	Period	
	1	2

PART A

Scheduled receipts			20
On hand			
Planned-order releases			

PART B

Gross requirements			
Allocated		20	
Scheduled receipts		18	
On hand	2	0	0
Planned-order releases		0	

REGULAR LOGIC

PART C

Gross requirements		0	
Allocated		18	
Scheduled receipts			
On hand	30	12	12

FIGURE 92   Regular update logic following release of order for item B.

the procedure that generates material requisitions. When some transient subassemblies are on hand, *two* requisitions will have to be generated, one for the quantity of the transient subassembly on hand, and one for the balance of the order, for the subassembly's component items. In the Figure 93 example, these quantities are 2 and 18, respectively.

PRODUCT MODEL DESIGNATIONS

A product line consists of a number of product models or product families. The marketing organization normally forecasts sales in terms of models, management thinks in terms of models, and the master production schedule

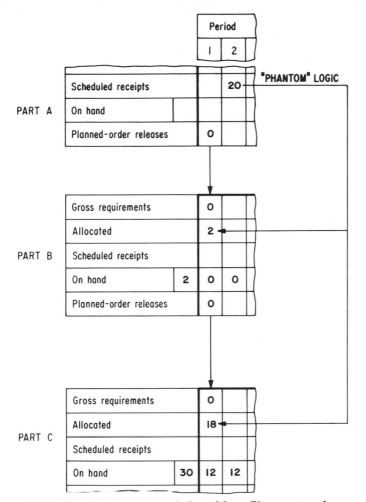

FIGURE 93   Simultaneous updating of item B's parent and component records.

may also be stated in terms of models. In cases of highly engineered products with many optional features, however, model identities are not fully meaningful for purposes of material requirements planning, because the model designations fail to provide a precise and complete product definition.

Model-code assignment is basically a matter of pointing up differences between products belonging to a product family. As a result of optional features of each line of product, in many cases there can be an almost endless variety of product buildup due to the large number of option combinations that are possible. For example, a farm tractor in a given model category might have the following optional features:

Function	Options
Wheel arrangement	■ Four-wheel construction
	■ Three-wheel construction, single front wheel
	■ Three-wheel construction, double front wheel
Fuel	■ Gasoline
	■ Diesel
	■ LP gas
Horsepower	■ 56 hp
	■ 68 hp
Transmission	■ Stick shift
	■ Automatic
Steering	■ Mechanical
	■ Power steering
Rear platform	■ Regular
	■ Low
Axles	■ Standard
	■ High-clearance
Hitch	■ Mechanical
	■ Hydraulic
Power takeoff	■ With, type A
	■ With, type B
	■ Without
Radiator shutters	■ With
	■ Without
Operator cab	■ With
	■ Without

Based on these options, it is feasible to build

$$3 \times 3 \times 2 \times 2 \times 2 \times 2 \times 2 \times 2 \times 3 \times 2 \times 2 = 6{,}912$$

tractors without any two being identical; each represents a unique configuration of optional features. In this case, it would be possible to use any number of model designations from 1 to 6,912. For instance, two models could be recognized based on horsepower, such as:

    Model A: 56 hp
    Model B: 68 hp

or six models could be recognized, such as:

    Model A: 56 hp, Four-wheel construction
    Model B: 56 hp, Three-wheel construction, regular
    Model C: 56 hp, Three-wheel construction, special
    Model D: 68 hp, Four-wheel construction
    Model E: 68 hp, Three-wheel construction, regular
    Model F: 68 hp, Three-wheel construction, special

The number of models could be raised to twelve by adding, say, axle clearance, or to eighteen by adding the fuel option, or to thirty-six if both were included. In each case, the model code would tell something—but not everything—about the features of the machine. Depending on which options are considered important enough to be reflected in model designations, creating model codes is an arbitrary matter.

A multitude of model designations is an otherwise harmless thing (it looks good in the sales catalog) except that all the models tend to get into the process of forecasting and master scheduling. Separate figures are then shown for each model, resulting in lengthy and cumbersome documents that are laborious to prepare, difficult to interpret, and even more difficult to evaluate. Furthermore, as each model represents a certain *combination* of optional features, any forecast expressed in terms of models will tend to be grossly inaccurate, necessitating constant revisions in the forecast and changes in the master production schedule.

It is difficult enough to forecast demand for any single option, but to forecast, with any degree of dependability, what other options it will be combined with is virtually impossible. In order to improve the quality of forecasting and to simplify the process of master scheduling, the number of models within each product family should be reduced (at least for internal purposes) to just a few, and ideally to one. It is much more difficult to forecast by model than by basic product and option. The basic product represents components, if there are any, common to all the possible product buildups and serves to indicate how many units of the product are expected to be sold, and how many are scheduled to be built.

This principle pertains only to forecasting, master scheduling, and planning for the procurement, fabrication, and subassembly of components. For purposes of final assembly scheduling, specific combinations of options must be specified for each unit to be built. Reducing or abolishing product models for purposes of internal planning does not mean that such model designations would necessarily have to be eliminated from price lists and sales literature. To implement the principle of forecasting and planning by basic product and option, the bill of material used by the MRP system would have to be modularized accordingly. The principles and techniques of modularization will be reviewed next.

MODULAR BILLS OF MATERIAL

A modular bill of material is arranged in terms of product modules, i.e., sets of component items each of which can be planned as a group. The process of modularizing consists of *breaking down* the bills of highest-level items (products, end items) and *rearranging* them into modules. There are two, somewhat different, objectives in modularizing a bill of material, namely:

1. To disentangle combinations of optional product features
2. To segregate common from unique, or peculiar, parts

The first is required to facilitate forecasting or, in some cases, to make forecasting at all possible under the material requirements planning approach. The second is aimed at minimizing inventory investment in components that are common to option alternatives, i.e., that are used in either optional choice. Demand for product options must be forecast, and this makes it necessary to plan safety stock in which the common components may be duplicated. The above two objectives, and the techniques used to achieve them, will be reviewed separately in the discussion that follows.

Disentangling Option Combinations

Under the material requirements planning approach, product variations or optional features must be forecast at the master production schedule level; i.e., it must be possible to forecast end items rather than their individual component items. When a product has many optional features, their combinations can be astronomical and forecasting these combinations becomes impractical. Furthermore, if separate bills of material were to be created for each of the unique end products that it is possible to build, the file would be enormous—too costly to store and maintain. But apart from that, a valid master production schedule could not even be established and stated in terms of such bills.

This problem is solved by means of a modular bill of material. Instead of maintaining bills for individual end products, under this approach the bill of material is restated in terms of the building blocks, or *modules,* from which the final product is put together. The problem, and its solution, can best be demonstrated by an example. The farm tractor discussed in the preceding section had eleven optional features with a total of twenty-five individual choices, making it possible to build 6,912 unique product configurations. There is no special difficulty in writing a bill of material for any one of these configurations, but it is not practical to store and maintain thousands of bills for a single product family.

Many of the 6,912 possible configurations may never be sold during the life of the product, and thus their bills of material would never be used. Furthermore, design improvements and engineering changes could add additional bills to the file. Consider this: The tractor, as described, has only one type of fender, but if the engineers create an option of special fenders with mudguards, the number of possible option combinations will *double* from 6,912 to 13,824. This means that another 6,912 bills would have to be added to the file. This is one reason why bills of material for end products should not be maintained in this case. But the other reason mentioned earlier is equally important; i.e., with these thousands of bills it would not be possible to state a valid master production schedule in terms of end products.

If the tractor manufacturer produces 300 of this type of tractor per month, which 300 out of the 6,912 possible configurations should he select as a forecast for a particular month? This is simply not a practical proposition. Note that volume is part of the problem. A product family with 100 possible option combinations constitutes a problem if volume is 20 per month. If volume were 10,000 per month, the forecasting problem would not be nearly as serious.

The solution of this problem lies in forecasting each of the higher-level *components* (i.e., major assembly units such as engines and transmissions) separately, and not attempting to forecast end products at all. This amounts to forecasting the various choices within the optional product features and translating such forecasts into the master production schedule.

Specifically, if 300 tractors of the type in question are to be produced in a given month, 300 so-called basic tractors (including fenders, hoods, rear wheels, etc.) would be scheduled. A bill of material for this "module" would be required to match the schedule. There are two choices of transmission, however, and let us assume that past demand has averaged, say, 75 percent stick shift and 25 percent automatic. Applying these percentages to the transmission option, 225 and 75 units, respectively, could be scheduled. But the batch of 300 customer orders in any one month is unlikely to break down exactly that way, and thus some safety stock would be desirable.

As previously mentioned, the proper way to handle safety stock under the material requirements planning approach is to plan it at the master production schedule level. Thus the transmissions would be deliberately overplanned (the statistical technique of determining standard deviations for a binomial population[1] may be used to establish correct safety stock), and transmission quantities such as 275 and 100 would be put into the master production schedule. This would not be done in every period, as unused safety stock is "rolled forward," i.e., applied in subsequent periods. The same approach would be followed for the other optional features. Each of the optional choices would have to be covered by an appropriate module of the bill of material, for use by the MRP system. Under this approach, the total number of bills of material would be as follows:

Basic tractor	1
Wheel arrangement	3
Fuel and horsepower	6
Transmission	2
Steering	2
Rear platform	2
Axles	2
Hitch	2
Power takeoff	3
Radiator shutters	1
Operator cab	1
Total	25

---

[1] In this case, the standard deviation is based on the *proportion* of the population's individuals who possess one of two qualities—male or female, Democrat or Republican, stick shift or automatic transmission.

This total of 25 compares with 6,912 if each tractor configuration had a bill of material of its own. Now if the engineers add special fenders, it would add only two bills to the file (regular fenders, part of the basic tractor, would become an optional choice and would have to have a bill of their own), instead of doubling it.

At this point in the discussion, the reader may be wondering how this type of problem is being handled in a real-life situation, if the manufacturer *does not* have bills of material set up in modular fashion. The chances are that there would be several bills, for *some* of the 6,912 possible configurations, covering the (arbitrarily established) models that are being recognized. These bills would be used for all other configurations also, by adding and subtracting optional components.

The add-and-delete technique solves some but not all of the problems. Its principal disadvantages are vulnerability to human error, slowing down order entry, and awkwardness in establishing proper historical data for option forecasting purposes.[2] Under this approach, the add-and-delete components would most likely be maintained under order points and safety stock. This is highly undesirable, because it deprives the user of some important benefits (discussed in Chapter 7) of an MRP system.

The Modularization Technique

The technique of restructuring end-product bills of material into a modular format will be demonstrated next. For this purpose, the previous tractor example will be scaled down, so that the solution may be seen clearly. Let us assume that the tractor has only *two* optional features, the transmission and steering, each of which has two choices. The customer can choose only between stick-shift and automatic transmission and between mechanical or power steering.

Figure 94 shows the four bills of material. The first combines stick shift and mechanical steering, the second, stick shift with power steering, and so on. In the product structure, the end-product (model) numbers, 12-4010, etc., are considered to be on level zero. The level-1 components, A13, C41, etc., represent assemblies, but *their* components are omitted from the chart to keep it simple.

To restructure these bills of material into modules, they are broken down, their level-1 components are analyzed and compared, and these components are then grouped by use. For example, it can be seen that the first component item in the first bill, A13, is common to all models, and it would therefore be assigned to the "common" group. The next item, C41, is found in stick-shift/mechanical and stick-shift/power combinations but not in the automatic transmission models. This indicates that C41 is unique to the stick-shift choice. The item that follows, L40, is used only with mechanical

[2]D. Garwood, "Stop: Before You Use the Bill Processor," *Production & Inventory Management*, vol. 11, no. 2, 1970.

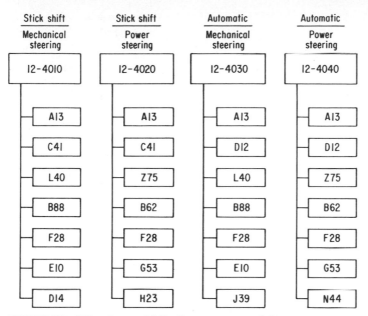

Stick shift	Stick shift	Automatic	Automatic
Mechanical steering	Power steering	Mechanical steering	Power steering
12-4010	12-4020	12-4030	12-4040
A13	A13	A13	A13
C41	C41	D12	D12
L40	Z75	L40	Z75
B88	B62	B88	B62
F28	F28	F28	F28
E10	G53	E10	G53
D14	H23	J39	N44

FIGURE 94   Bills of material for four tractor models.

steering. The remaining component items are similarly examined and assigned to groups. The result is shown in Figure 95.

Items Used Only with Specific Option Combinations

Note that the last level-1 component item, D14, does not fit into any of the groupings. When all four of the bills of material are broken down this way and their level-1 components are grouped by use, items D14, H23, J39, and N44 remain unassigned, because each of them is used only with one or the other of the option *combinations*. Here the process must be carried one step further. These items are broken down themselves, as illustrated in Figure 96, and *their* (level-2) components are assigned to the groupings by use. The final result is represented by Figure 97, where all the items involved in our example are grouped into the respective modules.

In this example, the entire problem has been solved by applying the technique of breakdown and group assignment. But if items D14, H23, etc., had not been subassemblies but single parts, it would have been impossible to break them down. In cases like that, the part that is used only with a certain combination of options should, if possible, be redesigned. This will not always be feasible, however, as illustrated by the engine in the original tractor example. Special engine-block castings are used for diesel, and the horsepower option entails different cylinder bores; the fuel and horsepower combinations cannot be disentangled. Either such combinations must be

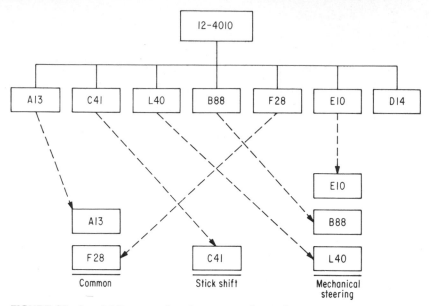

FIGURE 95   Level-1 items assigned to groups by option.

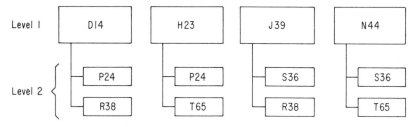

FIGURE 96   A breakdown of unassigned level-1 items.

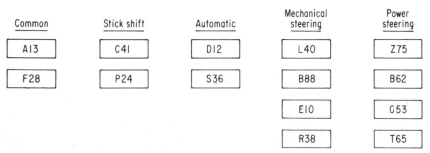

FIGURE 97   Completed modularization.

forecast (and form separate modules) or the items in question can be assigned to more than one grouping in the modularizing process. For example, item D14 (Figure 94) could be duplicated in both the stick-shift and the mechanical steering modules (Figure 97), ensuring that it would never be underplanned. Such duplicating is particularly indicated for inexpensive items of this sort, in preference to separate forecasting or redesign.

Options within Options

The *option-combination* items just discussed represent one type of complication from the modularization point of view. Another one is *options within options*. The tractor used in our example can have four-wheel or three-wheel construction, and an option in the latter is a single or double front wheel. This is an option within an option, and it calls for establishing three modules, i.e.:

1. Items common to the three-wheel-construction option
2. Items unique to the single-wheel suboption
3. Items unique to the double-wheel suboption

The proper treatment of optional product features is overplanning, i.e., forecasting and safety stock. This means that a suboption will have to be even more overplanned than an option. For example, the following sets of items might be scheduled when 300 tractors are to be produced:

- Basic tractors (common items):   300
  Option { - Four-wheel construction: 100
           - Three-wheel construction: 275
  Suboption { - Single front wheel: 200
              - Double front wheel: 125

Note that the option is overplanned by 75 sets of components, but when the suboption is taken into account, the overplanning amounts to 125 sets $(100 + 200 + 125 = 425)$. The suboptional parts are, by necessity, doubly overplanned. Breaking out suboptions is an alternative to treating the suboption as an option in its own right, i.e.,

Option { - Four-wheel construction   100
         - Three-wheel construction, single wheel: 200
         - Three-wheel construction, double wheel: 125

Under this approach, items common to the three-wheel options will be unnecessarily overplanned. In our example, 275 sets of items common to three-wheel construction would be planned under the option/suboption approach, and 325 sets under the straight option approach.

It can be seen that lack of modularization in *product design* (so-called integrated design), of which option combinations that cannot be disentangled and options within options are examples, entails more investment in safety-stock inventory and makes inventory management more difficult. This is due to a high forecast error in forecasting option combinations, and the necessity for double overplanning in the case of options within options.

Planning Bills

To return to the previous modularization example and to recap the steps taken up to this point: end-product numbers (codes) have been abolished, and their bills of material have been done away with as unnecessary for purposes of material requirements planning; where the final product formerly served as the end item in the bill of material, level-1 items (and in one case, level-2 items) have been *promoted* to end-item status. This procedure established a new, modular *planning bill,* suitable for forecasting, master scheduling, and material requirements planning.

The job of restructuring is not finished, however. The former level-1 items used with option combinations, D14, H23, etc., that have been excluded from the planning bill cannot simply be abolished. These items will eventually have to be assembled, and the production control system has to be able to place orders for these items, schedule them, and requisition their components. These bills must therefore be retained for the purposes just mentioned, as well as for industrial engineering and cost accounting purposes.

Manufacturing Bills

This represents another technique of bill of material structuring: the establishment of so-called *manufacturing bills,* or *M*-bills, that together constitute the *M*-bill file.[3] These bills of material are coded to distinguish them from the planning bills that the MRP system uses exclusively. *M*-bills are not involved in the process of component requirements planning, but are used for purposes of final assembly only. The inventory items defined by these bills (*M*-items) are built against the final assembly schedule, usually to customer or warehouse order, using the components planned and provided by the MRP system. The principle involved here is that in modularizing the bill of material at whatever product level, *end-product (level-0) bills can be abolished entirely but not any bills formerly on level 1 or lower.* These must be segregated in the *M*-bill file and retained for purposes of ordering, scheduling, costing, etc. In the example used, the total bill of material file would consist of

1. The planning-bill file, comprising bills shown in Figure 97
2. The manufacturing-bill file, comprising bills for D14, H23, J39, and N44

[3] In this exposition of the subject of bill of material structure, the terms *M-bills, S-bills,* and others are being used for lack of standard terminology, a condition attributable to an almost total neglect of this subject in literature.

Specifying options during order entry (or in scheduling a warehouse order) will call out and reconstruct, via the planning-bill file, the proper bills for individual end products but not for lower-level assemblies that have been eliminated from it, unless these have been made part of the *M*-bill file. How the latter is used in order entry and in final assembly scheduling will be shown later.

An *M*-item can only be a component of another *M*-item or of an end product. *M*-item components are either other *M*-items or end items. End items are defined as the highest-level items in the planning bill. Note that those purchased items that are being procured as a function of executing the final assembly schedule (rather than the master production schedule) are a logical adjunct of the *M*-bill file even when they are *not* components of an *M*-number. Such parts act as highest-level items in the *M*-bill file. They are excluded from the planning bill and are bypassed by the MRP system. Parts controlled by the final assembly schedule will be discussed later in this chapter and in Chapter 11.

Segregating Common from Unique Parts

Earlier it was mentioned that one of the two reasons for modularization is to disentangle option combinations, for purposes of forecasting and master production scheduling. The other objective of modularization, i.e., segregating common from unique (optional) parts for purposes of inventory minimization, however, has not been fully met in the example we have been working with.

In modularizing the bills of material, level-1 items in the example were assigned to groups, by option. But at least some of those items were assumed to be assemblies, and they may contain common components. For example, a subassembly that is only used with the stick-shift choice may have some common parts with another subassembly used only with automatic transmissions. Requirements for such common items will be overstated, as they are included in the safety stock of *both* options. In order to segregate such parts, the bills of material would have to be further modularized, that is, torn apart. In some cases it might be desirable to do that, but if this technique is carried to its extreme, the planning bill might end up containing single parts only and no subassemblies at any level. The ultimate module of the product is, of course, the individual component part.

Bill of material modularization may be a complex task if the product itself is highly complex, if it is engineered on the "integrated design" principle (nonmodular design), and if it entails a proliferation of optional features. Judgment must be used in deciding what should be modularized and how far. Particularly in attempting to segregate common or semicommon (an item used with diesel and gasoline choices but not with LP gas) parts, the approach should be conservative; i.e., excessive modularization should be avoided.

The Effects of Modularization

Modularization affects the timing of subassembly completion. A subassembly promoted to end-item status takes the place of its former parent in the master production schedule, which means that it will be finished later than had its lead time been offset from the timing of the parent. Each time an item is broken down one level and its original bill transferred to the *M*-file, its lead time must somehow be accounted for. While subassembly lead times are not significant in most cases, end items in the modular (planning) bill should, strictly speaking, be advanced in the master production schedule by the amount of their lead time if they have originally been on level 2 or lower. This would complicate master scheduling, and in practice it is not done when the lead times of the subassemblies in question are very short, as they usually are.

The crucial question in modularizing the bill of material is how far downward in the product structure to go. What is really being done is to determine the correct level in the (original) bill of material at which to forecast, master schedule, and plan material requirements. Whether a given subassembly should be forecast and planned or just its lower-level components — that is the fundamental question — depends on *when* it needs to be assembled.

There are two alternatives. One is to assemble it as a function of executing the master production schedule, via the MRP system. This means assembling to stock, or *preassembling*, before the end product itself is scheduled to be built, via the final assembly schedule, following the receipt of a customer (or warehouse) order. The other alternative is to defer making the subassembly until such time as the end product itself is scheduled to be built. Making the subassembly then becomes a function of executing the final assembly schedule. The choice between these two alternatives should be dictated by the nature of the product in question, and by the nature of the business. Lead times and the economics of subassembly operations (is it feasible to make the subassemblies one at a time?) will determine, in each case, whether the item should be preassembled or whether it can wait until final product assembly.

The master production schedule (further discussed in Chapter 11) is essentially a procurement, fabrication, and subassembly schedule. Its object is to furnish the component items required for the final assembly of the product. Different categories of subassemblies are under the control of this schedule and the final assembly schedule. When the bill of material is being modularized, a given subassembly is, in effect, being assigned to one or the other of these two schedules, i.e.:

1. To the master production schedule, by retaining it in the planning bill
2. To the final assembly schedule, by transferring it to the *M*-bill file

Thus the question of how far modularization should go tends to answer itself when the bill of material for a particular product is analyzed, and when the nature of the various subassemblies in a particular manufacturing environment is examined.

To conclude the present discussion, it may be proper to reflect on the objectives of modularizing the bill of material. In addition to the specific objectives brought out earlier, there is another, broader one. And that is to maintain flexibility of production with a minimum investment in component materials inventory. The goal is to be able to offer a wide choice of products and to give maximum service to customers, and at the same time keep component inventories low. Modular bills of material are designed to help achieve just that.

PSEUDOBILLS OF MATERIAL

When the bill of material is broken down in the process of modularization, various subassemblies are promoted and become end items, i.e., highest-level items with no parent in the planning bill. This tends to create a large number of end items. As it is the end item that has to be forecast, and as the master production schedule has to be stated in terms of end items, the hundreds (or thousands) of new end items would prove too many to work with. Fortunately, there is a simple solution to this.

The objective always is to have the smallest possible number of items to forecast, and the smallest possible number of end items shown in the master production schedule. To meet this objective, the technique of creating "pseudobills of material" is used. Going back to Figure 97, where the newly created end items are grouped by option, there is no obstacle to taking any such group and creating a pseudobill (assigning an artificial parent) to cover it. This is illustrated in Figure 98, where a new series of (pseudo) bills has been established.

These new bills of material, sometimes called *superbills* or S-bills, are an example of *nonengineering part numbers* being introduced into a re-structured bill of material. An S-number, such as S-101 in Figure 98, identifies an artificial bill of material for an imaginary item that will never be assembled. The sole purpose of the S-number is to facilitate planning. With the S-bills established, when the transmission option in the tractor example is being forecast, only S-102 and S-103 would be involved. These pseudo-bill numbers then represent this optional product feature in the master production schedule, and the MRP system will explode the requirements from this point on, utilizing the S-bills in the bill of material file.

Another pseudobill term in industrial use is the so-called *kit number* or K-number. This technique is used in some manufacturing companies where there are many small, loose parts on level 1 in the product structure. These

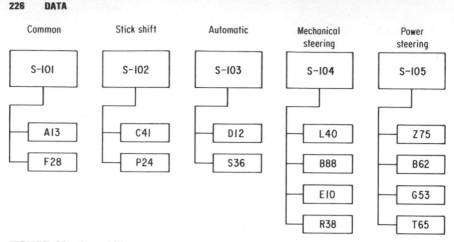

FIGURE 98   Superbills.

are often the fasteners — nuts, bolts, and cotter pins — used to assemble the major product units together. Under an MRP system, to deal with such items individually on the master production schedule level would not be practical. These parts are therefore put into an imaginary bag, as it were, and a part number is assigned to identify this bag, or kit. A (pseudo) bill of material is established for the kit, which is then treated as an assembly, for purposes of master scheduling and material requirements planning.

The principle involved here is the same as in the case of the S-bill, i.e., assigning a single new identity code to individually coded items that constitute a logical group, and employing the format of a bill of material to relate such items to one another. K-numbers may be used to advantage within a modular bill (to streamline material requisitioning, for instance), or they may be used even when there is no need for a modular bill of material. The K-number is another nonengineering part number. These artificial identity codes have little to do with the design of the product and are not part of product specifications, but are created for more convenient forecasting, planning, and master scheduling.

These newly created bills of material, along with the M-bills discussed earlier, represent a superstructure in the bill of material file which, once established, must then be maintained along with the rest of this file. This is a new function which increases the cost of file maintenance.

INTERFACE TO ORDER ENTRY

Procedures governing customer order entry and backlog management, called "order entry" for short, are outside the boundaries of the MRP system except in those cases where customer orders or contracts constitute the master production schedule itself, or where such orders are substituted for

items originally planned via this schedule. Otherwise order entry interfaces with the MRP system through the final assembly scheduling system.
The latter then calls on the MRP system for components and, where properly
implemented, checks the availability of these components by accessing the
respective inventory records during the course of the final assembly scheduling process.

To make this feasible, however, and to be able to back up the final assembly schedule with part numbers (bill of material numbers) of the highest-
level component items required for each specific unit of product being
scheduled, it is first necessary to *translate* customer or warehouse orders
into manufacturing language, i.e., bill of material numbers.

With most products of some complexity (assembled products), customers—and sales personnel—normally specify orders in descriptive
English, in terms of model numbers, or by means of a so-called *generic
code* that serves as shorthand for English description. An example of a
generic or product-description code is shown in Table 11.

TABLE 11 Product-Description Code

Example: 3 A G 1 1 A P 3

Position	Code	Option
1	1	Model 450 tractor
	2	Model 550 tractor
	3	Model 650 tractor
2	A	4-wheel construction
	B	3-wheel construction, regular
	C	3-wheel construction, special
3	G	Gasoline
	D	Diesel
4	1	56 hp
	2	68 hp
	3	76 hp
5	1	Stick-shift transmission
	2	Automatic transmission
6	A	Regular axles
	B	High-clearance axles
7	M	Mechanical steering
	P	Power steering
8	1	No power takeoff
	2	Power takeoff type A
	3	Power takeoff type B

The generic code is convenient to use in a marketing environment, and
it has the additional advantage of not being subject to variation between

models or to engineering changes. Power steering remains power steering, but the respective bills of material will vary between models, and their identity coding, as well as contents, will tend to change over a period of time. For purposes of manufacturing and costing, the generic code must be translated into a *specific code*, i.e., into bill of material and part-number terms.

In a modular bill of material situation, each generic code would have one or more *S*-number counterparts, and the generic-to-specific conversion could be effected either by means of decision tables or through *inverted bills of material* (another instance of pseudobills), as illustrated in Figure 99. In this example, a diesel option (letter D in position 3 per Table 11) coupled with 56 hp calls out S-bill 201, the engine, etc. In this way, the final assembly scheduling system can be integrated, or logically linked, with the MRP system.

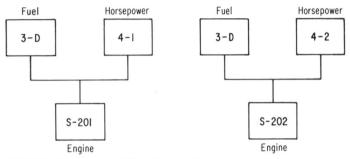

FIGURE 99   Inverted bills of material.

In conclusion, let us briefly discuss who does and who does not have to restructure bills of material as a precondition of successful MRP system operation. Where the product line consists of a limited number of items or models, modularizing the bill, or any other changes for the sake of bill of material structure, may be unnecessary. Master scheduling and material requirements planning *can* be based on models, and on their bills of material, provided the model codes define products uniquely.

On the other hand, bill of material restructuring is called for where the product line consists of a virtually unlimited number of end-product configurations, due to complexity of design and a proliferation of optional features. The study of how bills of material should be constructed then becomes a vital part of the work of designing and implementing an MRP system.

REFERENCES

Orlicky, J. A., G. W. Plossl, and O. W. Wight: "Structuring the Bill of Material for MRP," *Production & Inventory Management,* vol. 13, no. 4, 1972.
Structuring the Bill of Material, brochure form no. G320-1245, International Business Machines Corp., 1973.

PART SIX

MANAGING WITH THE NEW TOOLS

*[With computers] we can now explode
anything, and too often we do. The MRP
output can be only as good as the Master
Production Schedule we give it as input.*
ROMEYN EVERDELL *in* APICS News,
August 1972.

CHAPTER ELEVEN

THE MASTER
PRODUCTION SCHEDULE

A master production schedule is to an MRP system what a program is to a computer. The master production schedule is, technically speaking, only one of three principal inputs to an MRP system (Chapter 3), but whereas the other two, i.e., inventory status and product structure, supply reference data to the material requirements planning process, the master production schedule constitutes the input that "drives" it. It is the prime input on which an MRP system depends for its real effectiveness and usefulness.

Material requirements planning is the first step in the implementation of the overall manufacturing program of a plant, which is what the master production schedule represents. In the upstream/downstream relationship of information flow between systems, the master production schedule is furthest upstream, and it acts as a wellhead of the flow of manufacturing logistics planning information.

A given master production schedule is the determinant of future load, inventory investment, production, and delivery service. It is the cause of certain inevitable consequences in the areas just mentioned, and it may contain the seed of future problems and failures. As pointed out in Chapter 3, downstream systems are unable to compensate for deficiencies of their input. An MRP system will carry out its functions of inventory ordering, priority planning, and (indirectly) capacity requirements planning with great efficacy, provided that it is presented with a realistic, valid master production schedule to be processed.

MASTER PRODUCTION
SCHEDULING CONCEPTS

Does every manufacturing company or plant have a master production schedule? If such a schedule is defined as the overall plan of production, it would be difficult to conceive of a plant operating without it. In any manufacturing operation, the sum total of what a plant is committed to producing at any given point in time is equivalent to a master production schedule. What some manufacturing managers really mean when they say that they do not have a master production schedule is that in their case, the overall plan of production is not being expressed in one formal document. For purposes of material requirements planning, the creation and maintenance of a formal master production schedule is a prerequisite.

Definitions

A master *production* schedule should not be confused with a forecast. A forecast represents an estimate of *demand,* whereas a master production schedule constitutes a plan of *production.* These are not necessarily the same. A distinction should therefore be maintained between the functions of developing a forecast and laying out a schedule of production, despite the fact that in some cases the two may be identical in content.

A master production schedule is a statement of requirements for end items, by date (planning period) and quantity. In the preceding chapter, an *end item* was defined as the highest-level item (i.e., an item that is not a component of any parent) recognized in the bill of material that the MRP system uses for exploding requirements. There must be a correspondence between such items in the bill of material and the terms in which the master production schedule is stated. End items may be products, major assemblies, groups of components covered by pseudobills (Chapter 10), or even individual parts used at the highest level in the product structure. A component item may double as an end item when it is subject to service-part, interplant, or other demand from sources external to the plant. Orders and/or forecasts for all external-demand items are technically part of the master production schedule, although they are normally not listed in the formal document but exist in the gross requirements schedules of the respective inventory records.

Where the product line consists of complex assembled products with many optional features, it is not practical to state and maintain a master production schedule serving as input to the MRP system in terms of the products (product models) themselves, for reasons discussed at some length in the preceding chapter. In these cases, the schedule is expressed in terms of major components rather than end products. For example, a machine tool manufacturer would specify in his master production schedule the quantities of columns, knees, tables, beds, and other major assemblies from which individual machine tools will eventually be built to customer order.

The format of a master production schedule is normally a matrix listing quantities by end item by period. The meaning of these quantities in relation to the timing indicated is fixed by convention—in a given case, it may represent end-item availability, end-item production, or end-item component availability. Depending on which one it is, the form of interface between the master production schedule and the MRP system is affected, as previously discussed in Chapter 4.

For purposes of material requirements planning, the time periods of the master production schedule must be identical to those on which the MRP system is based—typically one-week periods. The sales forecast and the master production schedule that management and the marketing organization use are often, however, developed and stated in terms of months or quarters. They are usually also stated in terms of product models. The master production schedule must then be broken down and restated in terms of weeks and specific end-item numbers. Thus it may exist in two versions or layers, as illustrated in Figure 100.

The period of time that the master production schedule spans is termed the planning horizon (discussed previously in Chapters 3 and 8), and it may be divided into a *firm* portion and a *tentative* portion, also indicated in

Product \ Month	A	M	J	J	A	S	O	N	D	J	F	M	A	M	J
Hoist #35	50			50			50			60			60		
Hoist #45		100		80		75		60				50			
Hoist #55	200	200	200	150	150	100	100	100	150	150	200	250	250	250	250

End item \ Week	16	17	18	19
Motor 3848	60		60	
Motor 4002	30	30	30	30
Drum 12-305	25	50		

FIGURE 100   A master production schedule.

Figure 100. The firm portion is determined by the cumulative (procurement and manufacturing) lead time. It is not necessarily firm in the sense of being "frozen," but it does represent quantities of end items committed to, and started in, manufacture.

For the master production schedule, the frequency of maintenance (updating, revision) is usually geared to the forecasting cycle, which is almost always monthly. Between these "official" issues of an updated version of the schedule, however, there may arise a need for revision at any time, caused by the particular mix of new customer orders and by various unplanned developments in procurement and in manufacturing. It is highly desirable, therefore, for the MRP system to be able to process intervening and intermittent "unofficial" changes in the master production schedule on a more frequent basis than that afforded by the forecasting cycle. As discussed in Chapter 8, an MRP system loses much of its effectiveness if it is not used to replan once a week or more often. Arguments in favor of daily, or even continuous, replanning of material requirements have been presented in Chapter 5.

The Final Assembly Schedule

In order to comprehend the essence and the true function of the master production schedule, a distinction must be drawn between it and the *final assembly schedule*. This has been touched upon earlier in connection with other topics, but at this point a more thorough discussion is warranted. The distinction between these two schedules is a source of frequent confusion, because in some cases the schedules, although always different in concept, may be identical in reality; i.e., the final assembly schedule may serve as the master production schedule.

There may be no difference between these two schedules where the product line is limited or where the product itself is small and/or simple. Lawnmowers, hand tools, bicycles, vacuum cleaners, and clocks are examples of this situation in which the shippable product is the end item. Interestingly enough, the master production schedule and the final assembly schedule may be identical in the case of highly complex products that are engineered and manufactured to customer order, such as turbines or weapons systems.

But between these extremes there lies the broad middle ground of complex products assembled from standard components into a variety of configurations, often to specific customer order. In this category belong vehicles, machinery of all sorts, electrical equipment, and a long list of others. Here the two schedules are distinct. The master production schedule is expressed in terms of high-level components (assemblies, etc.) and, typically, because of the disparity between manufacturing lead time (long) and customer delivery time (short), it must be formulated and committed long before the final assembly schedule is prepared.

While the typical master production schedule extends a number of months into the future, the final assembly schedule usually only covers days or weeks. It is stated in terms of product models or specific configurations of optional product features, often in serial-number sequence. The master production schedule is based on *anticipated* customer demand. The final assembly schedule responds to *actual* customer demand, and is constrained by the availability of components provided by the master production schedule via the MRP system.

The master production schedule is essentially a procurement, fabrication, and subassembly schedule. Its function is to provide component availability, and it may therefore be viewed as a *component availability schedule.* In this context the term *component* means any inventory item below the end product level.

The master production schedule may be said to "produce" the mentioned components in support of the final assembly schedule. This is true to the extent that these components are part of the bills of material reflected in the master production schedule. The exceptions to this rule are items excluded from the planning bill during the process of modularizing the bill of material, as discussed in the preceding chapter. One of the points made there is worth repeating: A given subassembly may be assigned either to the planning bill (used by the MRP system) or to the *M*-bill (used by the final assembly scheduling system). This is tantamount to putting the item in question under the control of one or the other of these two systems. If the item is part of the *M*-bill, the final assembly schedule, rather than the MRP system, is "responsible" for producing it.

This rule extends to selected manufactured items and purchased items, which may be put under the control of the final assembly scheduling system. They will then be manufactured or procured as a function of executing the final assembly schedule, in correspondingly small lot quantities. Such items are characterized by

- High unit cost
- Short lead time
- Short assembly lead time of the item's parent (if any)
- Absence of significant setup or quantity discount considerations

Examples of component items governed by the final assembly schedule, related to products referenced in previous discussions, are as follows: A horizontal milling machine of certain design has a so-called overarm, required in the fourth week of the machine's final assembly. The overarm is a simple steel cylinder involving little machining with minor setup, but it is a massive and relatively expensive part. It is assembled into the milling machine by inserting it into the proper hole in the column and fastening it inside the column. Such an item is properly assigned to final assembly schedule control and is machined, in quantities perhaps as small as 1 or 2, during the final assembly cycle, for specific machines being built.

An example of a purchased part under final assembly schedule control is a tractor rear tire, a very expensive item. These tires (of which there are many varieties, makes, sizes, and tread patterns) are shipped by the vendor at very short notice, in any quantity needed to meet the current requirements of the tractor assembly schedule. Quantity discounts may apply to total annual consumption of all tire models, rather than to individual orders.

In both of the above examples, significant inventory investment is avoided or minimized, and the possibility of surplus is precluded, by gearing the manufacture or procurement of the items in question to the final assembly schedule.

Functions of Master Production Scheduling

A master production schedule serves two principal functions, namely:

1. OVER THE SHORT HORIZON
   To serve as the basis for the planning of material requirements, the production of components, the planning of order priorities, and the planning of short-term capacity requirements
2. OVER THE LONG HORIZON
   To serve as the basis for estimating long-term demands on the company's resources such as productive capacity (square footage, machine tools, manpower), warehousing capacity, engineering staff, and cash

These two functions relate to the "firm" and "tentative" portions of the master production schedule mentioned above. A well-implemented MRP system encompasses the entire planning horizon; i.e., both the firm and tentative portions of the master production schedule are reflected in the time-phased inventory records. While only the firm portion of the planning horizon is, strictly speaking, required for purposes of order release and order-priority planning, the system maintains data on tentative (but formally planned per the master schedule) requirements and planned orders, to provide visibility into the future on an item-by-item basis. These data can be put to a variety of uses, including lot sizing, projections of capacity requirements and inventory investment, serving to guide the negotiation of blanket-order contracts with vendors, determining inventory obsolescence and indicated writeoff, and others.

The master production schedule should strive to maintain a balance between the scheduled load (input) and *available* productive capacity (output) over the short horizon, and it forms the basis for establishing *planned* capacity over the long horizon. This represents long-term estimates of resources required to execute the master production schedule. Some of these resources, such as plant and new machinery, may take a year or more to acquire, and that is why a master production schedule should extend beyond the total cumulative production lead time. The long-horizon function of *resource requirements planning* will be reviewed in the next section.

MASTER PRODUCTION SCHEDULE DEVELOPMENT

The specific method of developing a master production schedule tends to vary from company to company. The general procedure, however, consists of a number of logical steps described below that can serve as the basic blueprint on which modifications are made depending on the nature of a particular manufacturing business.

Preparing a Master Production Schedule

A master production schedule represents, in effect, the future load on production resources. The load arises from requirements placed on the plant which reflect the demand for the product being manufactured. The method of establishing these requirements varies, depending on the industry. In the manufacture of products to stock, future requirements are generally derived from past demand. In the manufacture to order, the backlog of customer orders may represent total production requirements. In custom assembly of standard components, a mixture of forecasting and customer orders generates requirements. The organization of the distribution network and field inventory policy also directly affect production requirements. In most manufacturing companies, the requirements placed on a given plant derive from several sources. The identification of these sources, and of the demand they generate, constitutes the first step in developing a master production schedule. These sources are the following:

- Customer orders
- Dealer orders
- Finished goods warehouse requirements
- Service-part requirements
- Forecasts
- Safety stock
- Orders for stock (stabilization inventory)
- Interplant orders

Customer orders may constitute the master production schedule in the case of custom-engineered products, in contract manufacturing for the government, in industry-supplier situations, or in any case where the order backlog extends beyond the cumulative production lead time. In other cases, customer orders are filled by the plant but create requirements, via the final assembly scheduling system, on final assembly facilities only.

Requirements on the rest of the factory are conveyed by the master production schedule, which anticipates component-item demand.

Dealer and warehouse requirements for products constitute another
source of demand which, for purposes of master production scheduling,
may sometimes be treated the same way as customer orders. In most cases,
however, the difference lies in the practice of dealers and distribution warehouses of indicating their requirements (quotas) in advance of orders
being actually issued. These advance commitments are normally stated in
terms of product models without specific choices of optional features.
These then have to be forecast, for master scheduling purposes, by the
plant. In the case of simple products without optional features, planned-
order schedules of a time-phased order point system employed by the warehouse represent demand on the plant.

Service-part requirements by either customers or a service warehouse
normally bypass the master production schedule development process.
They are entered, in the form of either forecasts or orders, directly into
the respective inventory records. An exception might be the case of large,
expensive service-part assemblies that would be master-scheduled along
with regular products. Where a service warehouse uses the time-phased
order point, requirements are best conveyed via the planned-order schedules of the warehouse system.

Forecasts may, in some cases, constitute a source of requirements placed
directly on the plant. In many manufacturing businesses that either ship
directly to customers from a factory warehouse or assemble to order, a sales
forecast is the sole source of production requirements reflected in the
master production schedule. In many other cases, however, forecasting
also generates requirements that are being conveyed by the master production schedule. This pertains to product variations or to optional product features, which are usually forecast by the plant, even though the master
production schedule is based on commitments for product units by dealers
or field warehouses, as mentioned above. In these cases, the exact configurations of optional features are supplied just prior to shipment.

Safety stock, as mentioned earlier, should be planned on the master
production schedule level rather than on the component level. Safety-stock
requirements must therefore be viewed as a separate source of demand
on the plant. Safety stock, in terms of end items, is incorporated into the
quantities stated in the master production schedule.

Orders for stock may be the principal source of production requirements
in cases where the product is being stockpiled in anticipation of future

need. In businesses subject to highly seasonal demand, products and/or components are normally produced to stock during the off-season in order to be able to meet the peak demand, with a level load on productive capacity throughout the year. The resulting inventory is known as *stabilization stock*.

Interplant orders are normally confined to component items rather than products, which may include anything from single component parts to assembled end items appearing in the master production schedule. The treatment of these requirements parallels that of service parts. In cases where the "customer" plant uses an MRP system, this type of demand is more effectively conveyed via the planned-order schedules for the interplant items, as has been discussed in Chapter 4.

Demands from all the sources just reviewed, when consolidated, represent the so-called *schedule of factory requirements*. The creation of this schedule constitutes the second step in the development of the master production schedule. The latter is derived from the former but is not necessarily identical to it, for the following reasons:

■ A part of the demand expressed in the schedule of factory requirements may be met from plant inventory.

■ Product lot-sizing considerations, important from the manufacturing point of view, are obviously not reflected in the schedule of factory requirements. The demand is shown by quantity and date without regard for production economics. In the process of developing the master production schedule, product lot sizes are established that may deviate, in both quantity and timing, from the requirements of the various sources of demand. Additional lot sizing may subsequently take place at the component-item level.

■ The load represented by the schedule of factory requirements may either exceed productive capacity or be below the capacity to which the plant is committed.

■ This load may fluctuate excessively.

■ The schedule of factory requirements may be stated in terms of product models that will have to be translated into end-item bill of material numbers.

■ The schedule of factory requirements may not specify optional product features the demand for which must be forecast before being incorporated into the master production schedule.

The schedule of factory requirements serves as the basis for the final preparation of the master production schedule, which constitutes the third and final step in master production schedule development. Thus a specific manufacturing program is created which will then be processed by the MRP system to plan all subsequent component procurement, fabrication, and subassembly activity. In transforming the schedule of factory requirements into a master production schedule, the predominant consideration is that of capacity availability. The process and the techniques used to achieve a balance between load and capacity over the long horizon are described next.

Resource Requirements Planning

A master production schedule must be considered in relation to the load it places on available, or planned, resources including capacity, space, and working capital. If available resources are not adequate to meet the requirements represented by a given master production schedule, they must be increased or the schedule should be reduced. Unless solid planning of resource requirements takes place before the planning of production, there is a likelihood of failure in delivery service, a logjam in work in process, a disruption in the production control system, and increased manufacturing costs.

The resource requirements planning concept entails a long-range planning function intended to keep in balance the ability to meet demand and a reasonably level load on the company's resources. The technique of resource requirements planning consists of five steps, as follows:

1. Defining the resources to be considered
2. Computing a *load profile* for each product that indicates what load is imposed on what resources by a single unit of the product
3. Extending these profiles by the quantities called for by a proposed master production schedule and thus determining the total load, or *resource requirement,* on each of the resources in question
4. Simulating the effect of alternative master production schedules
5. Selecting a realistic schedule that makes the best use of (existing or planned) resources

Defining the resources to be considered is a management function. Resources range from drafting-room personnel to cash to capital equipment and plant square footage. In the discussion that follows, only one such resource, productive capacity, will be referenced. For purposes of resource requirements planning, productive capacity may be subdivided into individual capacity resources or groups. For example, the entire machine shop may be defined as a resource, and the impact of a given master production schedule is then measured in terms of total load on the shop. Or the shop may be defined as two or more resources, by function, such as heavy casting machining, miscellaneous machining, and sheet metal operations. Individual departments or groups of departments may constitute measured resources. A still finer breakdown would identify work centers or even individual machines. A single critical machine may legitimately be identified as a resource under this approach.

Resource requirements planning is, however, intended for relatively large groupings because its purpose is not to determine the exact load on an individual resource, but rather to evaluate the overall impact of a given master production schedule. Resource requirements planning is conducted on a "macro" level, using rough approximations of load, and a precise fit is not sought. The important thing is to be able to develop the alternative loads quickly, so that several different master production schedules may be tried out.

Computing load profiles for individual products is based on the simple proposition that each (quantity of) product in the master production schedule generates measurable load and that the same procedures that are used to arrive at a machine load report can be used to compute a product load profile. A given load profile consists, for instance, of the standard hours of fabrication required, by period, to produce one unit of product, measured against whatever fabrication resource is selected.

The load profile for a given product may be thought of as a load report for a simulated product lot of 1, computed on a relative time scale. In Figure 101, the end of period 10 corresponds to whatever period the product would appear in the master production schedule, and the overall fabrication load it generates is distributed over eight periods (the product's fabrication lead time) preceding the completion date. Figure 102 shows a load profile for the same product related to heavy presses, a critical resource or bottleneck.

A load profile is computed by using the MRP system as well as the operations scheduling and loading systems as simulators. The quantity of 1 each of the end items making up the product (using a typical combination of optional features), arbitrarily assigned to some future period, is processed

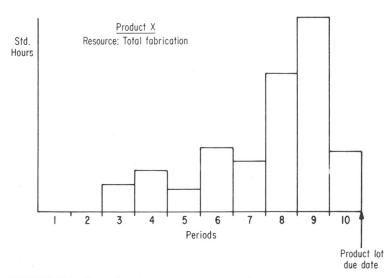

FIGURE 101   A product load profile for total fabrication.

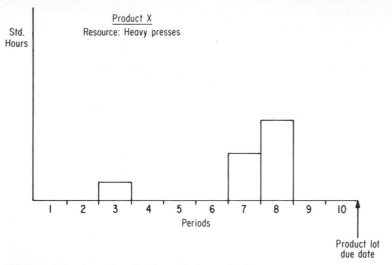

FIGURE 102   A product load profile for a single resource.

by the MRP system using blank inventory records or a special program routine suppressing the netting function. The gross requirement of 1 is exploded through all levels of the product structure, bypassing any lot-sizing computations. The resulting output are planned-order receipt schedules (all minimum quantities) for all items, at whatever level, that would be used in the production of one each of the end items in question.

These planned-order schedules then serve as input to the regular scheduling and loading systems, and using whatever scheduling rules and loading conventions are in effect, a special load report is generated. This load report, when summarized, represents the product load profile which is then stored for future use.

In developing the load profile, the treatment of setup time will vary, depending on whether setup standards exist, i.e., whether setup is considered direct labor or overhead. Where the routings contain setup standards, setup hours are part of the load profile created by the method just discussed. The setup load, however, is stored separately from run-time load because of the different treatment each will receive when the total load for a product lot is calculated. If setup standards are not maintained, empirical setup-hour data can be apportioned to the respective run times, or else the latter can be increased by some percentage to account for setup.

The final load profiles of all products are stored, so that they can repeatedly be used in resource requirements planning without a need for the detailed computation. The development of product load profiles is a one-time job. Unless the product in question is redesigned drastically, its load profile will serve throughout product life, because engineering changes would normally have only a trivial effect on the load involved.

Extending load profiles by the quantities called for by a given (version of the) master production schedule, and summarizing them by period, is a simple matter. It is accomplished very quickly with a computer that has access to the file in which the profiles are stored. The result is a report (printed or conveyed through a visual display device) showing the effect of the master production schedule, over the entire planning horizon, on the various resources for which profiles are maintained. These are called *resource requirement profiles*. They provide a fair indication of the loads that can be expected. The loads may be segregated by individual product lots, to show which of these are causing potential capacity problems. This is graphically portrayed in Figure 103. Note that load generated by service-part and interplant requirements is added to that derived from product lots. This could be an empirically verified percentage of the load, or it could be forecast, or it might be computed through separate load profiles if the service-part and/or interplant items are large and their demand significant.

Simulating the effect of alternative master production schedules is part of the selection-decision process. If the load generated by a proposed master production schedule is unsatisfactory (because of significant over-load or underload in one or more periods), the schedule is changed— usually on a trial-and-error basis—and the procedure is repeated. Note that in a business with a line of simple products made to, and shipped from, stock, planned-order schedules of a time-phased order point system may be used to represent the schedule of factory requirements. The latter would be converted into a master production schedule through the use of the firm

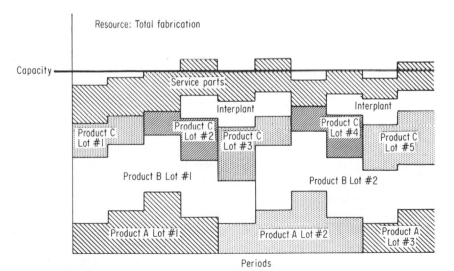

FIGURE 103   A resource requirement profile.

planned-order technique, which would also be used to modify the schedule. This is diagrammed in Figure 107 at the end of the next section.

In the absence of such a procedure, the MRP system will, of course, process any master production schedule, and load will subsequently be calculated. The load report (assuming it is based on both open and planned orders) then serves as a resource requirement profile, but if it proves unsatisfactory, the master production schedule would have to be changed and reprocessed—an unwieldy and costly procedure. Thanks to the availability of load profiles, a large number of potential master production schedules can be tried for fit in a very short time.

Selecting a feasible master production schedule is the final step in this process. This ensures that the schedule roughly fits capacity constraints. Further capacity adjustments will be made subsequently in the course of short-range capacity requirements planning (Chapter 7), when overtime, work transfer, subcontracting, etc., will compensate for the fluctuation of load from period to period. In the typical manufacturing business, the master production schedule decided on by management corresponds to some specific rate, or level, of production (sixty machines a month, eighty vehicles a day) to which all activities are then geared.

The purpose of resource requirements planning is twofold, as indicated earlier. Over the short horizon, it is to keep load within the bounds of available capacity. Over the long horizon, it is to help decide what additional capacity, if any, will have to be added and when.

CLOSING THE LOOP

In managing the master production schedule, and in using it to manage inventories and production, the following basic "law" should always be observed:

> *The master production schedule should be a statement of what can and will be produced, rather than what management wishes had been produced in the past and/or would like to be able to produce in the immediate future.*

This law, which stipulates that the master production schedule must be realistic, is still honored mostly in the breach. This is a result of long tradition, because in the past—before computers and before material requirements planning—the realism of a master production schedule was not easily ascertained or measured. The schedule simply set a goal that everyone in the plant was supposed to scramble to reach. The pressure that the master production schedule exerted to "get the product out the door" by keeping the manufacturing organization under pressure and off balance was considered by management to be beneficial, and it still often is.

This approach to managing production employs what an old machine-shop saying calls "brute force and ignorance." The master production schedule then acts as a brain that can transmit action commands to muscle-equipped members, but lacks feedback. It drives the organism blindly, because it is insensitive to obstacles and injury. This is, of course, extremely inefficient and costly. Today, it is also unnecessary.

The Plan and Reality

The relationship between the master production schedule (the master plan) and the many elements of its execution is clearly visible and in precise form, thanks to the modern MRP system (the existence of standard-variety scheduling, loading, and work-assignment subsystems is assumed). Such a system converts the master plan into a detailed plan of execution and helps to monitor the execution proper. The linkage between plan, execution, and *progress* of execution can now be maintained, and the connection can at all times be seen. This means that it has become both desirable and feasible to close the loop, something that has never been practical in the past. The situation in the real world of procurement and manufacturing can, and should, be fed back to the master plan so that it may be adjusted to better reflect reality.

In a manufacturing environment, most difficulties and problems are caused either by obstacles encountered in carrying out procurement and manufacturing tasks or by the master production schedule itself. For the overall manufacturing logistics system to function properly, the master production schedule must be realistic in three ways. What *can* be produced (as against what it would be *nice* to produce) is a function of the availability of:

- Material
- Time
- Productive capacity

and each one of these is equally important. A lack of critical material or lead time or capacity precludes production, and if the master production schedule insists on such production, it will incapacitate the MRP system in its priority planning function, leading to a collapse of the shop priority system. The manufacturing organization then reverts to form: staging, stockouts, assembly shortages, hot lists, expediting, confusion, increase in manufacturing cost. The informal system takes over because the formal system, of which the master production schedule is a critical part, is not doing its job.

In a manufacturing plant, probably the most commonly encountered problem is difficulty in, or inability of, meeting the monthly plan of shipments (shipping budget), caused by inability to complete final assembly due to a shortage of components. This problem is highly visible, but it is not of primary nature. Rather, it is a *symptom* of a variety of specific problems in earlier stages of the production process. These may be classified as follows:

- Problems in inventory planning
- Problems in procurement
- Problems in manufacturing

Inventory planning problems are represented by either lack of coverage of net requirements or lack of lead time to cover net requirements. Procurement problems consist of past-due deliveries, rejections of vendor shipments on the basis of quality, and a vendor's inability (usually temporary) to produce and deliver. Manufacturing problems take the form of past-due shop orders, scrap, inability (usually temporary) to proceed with manufacture due to a lack of tooling, machines or other facilities, and overloads. Every one of these types of problem affects the integrity of shop priorities (defined in Chapter 7), which is most important for the efficient and smooth operation of a plant.

As pointed out previously, the objective in managing inventories and production via the master production schedule is to establish and maintain a realistic relationship between plan and execution. Whenever a disparity develops between what the master production schedule calls for and the likelihood of being able to do it, an effort at reconciliation should be undertaken. The first step should always be to determine what, if any, extraordinary action can be taken to solve the problem at the execution level so that the master production schedule may remain intact. This is the usual course of action when overtime, subcontracting, expediting, etc., are resorted to—every effort is made to meet the schedule, and it is a completely proper effort as long as there is a reasonable probability that the schedule will actually be met.

A different case entirely is the situation when it develops that some part of the master production schedule cannot, and in fact *will not,* be met. Here the schedule must be promptly changed if it is to remain realistic. At this point, the question is exactly what in the master production schedule to change, and how. The answer can be accurately ascertained through the MRP system. The pegged requirements capability (discussed in Chapter 8) allows any of the specific problems enumerated above to be traced and related to the master production schedule.

Some problems may be solved below the master production schedule level, by revising planned-order data in parent-item inventory records, as has been shown in Chapter 8. In other cases, it will be necessary to use pegging to step through all the higher levels, to pinpoint the end-item lot (the quantity in a specific master production schedule bucket) that has to be changed to restore harmony between the schedule and reality.

Restoring the Schedule to Valid Status

The effect of any of the problems mentioned above, whether caused by the master production schedule itself or by unforeseen developments in the production process, is reflected in, and can be traced through, the time-phased inventory records. In a material requirements planning environment, these records provide the information that triggers all procurement and manufacturing activity, and obstacles encountered in the course of this activity can be related back to the respective records, as can inventory management problems. From the record in question, pegged requirements provide the trace to the master production schedule. This is illustrated in Figure 104.

Problems that are caused by the master production schedule itself (as contrasted with problems caused by poor performance in meeting this schedule) are the result of overstating the schedule. The latter may be overstated in its totality (exceeding overall capacity in every period), or it

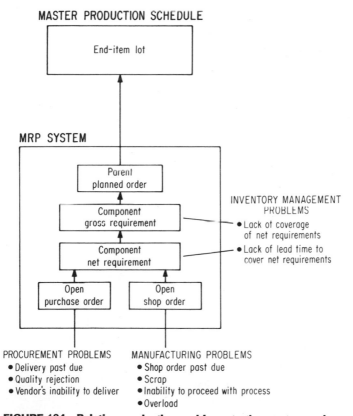

FIGURE 104   Relating production problems to the master production schedule.

End item	6-months average production per period	Period			
		1	2	3	4
A	100	180	100	90	100
B	200	480	200	160	180
Total	3000	6000	3000	3100	2900

FIGURE 105   A master production schedule overstated in the first period.

may be overstated in certain periods only, or it may be overstated in terms of specific capacities at a specific time (boring bars in weeks 45 to 51). Figure 105 shows a master production schedule that is obviously overstated in the first period, when a total of 6,000 units are scheduled, compared with an average of 3,000 in subsequent periods. An indicator of capacity is past output, which also averages 3,000 per period. The phenomenon of overstated current periods is quite common in manufacturing companies. Sometimes the first period carries a load equal to several periods' capacity!

Another way of overstating the master production schedule is to carry a behind-schedule backlog, as illustrated in Figure 106. Here this backlog

End item	6-months average production per period	Behind schedule	Period		
			1	2	3
A	100	150	100	100	90
B	200	180	240	200	160
Total	3000	4500	2900	3000	3100

FIGURE 106   A master production schedule overstated in the backlog.

amounts to 4,500 units, which is equivalent to 150 percent of capacity per period; in addition, a full load is assigned to the first period. Presumably the plant is supposed to get back on schedule—by producing 250 percent of its capacity in the current period! This example illustrates a situation that is even more common than the preceding one—the custom of carrying behind-schedule buckets in the master production schedule is prevalent. In reality, of course, nothing can be produced yesterday, only today and tomorrow. The master production schedule should reflect that reality. The behind-schedule column is best abolished, unless care is taken that the total of behind schedule and the first period does not exceed capacity for one period.

Both examples represent a gross overstatement of the master production schedule, which is disastrous to the shop priority system. In these cases, most orders are no doubt past due, and most jobs in process are behind schedule and marked "rush." Expedite lists are long, and because of that, there is a special expedite list *within* the expedite list. Work-in-process inventory is excessive. Manufacturing costs are high. Although the company has the ability to plan priorities (an MRP system is being assumed), the formal priority system has collapsed, if anyone ever took it seriously in the first place. When everything has high priority, nothing has high priority.

Disparities between the master production schedule and the realities of production will arise even when the schedule is not overstated. This is caused by a miscellany of unplanned events that tend to take place in the typical manufacturing operation. Delays in the progress of work due to the condition of tools and machinery are not uncommon. Neither is a temporary lack of adequate specific capacity. Neither is scrap, nor lack of material. There may be quality problems. Vendors fail to deliver. Interplant shipments get lost in transit. No system can prevent such obstacles from developing, but they can, and should, be adjusted for, compensated for.

With the aid of an MRP system, the remedy is straightforward. Whenever one of the mentioned difficulties occurs and when it becomes clear that some task (usually, an open order) will not, in fact, be completed as planned, the item in question is *traced* to the master production schedule (assuming the problem cannot be solved via pegging and firm planned order at an intermediate parent level), the schedule is *revised* and subsequently *reexploded* to establish up-to-date requirements and priorities. Note that it does not suffice to reschedule the order in question, because of dependent priorities. The example of scrap in Chapter 7 (Figure 66) illustrates this problem and its solution.

Failure to realign dependent priorities is the most common reason why shop personnel consider a formal priority system unreliable and may decide to work around it. If, for any reason, a given component item will definitely not be available at the time of need, the *real* relative priority of its co-component orders is, in fact, lower than it would be otherwise. The priority of these orders is dependent on the availability of the item in question, and if the formal priority system disregards this, it loses credibility in the eyes of shop people. They always find out. If these people cannot work according to the formal priorities *and* be satisfied that they are working on the right jobs at the right time, the priority system must be considered in a state of collapse.

To keep the master production schedule in harmony with the realities of production is a classic problem of manufacturing management. With older, conventional methods it is difficult or impossible to identify the specific end-item lot (or several lots that use a common component) that is linked to some minor disaster on the shop floor or on the receiving dock. With material requirements planning, all the tools are there.

The closed-loop approach made possible by the capabilities of an MRP system applies equally to master production schedule development (reviewed in the discussion of resource requirements planning) and to master production schedule implementation. This is illustrated in Figure 107, a logic diagram of the procedures described in the present chapter thus far.

Changing the Schedule for Marketing Reasons

The changes in the master production schedule discussed thus far have been related to problems of production. Changes will also be made, however, for reasons of marketing. It is common for a marketing manager to request, and for management to authorize, changes in the master production schedule so as to accommodate a customer or to make a sale. Such changes usually call for increasing the quantity or advancing the timing of an end-item lot. From the point of view of the company, these are desirable changes, but if they are made arbitrarily, the master production schedule may again become unrealistic, with all the adverse consequences discussed above.

Each schedule change of this type, whether merely intended or put into effect, represents the desire for *flexibility*, i.e., freedom in changing previous decisions. The flexibility is constrained, however, by the realities of *commitment*. Another way of expressing this is to say that the consequences (cost) of a previous decision constitute the practical limits of changing that decision. The limits of flexibility contract with passage of time, making it less and less practical to effect changes as the end item nears its scheduled completion date. The reality of commitment acts as a funnel with ever-narrowing walls that, as time goes on, leave less and less room for deviation from original plan.

If lead time is, say, four months, there is a world of difference in impact and cost of changing something in the master production schedule that is four months away from completion as against something that is three months away from completion. In the former case, the consequences of the previous decision (having placed the original end-item lot into the respective

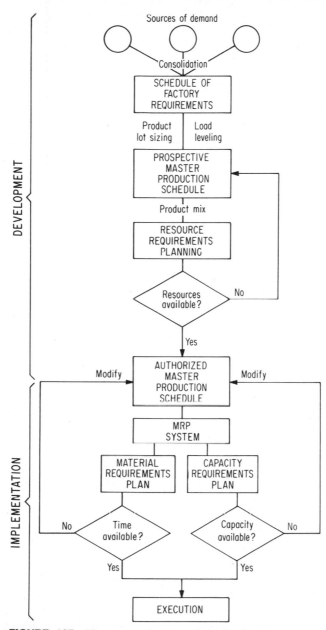

FIGURE 107   Master production schedule development and implementation.

master production schedule bucket) are negligible, as tangible commitments have not yet been made. In the latter case, only one month later, costs have already been incurred in the processing of requisitions and orders, as well as in purchasing and manufacturing activities. In addition, the action already taken entails a certain amount of committed-for investment for materials that it may not be possible to cancel.

This is related to the concept of firm and tentative portions of the master production schedule, mentioned earlier in this chapter. End-item quantities that appear in the firm segment of the schedule represent products in various stages of commitment, and corresponding degrees of amenability to change. The tentative portion of the schedule represents merely a plan for the execution of which money has not yet been expended or invested, as far as materials are concerned. The firm portion of a master production schedule is of the same length at any point in time, that is to say, it moves along the time scale with passage of time, progressively covering what had previously been the tentative area.

In order to avoid making marketing-motivated changes that would render the master production schedule unrealistic, the MRP system may be used to make a so-called *trial fit*. This means that the contemplated change is made in the schedule and exploded in a simulation mode. An MRP system has the inherent capability to act as a simulator, in that it will accept any version of a master production schedule and by processing it, will indicate the specific consequences—material availability, order action, and lead-time availability.

Special programming (or a modification of the regular program) would normally be used for this purpose, but an MRP system can always be used (less efficiently) as a simulator, without any modification. If the consequences of a trial fit prove unattractive, the system is restored to previous condition by simply reversing and reprocessing the trial entries.

In some manufacturing businesses where it is feasible to match incoming customer orders with the master production schedule or to incorporate them into it, trial fitting may be regular procedure. A *trial-fit report* then indicates which orders may be accepted with the customer's delivery-date request and which orders should be renegotiated for later delivery by a specific number of periods. The MRP system determines this based on the availability of component materials and lead time.

The Master Scheduler

A master production schedule, as mentioned earlier, may have two layers, the lower, more detailed of which serves as input to the MRP system. With the advent of such a system, the position of *master scheduler* in the production and inventory control department assumes special importance.

The master scheduler (and his staff, if any) is responsible for the creation and maintenance of the lower-layer master production schedule. He converts product models into specific end-item bill of material numbers, divides monthly into weekly quantities, and forecasts product options not specified in the (upper-layer) master production schedule or not forecast by Marketing. He keeps track of the use of safety stock provided at the master production schedule level, accounts for differences between quantities of end items produced via the master production schedule and those consumed by the final assembly schedule, and generally keeps the master production schedule up to date and valid.

An important function of his is to evaluate problems of priority integrity, as described earlier, that are brought to his attention by inventory planners who have traced a problem to the master production schedule by means of pegged requirements. He determines which end-item lot should be changed and how, and he initiates a recommendation to management that such a change be authorized.

The position of master scheduler may be a new one, necessitated by the introduction of material requirements planning. It constitutes an organizational link vital to closing the loop in the logistics planning system. Other organizational aspects of operation under an MRP system will be reviewed in the section that follows.

MANAGEMENT AND ORGANIZATIONAL ASPECTS

The master production schedule (or schedules, if there is more than one plant) documents the overall manufacturing program of a company. The development and administration of such a program, viewed as a broad function, should be the joint responsibility of all four of the basic functional divisions of a manufacturing enterprise, i.e., Marketing, Manufacturing, Finance, and Engineering. The first three of these are involved on a continuous basis, whereas Engineering enters the picture occasionally, when redesign or the introduction of new products affects the manufacturing program.

Assignment of Responsibilities

The general responsibilities, relative to the manufacturing program, of the three divisions that are continuously involved may be specified as follows:

MARKETING
- Responsibility for forecast of customer demand, which is basically the answer to the question as to what can be sold and when.
- In some instances, responsibility for finished goods inventory in terms of units, model mix, and storage location. This responsiblity is sometimes retained by Manufacturing or given to a special organization in charge of distribution.

FINANCE
- Responsibility for financing and control of finished goods inventory in terms of total investment, credit, and receivables.
- Responsibility for the financing of the manufacturing program.

MANUFACTURING
- Responsibility for the development of master production schedules within the constraints established by the above.
- Responsibility for performance to master production schedules.

While Finance is concerned with the broader aspects of its function and deals with the problem in terms of dollars within the framework of fiscal periods, Marketing and Manufacturing are involved more closely in that they must deal in terms of specific units of product and cope with the day-to-day problems of producing and selling. This means that once the broad plans for sales volume, supporting production, and overall financing have been made, responsibility for their administration and execution rests with Marketing (with the exceptions noted above) and Manufacturing. If the operation is to be successful, it becomes quite important to arrive at the proper *modus operandi* between these two divisions and to define and clarify their respective specific responsibilities in the following three areas:

1. Forecasting versus scheduling
2. Inventories of component materials versus inventories of finished product
3. Component materials for optional product features

Forecasting of demand is clearly a responsibility of Marketing, whereas the scheduling of production is (or should be) up to Manufacturing. A forecast and a master production schedule are two different things, but in practice they are sometimes confused in that, in some types of manufacturing business, the raw forecast is allowed to act as a master production schedule in disregard of production considerations. In other types of manufacturing business, marketing goals rather than a forecast of demand are reflected in the makeup of the master production schedule. The above remarks pertain also to (the statements of) these goals.

The authority for specifying and changing the contents of the master production schedule is sometimes improperly assigned or, perhaps even more typically, remains unassigned. In these cases, Marketing tends to influence and change existing master production schedules directly, possibly creating a number of undesirable consequences in production. The principle of separation of forecasting from scheduling production means that the only thing ever changed by Marketing should be the forecast or some other expression of marketing requirements. Such a change need not necessarily always result in a schedule change.

Inventories represent another area of responsibility that in many businesses can be divided between Marketing (or a distribution organization) and Manufacturing. In these cases, Manufacturing exercises control over, and is held responsible for, plant inventories of raw materials, work in process, and finished components carried to support current master production schedules. Marketing, on the other hand, assumes responsibility for both field and plant inventories of finished product.

The responsiblity for component materials of optional product features can often also be divided between Marketing and Manufacturing. In dividing this responsibility, management tries to apply the rule that whoever is in a better position to determine the quantities of materials to be ordered for a given optional feature should assume responsibility for it.

To determine how this responsibility is to be assigned, the options for each product are ranked according to their relative weight, i.e., the percentage of the total cost of the product. Options representing a significant portion of total product cost are then forecast by Marketing, the balance by Manufacturing. Marketing is in the best position to estimate the trend in future demand for major options, while Manufacturing typically has better historical statistics on the use of a host of minor options.

The logistics system that a manufacturing company needs to regulate the flow of materials through the entire cycle from vendor to finished-goods inventory to customer must act to coordinate activities of several functional divisions of the company. The master production schedule, which "drives" the entire system, serves as a basis for resolving the inevitable conflicts between the functional divisions and represents a *contract* between them.

That is why the various steps involved in the development and finalization of a master production schedule, reviewed earlier in this chapter, are in most cases carried out by a *master scheduling committee* or a hierarchy of committees, composed of representatives from the interested marketing, manufacturing, and finance organizations. The creation of a master production schedule is too important and critical a function to be entrusted to any one functional division of the company.

Management and the Master Production Schedule

On occasion it has been suggested that the master production schedule, i.e., its preparation and maintenance, could be automated and brought under complete computer control. This is envisioned as an extension of the process of automating systems and procedures in the area of manufacturing logistics. Where statistical forecasting of demand applies, so the reasoning goes, the automated forecasting procedures could be integrated into a program of master production schedule creation, including the preparation of the schedule of factory requirements, netting, product lot sizing, etc. The logic of the procedures can be clearly defined, and all the required data are available.

This notion, in the author's opinion, must be repudiated. All the required data are, as a matter of fact, not available. Information on a multitude of extraneous factors, current company policy, and seasoned managerial judgment—all of them bearing on the contents of a master production schedule—cannot be captured by a computer system. That is why management should be involved in the creation and maintenance of the master production schedule every step of the way.

The master production schedule represents the overall plan of production to which all subsequent detailed planning is geared. Inventory management action, procurement action, and manufacturing action—all these are directly or indirectly dictated by the contents of the master production schedule. Developing and maintaining the best possible master production schedule is the premise on which depends the success of the manufacturing logistics system. This, it would seem, will always be too important to entrust to a computer program.

The master production schedule represents the main point of management entry into the overall system. It is through this schedule that management provides (or can provide) direction, initiates changes in production, exercises control over inventory investment, and regulates manufacturing and procurement activities. It has been pointed out earlier that, given properly implemented and properly used systems for planning and execution, the master production schedule is virtually the sole determinant of what will happen in areas of capacity, production, and customer delivery service. Inevitable consequences flow from a master production schedule as it, in effect, contains within itself the scenarios that will later be acted out. Management has the opportunity, and responsibility, to manage all this through the master production schedule.

Coupled with a modern MRP system, the master production schedule constitutes a new tool for the solution of many problems that traditionally have had to go unattended to in a manufacturing operation. To take advantage of this tool, it is important to understand the relationship between factors of production, especially of open orders, and the master production schedule—and the desirability of maintaining a correspondence between this schedule and the realities of the manufacturing floor. The key to this is willingness, on the part of management, to change the master production schedule.

This calls for a departure from the traditional view of the master production schedule as representing a goal not subject to change, and one that, if somewhat overambitious, acts to spur the factory to greater efforts. In the modern view, a master production schedule should represent a *feasible* goal, subject to continuous review and adjustment. The master production schedule must no longer be considered a sacrosanct document—on the contrary, it should be treated as a flexible, living plan, adaptive to actual developments. Even in the presence of an MRP system, inventory, priority, and capacity planning will be invalidated in the face of an inflexible master production schedule.

This is a new situation, brought about as a consequence of applying the principles and techniques of time-phased material requirements planning. It calls for a new way of looking at things in a manufacturing business environment. Management has been given a new, powerful tool, and it should step up to its responsibility for using it well. Management is responsible for keeping the master production schedule valid, realistic, and up to date. Changes, additions, and adjustments in this schedule should be *managed,* because of their effect on inventory investment, manufacturing costs, and delivery service to customers.

REFERENCES

Everdell, Romeyn: "Master Scheduling: Its New Importance in the Management of Materials," *Modern Materials Handling,* October 1972.

Master Production Schedule Planning, Chapter 4 of Communications Oriented Production Information and Control System (COPICS), vol. 3, form no. G320-1976, International Business Machines Corp., 1972.

CHAPTER TWELVE

A NEW WAY OF
LOOKING AT THINGS

In the introduction to this book, the author remarked that the availability of computers in the 1950s represented a lifting of the previous information-processing constraint, which presaged the impending obsolescence of older methods and techniques of production and inventory management. Before the advent of the computer, production and inventory control methods and systems were relatively ineffective. These methods and systems had been devised in light of the information-processing tools available at the time, and they suffered from a lack of ability to correlate and handle data on the massive scale required. This *constraint of the tools,* which affects the efficacy of methods and systems, also governs the way people look at things, perceive problems, and formulate solutions to these problems at a given point in time. The constraint of the tools is reflected in the thought and literature of an era.

The introduction of computers into production and inventory control work represented a sudden increase—by orders of magnitude—in the power of available tools. In the late 1950s the constraint of the tools was lifted and a new era began. The new tools were applied toward solving old problems, and eventually solutions were devised for even those that in the past had been the most baffling and stubborn. Today there exist solutions to problems that not only could not have been solved in the past but that no one at the time could conceive how *ever* to solve.

The essence of the production and inventory control problem in the past was not so much a lack of ability to plan as to *replan,* to respond to change. Today, there exists the capability to update for change easily, quickly, and correctly, thanks to the computer and the techniques of time-phased material requirements planning. This capability of timely replanning in response to change must now be examined in all its implications. The time has come to rethink certain traditional concepts, axioms, and theorems. Many of these are no longer relevant or valid, because they fail to take into account the recent great enhancement in the ability to update for change. Traditional views that now must be revised pertain to the following topics:

1. Manufacturing lead times
2. Safety stock
3. Queue analysis and queue control
4. Work in process
5. Forecasting of independent demand

These now appear in a new light, which the discussion in this chapter will attempt to establish.

PLANNED VERSUS ACTUAL MANUFACTURING LEAD TIME

In the classic problem environment of a job shop or general machine shop, the queue-time element of lead time may account for 90 percent or more of the total time elapsed. It is by compressing queue time that the overall lead time can be reduced. In the case of an individual shop order, it is important to distinguish between

- Planned lead time
- Actual lead time

Planned lead time is the value supplied to the MRP system, and it is this lead time that the system uses for planning order releases. The original due date of an order reflects the planned lead time.

Actual lead time reflects a revised due date which coincides with the date of actual need, if the latter has changed since the time of order release.

The difference between the two lead times, planned and actual, can be major. The author learned this early in his production and inventory control career, although he did not grasp its full implications at the time. It was at a plant producing a line of machinery, where all fabricated parts, large or small, had traditionally been allowed a 12-week lead time. The largest component items that required the most machining operations were a group of large steel shafts. The several product models required one such shaft each, different shafts being used in the assembly of different models.

One day an assembly-line foreman noticed that the available supply of shafts used on the model being built at that time was low. A quick count indicated that the supply would run out by about ten o'clock the next morning. An expediter was sent to look for a replenishment order in the machine shop but could find none. He called the responsible inventory planner, who, upon consulting his records, informed him that for some reason or other there were no outstanding orders for the shaft in question.

Everyone understood that if more shafts could not be produced by the next morning, the assembly line would have to be shut down. Some 100 men would have to be sent home, at full pay according to the union contract, not to mention the loss in production. The reaction to this threat was swift and decisive. While the shop-order paperwork was being prepared, a truck was dispatched to the nearest steel warehouse to pick up raw material for the shafts. An emergency order was promptly launched in the shop, and an expediter was assigned to stay with the order and see that it moved from operation to operation without delay.

The shafts were produced overnight. They were rather expensive shafts because the way had been cleared for them in the shop by tearing down existing setups on all the machine tools required for performing the work — but the assembly line was kept going.

At that time, the shaft that had a planned lead time of 12 weeks was made in one day. At another time, the same shaft had been in process for six weeks when management changed the master production schedule and moved the respective product lot six months back. The shaft's actual lead time then turned out to be 30 instead of 12 weeks. Still later, another product lot was rescheduled into the next fiscal year, when a new model design would be effective and the particular shaft would no longer be used. The shafts in process at the time of the schedule change were never finished (they were eventually scrapped and written off), and thus their actual lead time proved to be infinite.

The planned lead time was 12 weeks, but actual lead time varied from one day to infinity. What determined actual lead time was, of course, *priority*. When the shaft was being manufactured overnight, it had the highest priority in the house. The following definitions may be formulated by generalizing from this example:

■ Individual *planned* lead time represents an estimate of the time that will elapse between start and completion of an order. This lead time is used in the planning process, and it determines order release.

■ Individual *actual* lead time is a function of order priority.

With material requirements planning, individual actual lead times are determined by the order due dates established, and revised, by the system. The need for revision is detected as early as it arises, which mitigates extremes in the lead time, such as those related in the above story. While it is true that individual actual lead time is a function of priority, it must be remembered that priority is relative. The lead time of only a small number of orders (those with highest priority) can be significantly compressed at any one time, in view of limited capacity. *Individual* actual lead time (for a specific order) should therefore be distinguished from *average* actual lead time.

The average actual lead time of successive orders for a given item should, with adequate capacity planning, approximate planned lead time. The average actual lead time of all orders that are simultaneously in process is a function of capacity and the level of work in process. Care must be taken when determining this lead time for purposes of projecting work-in-process levels or of expressing the relationship between capacity, work in process, and lead time algebraically, as average actual lead time, when simply measured historically, will tend to be distorted. It will be inflated to the extent that it includes orders with priorities that have significantly dropped subsequent to release, i.e., orders for items that had requirements deferred into the far future, or for which requirements disappeared entirely. More will be said on this later.

The point of this discussion is that the old concept of a "good" or "accurate" lead time, that is to say, an accurate planned lead time, must be discarded. Planned lead times need not, and should not, necessarily equal actual lead times. Actual lead time is flexible.

SAFETY STOCK IN A NEW LIGHT

The venerable concept of safety stock needs to be rethought in light of the fact that actual lead time is flexible and that modern inventory management systems—material requirements planning and the time-phased order point—have the ability to realign open-order due dates with shifting dates of need. The traditional approach to inventory control assumes that lead time is fixed and known and that only demand is variable. But what happens to this approach when it turns out that actual lead time is, in fact, flexible— when it can be made to expand and contract *with* demand? What is to become of safety stock, and how is it to be calculated now?[1] When there is a system capable of replanning priorities by revising open-order due dates, there certainly is no longer any need for safety stock to cover the period of *planned* replenishment lead time.

It would seem that the traditional techniques of determining safety stock are obsolete and that new techniques and a new theory are needed. Safety stock, where it applies, should be susceptible to reduction, across the board, without an adverse effect on service.[2] Safety stock on the item level is not, of course, normally planned by an MRP system, and is not intended to be.

---

[1] O. W. Wight, *Oliver Wight Newsletter No. 12,* May 1972.

[2] A. O. Putnam, E. R. Barlow, and G. N. Stilian, *Unified Operations Management,* McGraw-Hill, 1963, p. 183.

It is, however, planned under a time-phased order point. In either case the material requirements planning logic, common to both types of system, tends to defeat the purpose of safety stock by preventing it from ever actually being used—if the system can help it. This will be demonstrated in an example illustrated by Figures 108, 109, and 110.

The item in the example has a planned lead time of four periods, demand during lead time is forecast as 40 units, and safety stock is 20. Order point is therefore 60. Figure 108 shows, in graphic form, the inventory projection and the position of the replenishment order at the time order point is reached. Depending on whether the item is under statistical order point or time-phased order point (equivalent to material requirements planning), the projection of safety stock and the position of the replenishment order will vary if actual demand exceeds forecast.

This is shown in Figure 109, where actual demand in the first period has turned out to be 20 rather than the forecast 10. Under statistical order point, the excess demand is thought of as having been met from safety stock; the timing of the replenishment order continues unaffected. Under time-phased order point, the system has reacted by moving the due date of the order one period forward, which keeps the safety stock at the original 20.

Figure 110 shows what happens if actual demand exceeds forecast in the second period also. Under statistical order point, safety stock is considered used up and the order due date remains firm. Under time-phased order point, the replenishment order is rescheduled again and safety stock remains at 20. It can be seen that if demand in periods 3 and 4 is as forecast,

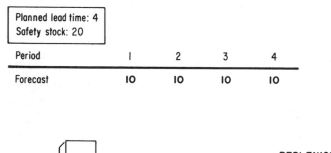

Planned lead time: 4 Safety stock: 20				
Period	I	2	3	4
Forecast	10	10	10	10

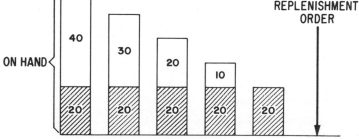

FIGURE 108   Implications of safety stock.

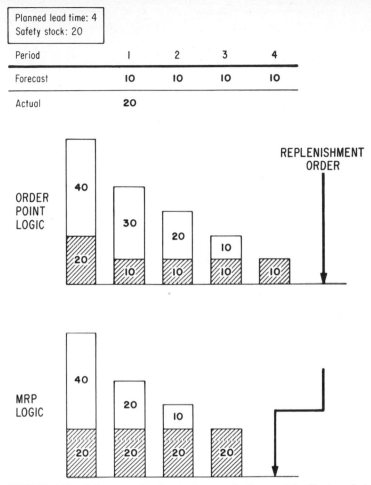

| Planned lead time: 4 | | | | |
| Safety stock: 20 | | | | |

Period	1	2	3	4
Forecast	10	10	10	10
Actual	20			

FIGURE 109 Safety stock: demand exceeds forecast in first period.

inventory under statistical order point will be depleted but not under time-phased order point. The latter technique strives to preserve safety stock intact. Provided that the replenishment order can actually be completed as rescheduled, safety stock proves to be "dead" inventory that could be drastically reduced if not eliminated.

A FRESH LOOK AT QUEUES

Queue analysis and queue control appear in a new light once the new ability of maintaining valid work priorities is taken into account. Figure 111 depicts the familiar tank (sometimes a funnel) that has frequently been used to illustrate the phenomenon of a queue and, by extension, work in

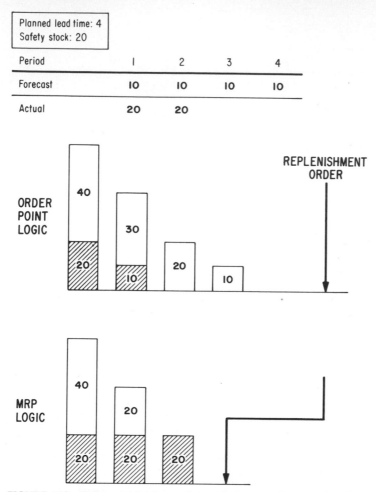

| Planned lead time: 4 | | | | |
| Safety stock: 20 | | | | |

Period	1	2	3	4
Forecast	10	10	10	10
Actual	20	20		

FIGURE 110   Safety stock: demand exceeds forecast in second period.

process. On closer scrutiny, this tank example is found to be rather badly oversimplified. Consider the assumptions in this analogy: The jobs in the tank are homogeneous and interchangeable, first-in/first-out, and the total queue determines average actual lead time. The above holds true for water in a tank but not for units of work in a factory, which are stratified by priority.

Figure 112 shows an up-to-date version of the tank example, in which there are priority strata including "sludge" at the bottom. The total queue is composed of "live," "dormant," and "dead" elements. Only the live portion of the queue is meaningful, and only this portion determines average actual lead time (see next section). The "liquid" is pumped always from the top of the surface, and sludge is drained (scrap and writeoff) through a separate hole in the bottom.

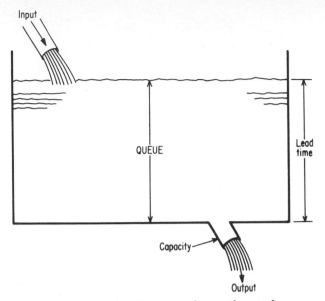

FIGURE 111   Analogy of queue and water in a tank.

Let us now consider a queue in front of a work center. Figure 113 illustrates the two faces of such a queue. The traditional view is from the left-hand side, and the six jobs supposedly represent current load. The assumption is that every one of the jobs is eligible, in priority sequence, to be worked on in the current period. In reality, this is not necessarily so. For

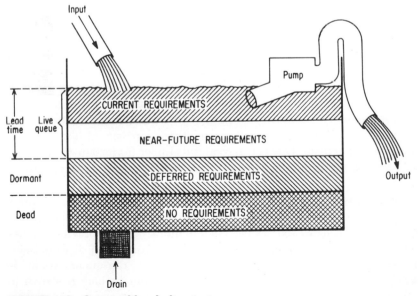

FIGURE 112   Queue with priority strata.

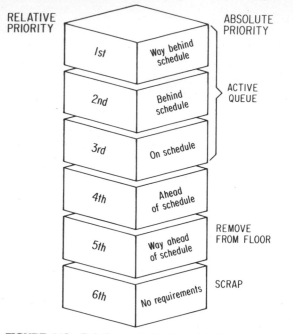

RELATIVE PRIORITY

ABSOLUTE PRIORITY

1st — Way behind schedule

2nd — Behind schedule

3rd — On schedule

4th — Ahead of schedule

5th — Way ahead of schedule

6th — No requirements

ACTIVE QUEUE

REMOVE FROM FLOOR

SCRAP

FIGURE 113   Relative and absolute priority.

purposes of valid queue analysis it is not sufficient to stratify the queue by merely *relative* priority—*absolute* priority must also be taken into account. Relative priority is determined by the ranking of a group of jobs. Absolute priority is given by the relation of a job to its date of need. This is reflected in the right-hand view of the blocks in Figure 113, which shows that the *active queue* consists, in this case, of only one half of the jobs.

The conventional notion of queue control, represented by Figure 114, must be reconsidered once priorities are taken into account. The traditional theoretical approach to this problem is to measure a queue at a work center over a period of time (e.g., minimum 60, maximum 100 standard hours) and to remove its fixed portion (60 standard hours) through overtime, sub-contracting, etc. The "controlled" queue then consists of the variable portion which fluctuates between zero and its upper limit (0 to 40 standard hours). This is the minimum queue required to prevent running out of work.

In reality, it would be foolhardy to assume that standard hours of work adequately describe a queue. The units of work are not necessarily homo-geneous and interchangeable, as has been demonstrated in previous exam-ples. If the fixed portion of the queue were to be worked off, it would cer-tainly be the jobs with highest relative priority; i.e., the queue would be reduced from the "top" rather than from the "bottom," which is shown in

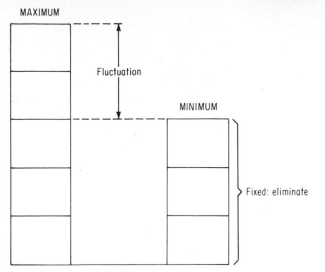

MAXIMUM

Fluctuation

MINIMUM

Fixed: eliminate

FIGURE 114   Queue control: conventional view.

Figure 115. When looked at this way, this entire approach to the problem proves nonsensical, as what is left at the work center are the dormant and dead portions of the queue.

WORK IN PROCESS REVISITED

Work in process, in its relation to lead time, has traditionally been viewed as conforming to the following theorem:

$$L = \frac{W}{R}$$

where L = lead time (in days, weeks, or months)
W = work-in-process inventory (in units, hours, or dollars)
R = rate of output (per period of L, in units of W)

$$L = \frac{1,200 \text{ units}}{200 \text{ units per week}} = 6 \text{ weeks}$$

The average lead time arrived at this way is not always meaningful. When work in process is stratified by priority, the formula will be seen to be ·in need of modification. For example:

Active queues:	800
Deferred requirements:	300
No requirements:	100
Total:	1,200

$$L = \frac{800 \text{ in (active) process}}{200 \text{ units per week}} = 4 \text{ weeks}$$

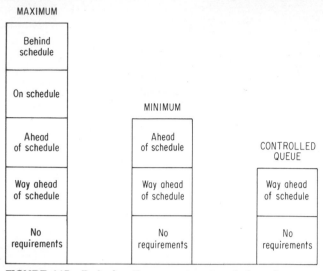

FIGURE 115   Reducing the queue to unneeded work.

Average actual lead time is a function of the live portion of work in process and of the rate of production.

Work in process and lead time codetermine one another. This is a kind of chicken-and-egg relationship, and the difficulty with the above equation is that it assumes that work in process (or, in another version, lead time) is given. In reality, of course, work in process is variable, and its level is a function of the relationship between input to, and output from, the shop. It is obvious that when input exceeds output, work in process (and lead time, with the exception noted above) goes up, and vice versa.

It follows, therefore, that in order to reduce work in process and lead times, output must temporarily exceed input. In order to control work in process so as to keep it from exceeding a given level, input must be held to the existing rate of output. In a material requirements planning environment, input to the shop is represented by the work (and cost) contents of the shop orders being released (actually, being recommended for release) by the system. The flow of these orders, however, must not be held to the rate of current production.

The flow of orders being generated by an MRP system actually cannot be directly controlled or regulated by anyone. It will not be possible to release an order prematurely if the system has planned the component materials to become available only at the time of need. To hold back on orders that the system is trying to release may create an increasing backlog of orders past due for release. All such orders will later have to be released with less-than-planned lead time, which is likely to cause difficulties in the shop and missed order due dates.

With material requirements planning, unimpeded order release is required. The system is releasing orders with correct priorities, in correct sequence, and at what is, by definition, the right time. Priority, i.e., need, rather than the work-in-process level or any other consideration, should govern the releasing of orders. When the priority strata of work in process are taken into consideration (work with deferred or nonexistent requirements is, at any given time, "immovable" regardless of current input and output), the level of work in process assumes secondary importance. What is important are priorities, order completions, shipments, and customer delivery service.

When there is a significant change in requirements as a result of revising the master production schedule, the MRP system may pump a large number of new orders into the shop, on top of an already-high work in process. As long as the master production schedule is valid in terms of both marketing needs and capacity, let work in process be what it will and let the MRP system do its job, without interference at the order-release point.

When input to the factory exceeds output, it is an indication of the fact that the master production schedule is overstated in terms of capacity and should be changed, unless capacity can be promptly increased. An updated view of the relationship between input and output is presented in Figure 116. The desired balance between the rates of input and output should exist not at the point of the MRP system's output but at the point of its input. What should be regulated in relation to the factory's output is the amount of future work implicit in the master production schedule.

LIVING WITH BAD FORECASTS

Forecasting of independent demand, a classic problem of inventory management, appears in a decidedly different light in view of the new capability

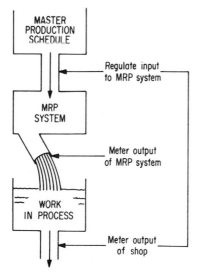

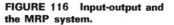
FIGURE 116 Input-output and the MRP system.

to update for change. A forecast is required when an advance commitment (to procure or to manufacture) has to be made. The less flexibility there is in subsequently modifying the original plan, the more important the dependability of the forecast is. When it is easy to modify that plan, however, and to keep modifying it correctly and continuously based on *actual* developments, the quality of the forecast loses in importance.

Material requirements planning and the time-phased order point have the ability to replan and to keep replanning, quickly, accurately, automatically. The time-phased order point, particularly, replans with equal ease whether the replanning is due to a change in the forecast or a disparity between forecast and actual demand. The self-adjusting capability of this technique makes the relative forecast accuracy almost unimportant. The time-phased order point depends on a forecast of demand for being able to function, but it does not depend on this forecast's accuracy for its effectiveness.

This is a highly significant, and fortunate, development as forecast accuracy, regardless of the technique used, remains generally unsatisfactory. Over the past decades, there has been improvement in forecasting as far as *sophistication of technique* is concerned. Improvement in forecasting *effectiveness*, on the other hand, has been rather modest. Working with poor forecasts is still the order of the day, and will likely continue to be. If so, refinements in forecasting technique are a lot less important than the development of planning methods that enhance the ability to live with poor forecasts.

The time-phased order point provides an excellent example of an inventory control technique that "works," almost independently of the quality of the forecast. The next example will illustrate this point. Figure 117*A*, an inventory record of an item under time-phased order point, shows a forecast of 30 in every period and a quantity currently on hand of 140. Safety stock is 15, and it is projected to be reached in period 7. The next replenishment order is scheduled for release in period 4.

Suppose that actual demand in the first period turns out to be zero rather than the forecast 30, as shown in Figure 117*B*, which portrays the status of the item at the beginning of period 2. On-hand inventory at that time will then be 140 instead of the previously projected 110. This will affect net requirements and coverage. Note that both the open order and the planned order have been moved back one period, as the date of need has receded. If there is no demand in period 2, these orders will again be moved back; if demand equals forecast, the orders will stay as presently scheduled, but if demand exceeds forecast (in our case, by 6 or more units) they will be moved forward.

Suppose that actual demand for the same item turns out to be 90 in period 1 instead of the forecast 30, as shown in Figure 118*B*. This will, of course, have changed the quantity on hand at the end of period 1 to 50, as against

Lead time: 3 Safety stock: 15		Period							
		1	2	3	4	5	6	7	
Gross requirements		30	30	30	30	30	30	30	A
Scheduled receipts						80			
On hand	140	110	80	50	20	70	40	10	
Planned-order releases					100				

ACTUAL DEMAND
IN FIRST PERIOD: 0

Gross requirements			30	30	30	30	30	30	B
Scheduled receipts						→80			
On hand	140	110	80	50	20	70	40		
Planned-order releases					→100				

FIGURE 117   Time-phased order point: actual demand is less than forecast.

the previously projected 110. This, in turn, changes both the open-order and planned-order schedules. As the date of need has advanced, all orders have been moved forward and the first planned order will be released in the current period, which would not have been the case if actual demand had equaled forecast.

These examples show that no matter how large the forecast error may prove to be, the time-phased order point technique makes an automatic adjustment and goes on from there. The self-adjustment characteristic of this technique, as it applies to open orders, is particularly significant, as the gross and net requirements for independent-demand items are *expected* to keep changing due to forecast error. In the first of the two examples, it is important to note that should there never be any more actual demand, the open order will never be finished (no more cost incurred) and no planned order will ever be released.

The time-phased order point is able to work with a "bad" forecast. An MRP system is able to work with "inaccurate" item lead times. This is something entirely new. Older techniques were wedded to demand and lead-time values with a basic assumption of their validity and accuracy. Their effectiveness suffered primarily because these values have always been, and continue to be, inherently volatile. The new techniques use forecast demand and planned lead time merely as *points of departure*. These data serve

Lead time: 3 Safety stock: 15		Period							
		1	2	3	4	5	6	7	
Gross requirements		30	30	30	30	30	30	30	A
Scheduled receipts					80				
On hand	140	110	80	50	20	70	40	10	
Planned-order releases					100				

ACTUAL DEMAND
IN FIRST PERIOD: 90

Gross requirements		30	30	30	30	30	30	B
Scheduled receipts		80◄———						
On hand	50	20	70	40	10	-20	-50	
Planned-order releases		100◄———			100◄—			

FIGURE 118   Time-phased order point: actual demand exceeds forecast.

as the rawest of raw materials for the construction of a preliminary plan, which is then modified and modified again in the face of reality. These techniques depend more on what *is* happening than on what was *planned* to happen—they are truly adaptive.

RESEARCH OPPORTUNITIES

There is ample opportunity and a genuine need for further research into material requirements planning and related areas. Thus far, the subject has received minimum or no attention—except for questions of order quantity—in hard-cover literature, research papers, and academic curricula. Operations research in general has consistently shown a predilection for inventing *techniques* (algorithms), but practicing managers have little interest in the results of research that produces mathematically elegant "solutions" to trivial or nonexistent problems. Those who represent the industry point of view (the author included) have had occasion to wish for the researcher to address what *needs* to be researched, as against what is eminently *researchable,* and for the educator to teach what *needs* to be taught, as against what is eminently *teachable.*

An improvement on both sides of this question can only come from better cooperation and dialogue between academia and industry. The inhabitants of the "real world" must in the future take the initiative in articulating and communicating their problems to researchers and educators, and they should actively support valid research. Researchers, on the other hand, should make an attempt to *validate* their research targets before actually proceeding with projects. This is not at all difficult to do—the researcher will find industry people helpful and cooperative in answering his question: "Is this one of your more pressing problems, and should I be working on it?" In the area of material requirements planning, the author suggests the following as affording opportunity for productive research:

1. THEORY
   - Manufacturing lead time
   - Safety stock for independent-demand items
   - Links between the MRP system and execution subsystems
2. JUSTIFICATION
   - Applicability of material requirements planning
   - Costs of an informal system
3. SYSTEM DESIGN
   - Design criteria for different business environments
   - Bill of material modularization
   - Alternatives in the treatment of optional product-feature data
4. SYSTEM IMPLEMENTATION AND USE
   - Analysis of implementation problems
   - Master production schedule development and management
   - Operational aspects of MRP system use
5. EDUCATION
   - Curricula design and teaching tools

Manufacturing lead time (see Chapters 3, 4, and 12) of an item planned by an MRP system has two distinct values, at least in concept: planned versus actual. Planned lead-time values must be supplied to the system by the user, but their validity is not verifiable. What should planned lead times be in a given situation? Excessive planned lead times inflate the investment in work in process—this we know, but we do not know what their optimum values should be and by what method to arrive at them. It seems clear that optimum lead-time values cannot be constant, as they are a function of capacity and the load pattern resulting from a particular product mix that is in production at any given time. The precise relationships remain to be discovered and defined.

Safety stock for independent-demand items (see Chapters 4 and 12) no longer serves its former primary function of compensating for forecast error, once the item comes under the control of material requirements planning logic (time-phased order point). When it becomes possible routinely to update the priority of the replenishment order, it becomes feasible to reduce safety stock, individually and across the board. What, then, should the level of safety stock be? Should it be reduced to correspond to the limits of lead time compression? What are these limits in a given set of circumstances?

Links between the MRP system and execution subsystems (See Chapter 7) need to be better defined and the systems better integrated. We need better techniques for answering the crucial question of whether the material requirements plan can actually be met, as far as its timing is concerned, on an order-by-order basis. Confusion and controversy about techniques such as operations sequencing simulation, finite capacity scheduling, and input-output control need to be resolved.

Applicability of material requirements planning methods (see Chapters 1 and 2) is a subject that calls for exploration. The perceived limits of applicability have been receding during the past years, as industry has gradually been gaining experience with MRP systems. Can these systems be adapted for use in continuous-process manufacturing? In high-volume appliance manufacturing? Can they be expanded to cover inventories of tooling, supplies, etc? Can the use of these systems be expanded still further by adapting them for the planning of nonmanufacturing operations? What are the criteria of *advantageousness,* as contrasted with *applicability,* of the application of material requirements planning methods in a specific case?

Costs of an informal system (see Chapter 7) are unquestionably high but no one seems to know how high, because conventional accounting methods are ill-suited for capturing costs in this category. The ledger does not include accounts for costs of confusion, unnecessary handling of excessive material, mistakes made by operating management due to lack of valid information, inefficiencies of component staging and expediting, missed schedules, time spent by supervisory personnel on "chasing" parts, machine teardowns due to rush work, inventory write-off attributable to poor planning—the list seems endless. Note that to the extent that the informal system is being maintained *parallel* with, and *because* of, a formal system that does not function satisfactorily, the costs of an informal system are avoidable. Is this a serious problem? It is indeed, despite the fact that its dimensions are hidden under a bushel. Field research into this problem would produce startling results.

System design criteria for different business environments (see Chapters 8 and 10) have not yet been developed, at least not formally, in literature. Questions of planning-horizon length, time-bucket size, time phasing of allocated quantities, replanning frequency, etc., are being answered empirically and intuitively. What is the optimum design of an MRP system for a given environment? Can factors bearing on elements of design be isolated and quantified?

Bill of material modularization (see Chapter 10) and other techniques of bill of material structuring have thus far received only the scantest attention in literature. The information is contained in anonymous system documentation of scattered MRP system users. Principles and ground rules for the guidance of prospective MRP system users have yet to be formulated. This subject invites and requires research. The most intriguing question is this: can the logic of bill of material structuring be formally described, captured, and programmed for a computer to execute? Can software be developed that would analyze and restructure a bill of material file correctly, in optimum fashion for purposes of material requirements planning in a specific case?

Alternatives in the treatment of optional product-feature data (see Chapter 10) need to be explored, evaluated, and documented in literature. This problem area is related to bill of material structuring as well as to product design and the organization of product specifications data. Phenomena of "nested" options (option within option within option) and suboptions invite inquiry. The comparative merits of "add-and-delete" techniques (reduced file storage and maintenance requirements but problems of identification) versus the creation of distinct complete bills (clean identification, retrieval, historical statistics, etc., but large storage capacity) whenever a new option is added, need to be analyzed and evaluated.

Analysis of MRP system implementation problems, that is to say, management and operating problems encountered in implementing (installing) MRP systems, would serve a very useful purpose, as it would act to reduce both system implementation cost and the rate of system failure. The author knows, from his own experience, that the most serious obstacles to MRP system success lie outside the (technical) system boundaries. The problems must be sought not in computer hardware and software but in people, their attitudes, habits, and knowledge level.

Master production schedule development and management (see Chapters 7 and 11) represent the area of probably the richest research "pay dirt." Master scheduling is just beginning to come into its own, as a direct result of increased MRP system use in the past few years. The MRP system acts as a mirror being held up to the master production schedule—it illuminates its quality by translating it into specific consequences in terms of material, lead time, and capacity availability. Once an MRP system is installed, it tends to force management to reexamine the entire process of master scheduling, including the procedures of schedule development, maintenance, and revision. Management of the manufacturing operation *through* the master production schedule becomes feasible—an opportunity and a responsibility. Much more needs to be learned about this area. How should master production schedules be developed and what should they consist of in different business environments? What are the organizational implications? What are the limits of master production schedule changeability? What techniques should be employed to ensure and safeguard the integrity of shop priorities?

Operational aspects of MRP system use (see Chapter 8), despite their importance, have not been adequately investigated and documented in literature. How does an inventory planner, capacity planner, master scheduler, and manager make optimum use of the tool represented by an MRP system? What *are* all the latent capabilities of an MRP system? What are the limits of information that the system can provide? What is the set of situations that a planner may potentially face, and what is the correct response to each one of these? In what respects are MRP systems found lacking, from the user's point of view? Answers to many of these and similar questions may be found, case by case, in the field. Their analysis, classification, and compilation would provide a much needed generalized guide to the use of MRP systems.

Curricula design and teaching tools are, at this time, still largely undeveloped. As this book is being written, few collegiate-level courses on operations management, production management, and inventory management even include the subject of material requirements planning. Where the subject is included it tends to be given cursory treatment, in part due, no doubt, to a dearth of teaching materials. Thus far, only a handful of case studies have been written and reading has by necessity been limited to trade-press articles and scattered papers. This area is wide open to creative research and development. Much work is needed in curricula redesign, development of teaching materials, classroom examples and exercises, writing of case studies, and the construction of computer-based simulators suitable for student use. Here academic-industry cooperation would foster rapid progress. Prospects for such progress have brightened since the forming, in 1973, of an Academic MRP Interest Group by certain members of the American Institute for Decision Sciences (AIDS), whose objective is closer future cooperation with the American Production and Inventory Control Society (APICS).

IN CONCLUSION

As this book is being written, the author's association with the field of manufacturing logistics as student, practitioner, teacher, and consultant spans almost a quarter of a century. During this time of work on the formidable problems of production planning and manufacturing inventory management he has witnessed many profound changes taking place:

- An increased management concern, and the increasing importance management attaches to production and inventory control
- A growth in our knowledge of the subject
- A professional approach steadily replacing traditional methods of "brute force and ignorance"
- The emergence of computers which ended the former information-processing constraint and thereby revolutionized methods and systems of planning and control
- The development of time-phased material requirements planning, both as a powerful tool and as an area of knowledge
- The closing of the loop, via the MRP system, between orders and capacities on one hand and the master production schedule on the other
- The structuring of what had always been an ill-structured problem
- The fashioning, for the first time ever, of a formal planning system that can actually function in a manufacturing environment without a parallel informal system
- Changes in thought and in the perception of the entire manufacturing logistics problem

As a young practitioner, the author was convinced that he could develop a virtually perfect, detailed plan of production and material supply for his company if he were given the pertinent data, some sharp pencils, and time to work out the plan, and if subsequently everyone would hold still so that the plan could be executed. He soon learned, however, that even before the planning could be completed, management was likely to change the master production schedule, the engineers would change the makeup of the product, the sales department would change the forecast, and the industrial engineers would change the manufacturing process.

The problem was not one of planning but of *replanning*. Replanning at the rate changes were taking place was impossible, however. The author, at that time, perceived the solution to lie in stabilizing the master production schedule, in making the marketing people live with the original forecast, in freezing the design of the product—ending the volatility of the environment and stopping the turbulence. Needless to say, that never happened.

From today's vantage point, it is clear that such thinking is invalid and the perception false. The manufacturing business environment, in most cases, is inherently unstable and turbulent. Change is the rule. Change, in fact, is "the name of the game." The solution lies not in methods to stabilize and freeze, but rather in an enhancement of the ability to *accept* change and to respond to it promptly and correctly—and do it routinely, as a matter of course. In the future, instability and propensity to change will, if anything, increase. An ability to accept change fosters more change.

The future should bring further enhancements in the ability to respond to change through expanded use of computer-based methods of time phasing, i.e., material requirements planning and time-phased order point, and through a linkage of such systems between vendor, manufacturer, and distributor. Both the shop and the vendor will need to be reeducated to the volatility of need and to formal, routine methods of conveying the information, in contrast with traditional expediting. Expediting, a symptom of inability to maintain a valid plan, and the most inefficient method of gathering and conveying information (this is what expediting really is), is on the wane. Formal systems are bound to displace informal systems because they can be vastly more efficient—and we now have formal systems that can do the job.

At the beginning of this book, the author pointed out that the availability of computers and their first uses for manufacturing applications ushered in a new era representing a sharp break with tradition in inventory management and production planning. Although not evident at the time, most of the previous techniques and systems approaches were marked for discard. New concepts, techniques, and systems have evolved since then. They matured in the past few years and are now in the process of being standardized. Many represent areas that are underresearched and underdocumented. More work still needs to be done, but there can be little doubt that the concepts, techniques, and systems approaches described in this book will see progressively increasing acceptance and use in the future. The author hopes that his present effort will further such acceptance and contribute to the effectiveness of such use.

INDEX